The MAILBOX®

Organi[...] FEBRUARY Now!

grades

Everything You Need for a Successful February

Monthly Organizing Tools

Manage your time, classroom, and students with monthly organizational tools.

Essential Skills Practice

Practice essential skills this month with engaging activities and reproducibles.

February in the Classroom

Carry your monthly themes into every corner of the classroom.

Ready-to-Go Learning Centers and Skills Practice

Bring February to life right now!

Managing Editor: Sharon Murphy

Editorial Team: Becky S. Andrews, Kimberley Bruck, Karen P. Shelton, Diane Badden, Thad H. McLaurin, Kimberly Brugger-Murphy, Gerri Primak, Karen A. Brudnak, Hope Rodgers, Dorothy C. McKinney, Randi Austin, Cindy Barber, Janet Boyce, Catherine Broome-Kehm, Rebecca Brudwick, Jill Davis, Stacie Stone Davis, Nichole Dirks, Margaret Elliott, Cynthia Holcomb, Angie Kutzer, Andrea Singleton, Leanne Stratton, Sharon Vandike, Susan Walker, Katie Zuehlke

Production Team: Lisa K. Pitts, Pam Crane, Rebecca Saunders, David G. Bullard, Jennifer Tipton Cappoen, Chris Curry, Sarah Foreman, Theresa Lewis Goode, Clint Moore, Greg D. Rieves, Barry Slate, Donna K. Teal, Zane Williard, Tazmen Carlisle, Cat Collins, Marsha Heim, Amy Kirtley-Hill, Lynette Dickerson, Mark Rainey, Angela Kamstra, Sheila Krill

www.themailbox.com

ISBN10 #1-56234-683-0 • ISBN13 #978-156234-683-6

Manufactured in the United States
10 9 8 7 6 5 4 3 2

Table of Contents

Monthly Organizing Tools

A collection of reproducible forms, notes, and other timesavers and organizational tools just for February

Essential Skills Practice

Fun, skill-building activities and reproducibles that combine the skills your students must learn with favorite February themes

February in the Classroom

In a hurry to find a specific type of February activity? It's right here!

Ready-to-Go Learning Centers and Skills Practice

Two center activities you can tear out and use almost instantly! Plus a collection of additional reproducible skill builders!

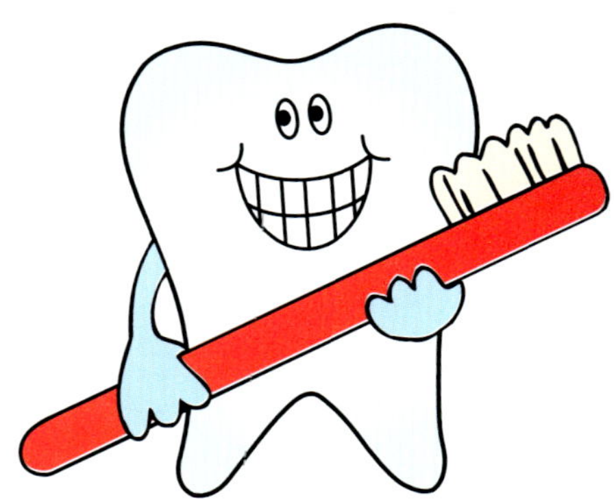

Skills Grid

	Groundhog Day	Valentine's Day	Presidents' Day	Dental Health	Centers	Games	Time Fillers	Writing Ideas & Prompts	Learning Center: Suppertime Serenade	Learning Center: The Sugar Shop	Ready-to-Go Skills Practice
Literacy											
ABC order		31									
uppercase and lowercase letters			40								
initial consonant: *h*											90
ending consonants: *b, f, m*		30									
beginning sounds				42							
ending sounds: /g/, /l/, /t/									74, 81		
ending sounds: /d/, /k/, /n/											91
long vowels	20										
short vowels: *i, u*											92
short and long vowels					59						
onsets and rimes						62					
blends with *l*		25									
word formation		22									
sight words					58						
syllables				43							
positional words	18										
rhymes		23									
spelling				44							
capitalization			35								93
writing		24	36				69				
journal prompts								70			
writing sentences								70			
creative writing								71			
writing and illustrating a story								71			
reading motivation			37								
following directions							68				
skill review		26									
Math											
ordering numbers		22									
number order to 20				49							94
place value											96
compare numbers			37								
compare sets						62					
building numbers				44							
estimation		23									
counting		24				63					
addition					59						
addition and subtraction			34								
subtraction facts to 12			41								
fact families		25		48							
nonstandard measurement			36								
comparing lengths				43			69				
coin value										82, 89	
coin combinations		26								82	
coin identification		32	35								
coin amounts to 50¢		33									
counting pennies					58						95
graphing	18										
patterns	21										
word problems				45							
skill review		26									
Social Studies											
presidential facts			34								
Health											
healthy dental habits				42, 45		63					

Medallion

Program with a child's name. Tape to a student's clothing or backpack.

Brag Tag

Use a child's words to finish the sentence starter.

Award

____
student

had
sweet
success
today!

____________________ ____________________
teacher date

Medallion, brag tag, and award: Copy onto colorful construction paper, cut out, and use as desired.

February

Sunday	Monday	Tuesday	Wednesday	Thursday	Friday	Saturday

Center Checklist

Name	Center												

Class List

Name													

Classroom News

From ______________________ Date ______________

Sweethearts

Look What We Are Learning

Help Wanted

Please Remember

Special Thanks

Classroom News

From ______________________________ Date ____________________

Clip art: Use the artwork on student papers and on correspondence such as announcements, forms, and parent notes.

Name ______________________________

Goal ______________________________

Name ______________________________

Goal ______________________________

Name ______________________________

Goal ______________________________

____

Incentive charts: Have students track their progress as they work toward a variety of goals.

Name

Journal cover: Make this page the front cover of your students' writing journals.

Materials to Collect:

To Do:

♥ ____________________

♥ ____________________

♥ ____________________

♥ ____________________

♥ ____________________

♥ ____________________

♥ ____________________

♥ ____________________

♥ ____________________

♥ ____________________

♥ ____________________

♥ ____________________

Duties This Month:

Themes:

Meetings:

Birthdays & Special Dates:

Monthly planning form: Use this handy form to stay on top of February's school-related responsibilities.

Open: Use this page for parent correspondence and use it with students too. For example, ask each child to create a list of words that he would like to appear on candy hearts. Or give each child candy hearts to show addition or subtraction problems, using the page as a workmat.

date

Dear Parent,

Please remember

Parent reminder note: Use this note to remind parents of supply requests, field trips, and special events such as a classroom party, a school program, or a guest speaker.

SCHOOL NOTE

SCHOOL NOTE

School notes: Use these notes for parent communications such as announcing an upcoming event, requesting supplies or volunteers, and writing messages of praise.

Family Fun

This personalized project gives your child a chance to showcase his or her family. Have your child cut out the heart. Help your child write his or her name and the names of family members on one side of the heart. Then have your child decorate the other side of the heart using stickers, crayons, markers, or small pieces of construction paper or gift wrap.

We hope to see your completed project by ______________.

Sincerely,

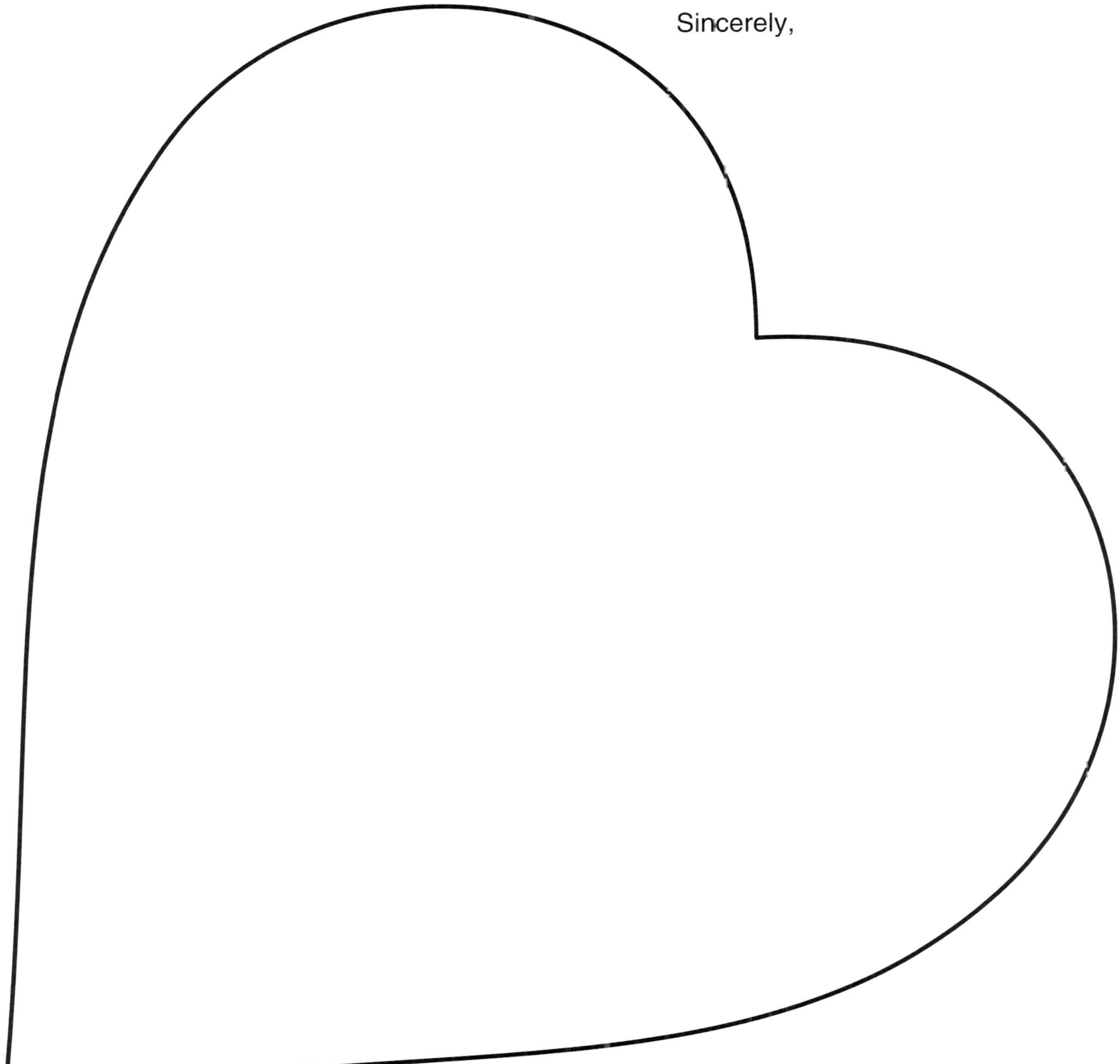

Learning Links: fine-motor skills, writing

Note to the teacher: Date and sign a copy of the page. Then make student copies on red or pink construction paper. When a child returns her project, invite her to share her heart with the class. Then bind the hearts together behind a tagboard heart titled "We Love Our Families."

Groundhog Day

No matter what type of weather the groundhog predicts on February 2, these ideas are sure to brighten your classroom!

Literacy • • • • • • • • • • • • • • • *Positional words*

Where's the Groundhog?

Have each child color and cut out a copy of the groundhog pattern on page 19. Then have her place it in a brown paper lunch bag that she has rolled down to make a hole. Announce a positional word and use the word in a sentence relating to the hole, such as "The groundhog jumped *over* his hole." Have youngsters manipulate their groundhogs to show the position. For more advanced students, place positional word cards at a center and encourage youngsters to read the words, and then use their groundhogs to show the position.

Graphing • • • • • • • • • • • • • • • • • • • Math

Shadow Seekers

Prior to February 2, ask students to predict whether or not the groundhog will see its shadow. Have each child color a copy of the recording sheet on page 19. If a student predicts that the groundhog will see its shadow, have him glue the sun where indicated and draw the groundhog's shadow. If he predicts that the groundhog will not see its shadow, instruct him to glue the cloud where indicated. Display the completed recording sheets to make a two-column graph. Have youngsters make observations of the graph results. When the big day arrives, revisit the graph to check students' predictions.

Find reproducible activities on pages 20–21.

Use with "Where's the Groundhog?" on page 18.

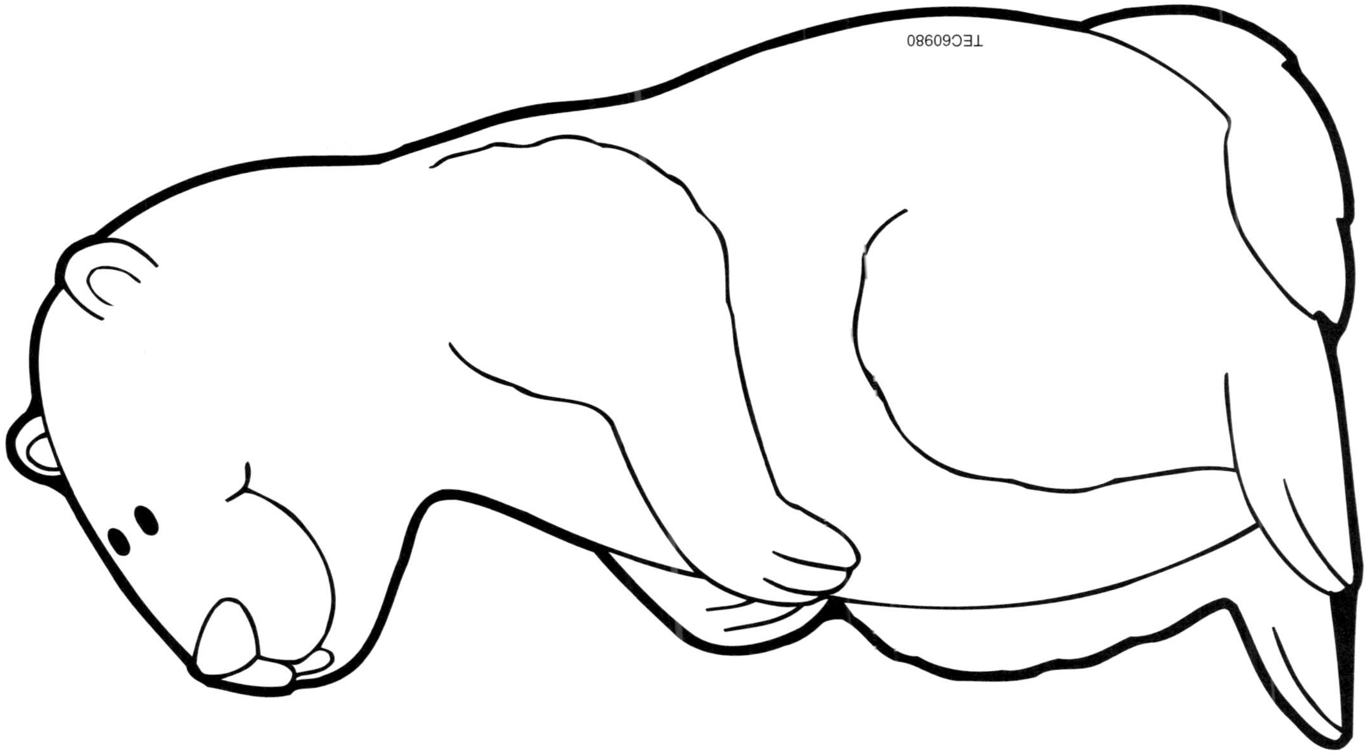

Recording Sheet

Use with "Shadow Seekers" on page 18.

Gus the Groundhog

Name ________________________________

Cut.

Glue to match the vowel sounds.

ā 		
ō 		
ī 		
ē 		

Use the word bank to complete each sentence.

1. Gus's favorite flower is a ________ .
2. Gus sleeps at ________ .
3. Gus watches ________ fall from the sky.
4. Gus listens to the ________ buzz.
5. A ________ gives Gus shade from the sun.

Long Vowels

What's the Weather?

Name ______________________________

Cut.

Glue to complete the pattern.

Valentine's Day

Literacy • • • • • • • • • • • • • • Word formation

Just Buggy!

The lovebugs in this activity provide your class with a unique spelling reference! Assign each child a different sight word or spelling word. Instruct her to write each letter of the word on a different heart cutout and then mix up the letters. To make a lovebug, have her decorate another heart to resemble a bug's face and add pipe cleaner antennae. Next, instruct her to glue the hearts on a tagboard strip, as shown, to spell the word. Display the lovebugs within students' view.

Ordering numbers • • • • • • • • • • • • • • Math

Which Order?

This center provides practice with ordering numbers from least to greatest and greatest to least! Copy the spinner pattern on page 27 onto tagboard; then use a brad to attach a large paper clip. Also, program a supply of blank cards, with each card having a different number. Store the cards in a resealable plastic bag. Place the bag, the spinner, and a supply of recording sheets (page 27) at a center.

When a child visits the center, he removes three number cards from the bag, spins the spinner, and orders the numbers as indicated. Then he writes the numbers in the appropriate section of the recording sheet and returns the cards to the bag. He repeats the activity to complete each side of the recording sheet or as time allows.

Youngsters are sure to develop a love for literacy and math when you use the following heartfelt ideas!

Math

Estimation

Full of Cookies

Just how many valentine cookies will fit on a cookie sheet? Invite youngsters to help find out! Give each child a few small construction paper hearts (all equal in size) so that there are more than enough total hearts to cover a cookie sheet. Invite each youngster to decorate his hearts to resemble valentine cookies.

Next, present a cookie sheet to the class. Ask each youngster to estimate how many cookies will fit on the cookie sheet without overlapping. Direct him to write his prediction on a copy of the estimation strip on page 28. Then have students bring their cookies to the large-group area, help cover the sheet with cookies, and count the total amount. Have each child return to his seat and complete his estimation strip by writing the actual amount and circling the correct phrase. If desired, help students categorize their estimates on a chart.

Literacy

Rhymes

Candy Box Memory

This partner center looks good enough to eat! Program 12 three-inch cupcake liners with different rhyming pairs. Glue the liners to a large poster board heart to create a candy box. Then set a large brown pom-pom (candy) in each liner and place the candy box at a center. To play, a student removes two candies from the box and reads the words aloud. If the words rhyme, she keeps the candies and takes another turn. If they do not rhyme, she returns the candies and it becomes her partner's turn. Play continues until all rhymes have been matched.

Literacy • • • Writing

Kindness Counts!

Cut a large heart from bulletin board paper and place it on a table along with markers. Invite a few students at a time to gather around the heart, and have each child write a kind message. After each youngster has posted a message, invite each student, in turn, to toss a counter onto the heart and point to the message that is closest to the counter. Have the youngster who wrote the message read it aloud to the other students.

Counting • • • Math

Matchmakers

For this whole-group activity, cut out a class supply of construction paper hearts. Program half of the hearts with different grade-appropriate numbers and the other half with corresponding numbers of dots. (If you have an odd number of students, include yourself in the count.) Randomly distribute the cutouts. Instruct the students with numbered hearts to line up side by side, holding their hearts with the numbers facing out. Then direct the other youngsters to count the dots on their hearts and then go stand next to the student holding the matching number. After all students are paired, collect the hearts and redistribute them for another round of play!

Fact families • • • • • • • • • • • • • • • • Math

House of Love

Have each child trim the top corners off a sheet of construction paper and decorate it to resemble a house. Then direct him to glue on three small heart cutouts that you have programmed with the numbers in a chosen fact family. After the glue is dry, collect students' houses and then redistribute them, giving each youngster a different house. Have him label a sheet of paper with the three numbers on his house and then write the corresponding facts. If desired, place the houses at a center for independent practice.

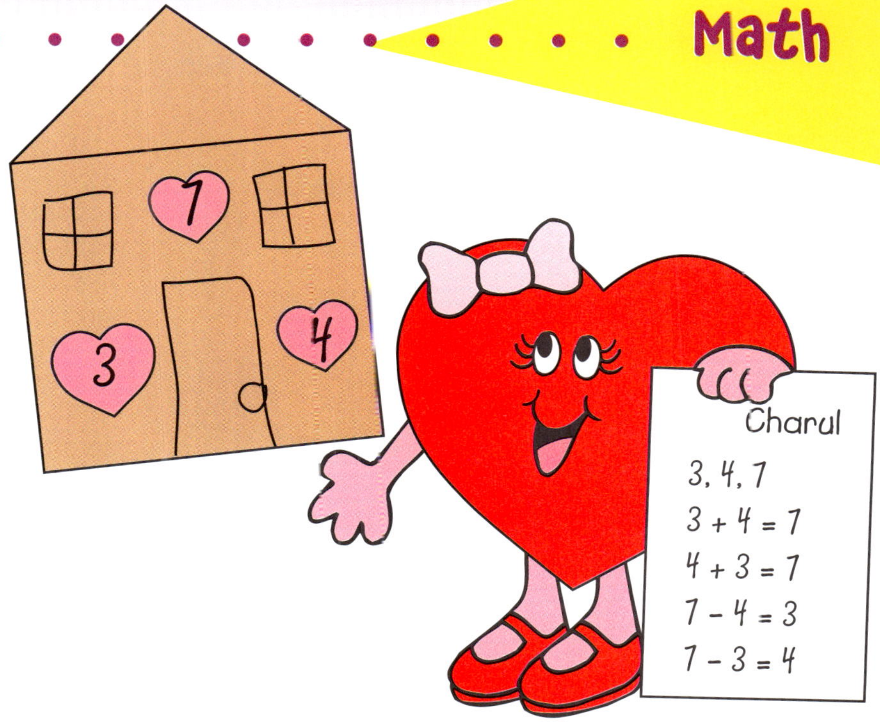

Literacy • • • • • • • • • • • • • • • • Blends with l

Sweet Sorting

For this taste-tempting center, obtain three empty heart-shaped candy boxes with lids or prepare three poster board heart cutouts. Label the lid of each box (or the bottom of each cutout) with a different blend: *fl, gl,* or *cl.* Color and cut out a copy of the picture cards on page 28; then store the cards in a container. At a center, place the container and candy boxes with each lid propped up behind its matching box. When a youngster visits the center, she removes a card, names the picture, and places it in the appropriate box. She continues in this manner for the remaining cards.

Math

Coin combinations

Valentines for Sale!

Put old valentine cards to use with this small-group activity! Mount a supply of valentine cards on separate pieces of construction paper. Then label each paper with a different number and a different grade-appropriate price. Gather a small group of students around the cards. Give each child an assortment of real or imitation coins and a copy of the recording sheet on page 29.

To begin, ask each child to take a card and count out coins that equal the corresponding price. After checking his work, have him write the information on his recording sheet and color the cards and coins if desired. Then invite him to "buy" more cards in this manner to complete his sheet.

Skill review

Literacy & Math

Special Delivery

This versatile center delivers a unique way for youngsters to practice just about any sorting skill! Prepare three shoeboxes by covering them with colorful paper and cutting slots in the lids to resemble mailboxes. Program the mailboxes and a supply of heart cutouts with a corresponding sorting skill. Consider sorting by sums, word families, rhymes, vowels, initial consonants, ending punctuation, or coin combinations. A child sorts the hearts into the mailboxes according to the chosen skill.

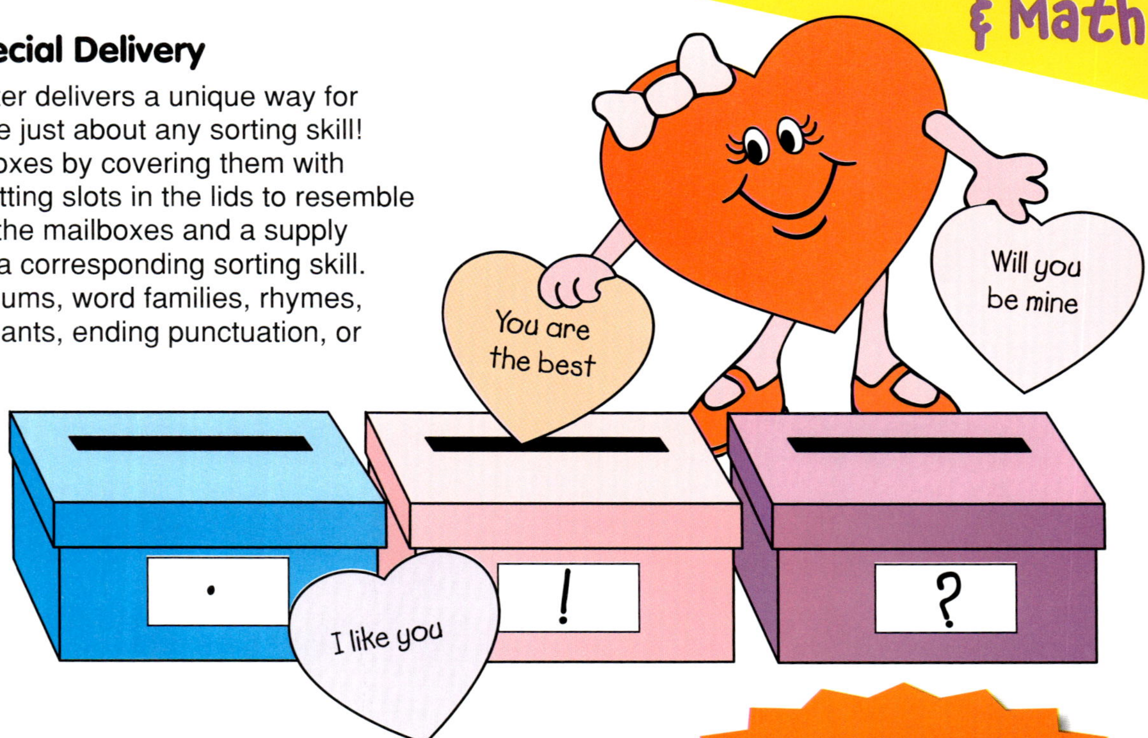

Find reproducible activities on pages 30–33.

Spinner Pattern

Use with "Which Order?" on page 22.

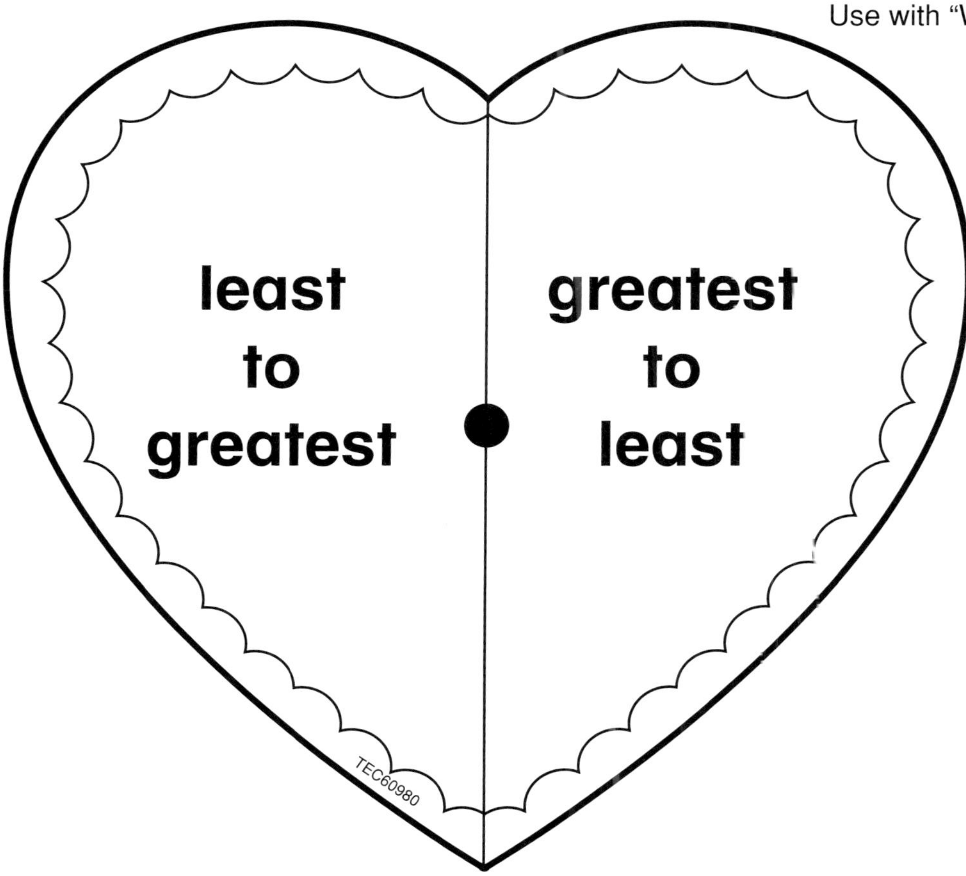

Name ____

All in Order

Least to Greatest	Greatest to Least
A. ______, ______, ______	A. ______, ______, ______
B. ______, ______, ______	B. ______, ______, ______
C. ______, ______, ______	C. ______, ______, ______
D. ______, ______, ______	D. ______, ______, ______
E. ______, ______, ______	E. ______, ______, ______

Note to the teacher: Use with "Which Order?" on page 22.

Estimation Strip

Use with “Full of Cookies” on page 23.

How many valentine cookies will fit on a cookie sheet?

My guess is ______ cookies.

There are ______ cookies.

My guess was **less than** **greater than** **the same as** the actual amount.

Picture Cards

Use with “Sweet Sorting” on page 25.

Be Mine

Name ______________________________

Valentine Card Number	Price	Coins
____		
____		
____		
____		

Note to the teacher: Use with "Valentines for Sale!" on page 26.

Valentine Mail

Name ______________________________

Name each picture.

Write the ending letter.

we _____

lea _____

dru _____

cra _____

broo _____

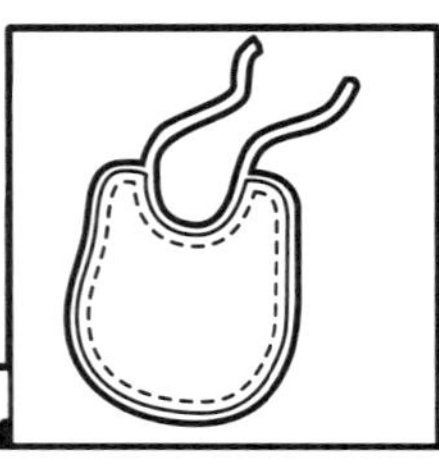

bi _____

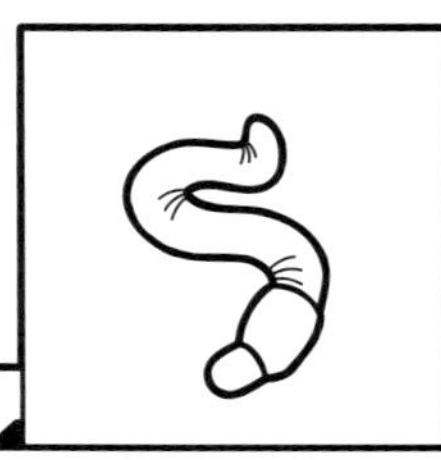

wor _____

el _____

Hogs and Kisses

Name ____

Write each group of words in ABC order.

1. ________________ 1. ________________

2. ________________ 2. ________________

3. ________________ 3. ________________

1. ________________ 1. ________________

2. ________________ 2. ________________

3. ________________ 3. ________________

Lovebugs

Name ______________________________

Color the coins by the code.

Cut. Glue to match.

Color Code
1¢ — red
5¢ — yellow
10¢ — purple
25¢ — orange

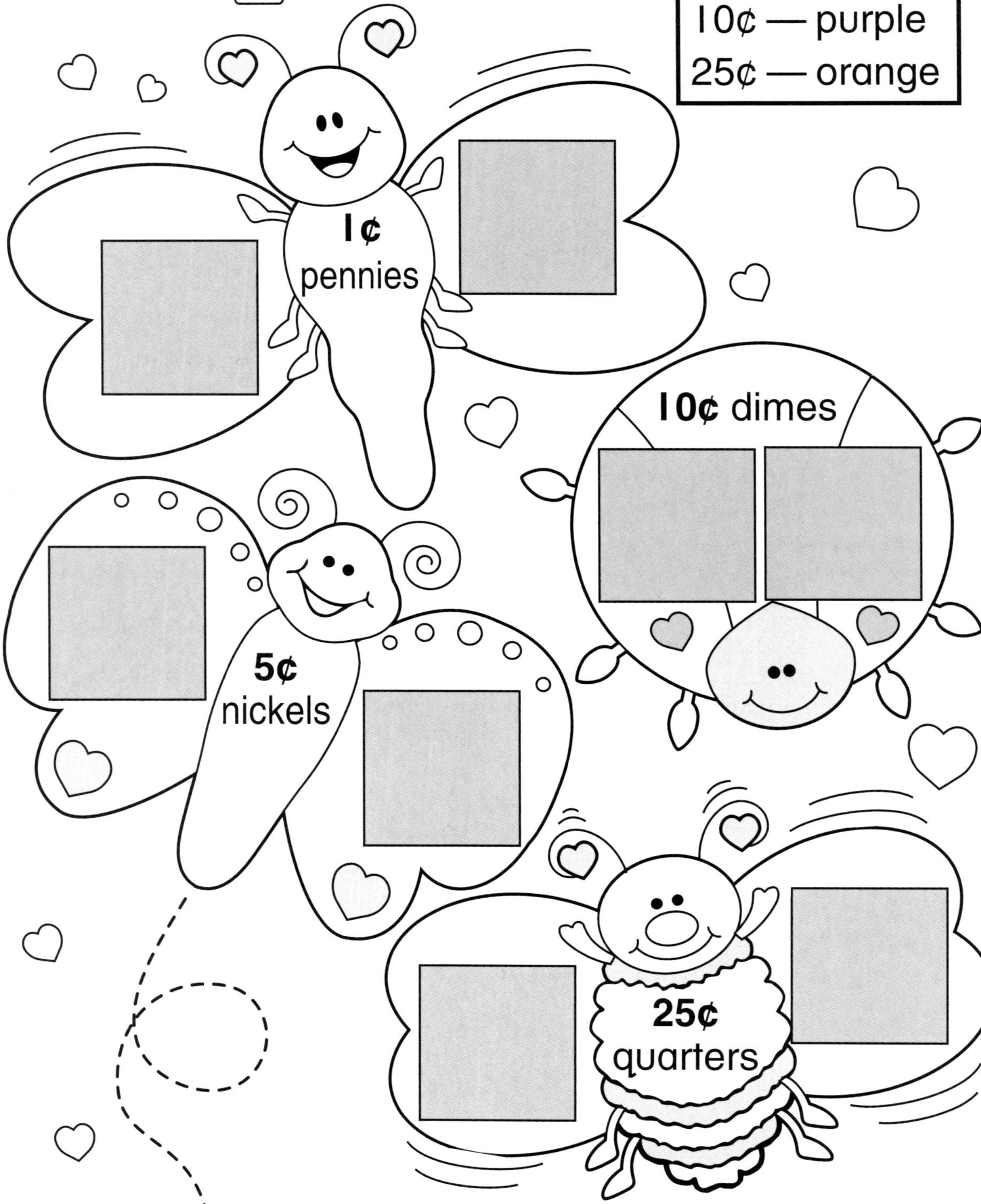

Goody Bag

Name ______________________________

Write each amount.

Cut. Glue to match the amounts.

______¢

______¢

______¢

______¢

______¢

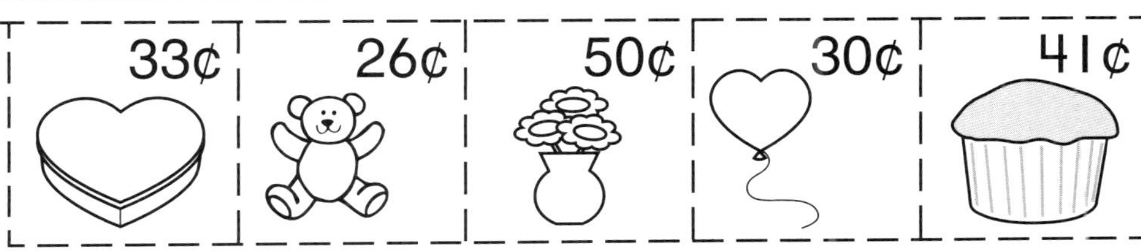

Presidents' Day

Math

Addition and subtraction

In the Hat

Pull math facts practice out of a stovepipe hat! Abraham Lincoln, who had a habit of tucking important papers inside his hat, would certainly approve! To prepare this center, create two stovepipe hats by covering two oatmeal containers (or other cylindrical containers) with black paper and taping the bottom of each container to a separate black poster board circle. Label one hat "Correct" and the other hat "Incorrect." Also program each of several cards with either a different correct or incorrect math fact. Label the back of each card for self-checking. Place the cards and the hats at a center. When a child visits the center, she chooses a card, checks the sum or difference, and then places the card in the appropriate hat. She continues in this manner for each of the remaining cards. She then removes each card and flips it over to verify her work.

Social Studies

Presidential facts

Who Was the President?

Presidents' Day was originally designated to observe the birthdays of George Washington and Abraham Lincoln, but now it is a day to recognize all presidents. Use the presidential facts on page 35 to introduce youngsters to other former presidents. Then lead students in the song shown, inserting substitutions as desired.

(sung to the tune of "London Bridge")

Who was our [first] president, president, president?
Who was our [first] president? Do you know?
[George Washington] was the [first] president, president, president.
[George Washington] was the [first] president.
This I now know!

The third Monday in February is a day to commemorate all presidents. Elect to use the following skill-based ideas and you are sure to earn youngsters' seal of approval!

Capitalization • • • • • • • • • • • • • • • **Literacy**

Happy Birthday, Mr. President

Use this center as a follow-up to a review of capitalization rules. To prepare, use the Presidential facts on this page as a reference to program six paper strips with presidents' names and birthdays, omitting all capitalization. Also color, cut out, and laminate a copy of the birthday cake pattern on page 38. Place the cake, the programmed strips, and a wipe-off marker at a center. When a child visits the center, he chooses a strip and uses proper capitalization to write the president's name on the first line of the cake and the president's birthday on the second line. He then wipes the cake clean and continues in this manner with the remaining strips.

Presidential Facts

George Washington—1st president; born February 22, 1732
Thomas Jefferson—3rd president; born April 13, 1743
Abraham Lincoln—16th president; born February 12, 1809
Ulysses S. Grant—18th president; born April 27, 1822
Theodore Roosevelt—26th president; born October 27, 1858
John F. Kennedy—35th president; born May 29, 1917

Math • • • • • • • • • • • • • • • *Coin identification*

Presidential Race

For each child, cut out a construction paper copy of the spinner on page 38. Secure a large paper clip to the spinner with a brad as shown. To begin, explain to students that the United States honors some of the most admired presidents by putting their images on coins. Give each youngster a real or imitation penny, nickel, dime, and quarter to examine. Also give each child a prepared spinner and a copy of the gameboard on page 39.

To play, a child places the appropriate coin at the beginning of each row, spins, and moves the corresponding coin one space in its row. She continues in this manner until one coin reaches the finish line. After all students finish their games, invite youngsters to compare which presidents won their races!

Literacy • • • • • • • • • • • • • • • • *Writing*

Truthful Tales

According to legend, young George Washington was so honest that he admitted to cutting down one of his father's beloved cherry trees. (This legend was actually fabricated by a writer to showcase Washington's honesty.) Encourage each youngster to think about a time when she was honest, even when it may have been difficult to tell the truth. Help her write about an honest experience on a round sheet of paper. Then staple the paper between two slightly larger red construction paper circles. Direct each youngster to glue on a construction paper stem and label the front cover like the one shown. Post the cherries on a large paper tree for all to see!

Nonstandard measurement • • • • • • • • • • • • Math

How Tall?

At six feet four inches, Abraham Lincoln was the tallest president of the United States of America! Help youngsters understand just how tall Lincoln was with this small-group activity. For each group of students, cut a length of adding machine tape or bulletin board paper to measure six feet four inches. Tape each length to the floor. Give each group a different set of nonstandard measurement tools, such as markers, unsharpened pencils, glue sticks, or craft sticks. Have each group use its objects to measure Lincoln's height and write the result on its strip. After each group completes the activity, invite youngsters to share their results and discuss why different groups obtained different measurements.

Compare numbers • • • • • • • • • • • • • • • Math

Cherry Comparing

This partner center is inspired by the legend of George Washington cutting down his father's cherry tree. Place two construction paper tree cutouts at a center along with a supply of red pom-poms or counters (cherries) and two dice. When a twosome visits the center, each player takes a turn rolling the dice and placing the corresponding number of cherries on her tree. Then students compare their numbers using terms such as *greater than, less than,* or *equal to.* Players continue in this manner as time allows. For more advanced students, program each of three cards with a different comparison symbol (<, >, or =) and have students use the cards to show the numbers' relationship.

Literacy • • • • • • • • • • • • Reading motivation

Get Into Books!

Nurture your youngsters' love of reading with this bookmark-making project. Tell students that Abraham Lincoln was known to say, "The things I want to know are in books." Give each child a 2" x 9" tagboard strip and a three-inch black construction paper square. Help him trim the square into the shape of a stovepipe hat and glue it to one end of the strip. Then direct him to draw Lincoln's face and body. Encourage each child to read a favorite book with his bookmark buddy, Abe!

Find reproducible activities on pages 40–41.

Cake Pattern

Use with "Happy Birthday, Mr. President" on page 35.

Spinner Pattern

Use with "Presidential Race" on page 35.

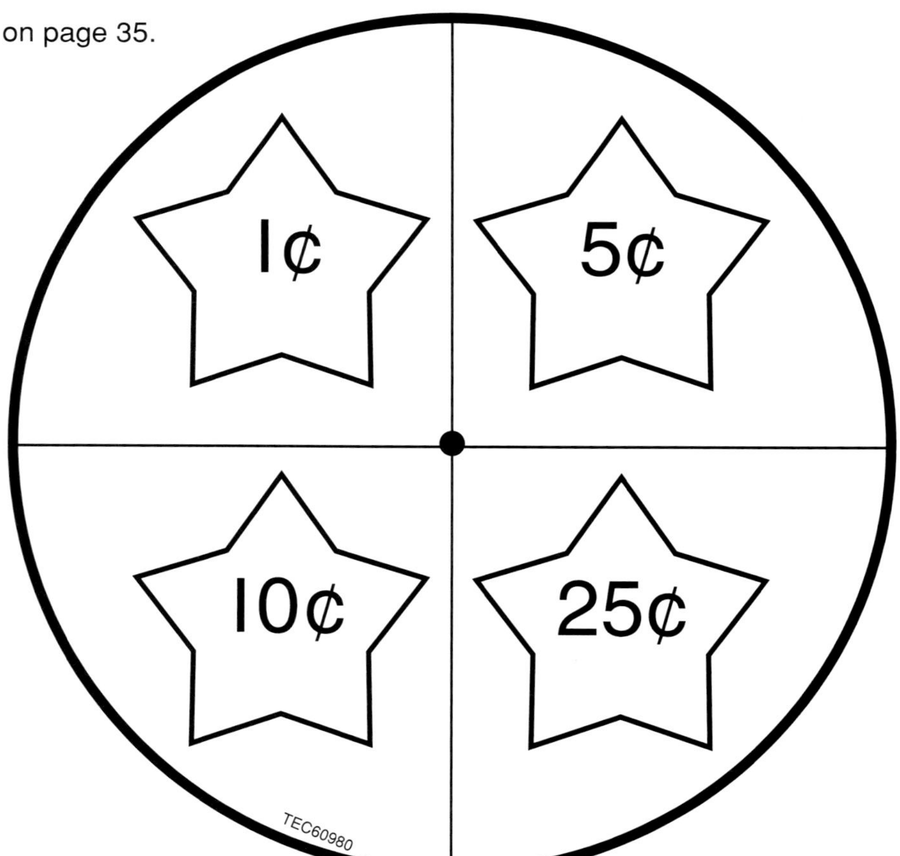

Presidential Race

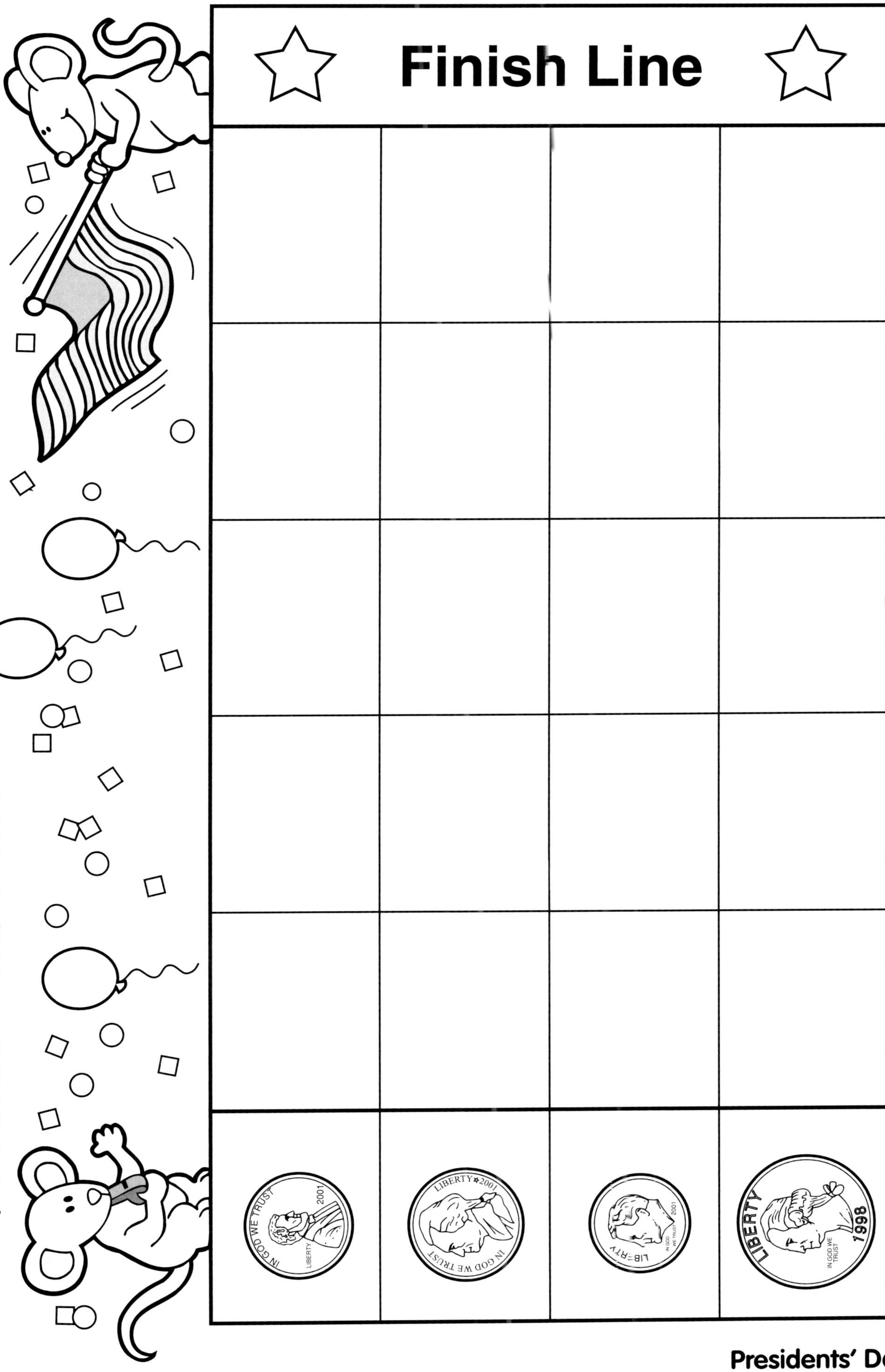

Note to the teacher: Use with "Presidential Race" on page 35.

Lincoln's Letter Logs

Name ______________________

Write the matching uppercase letter.

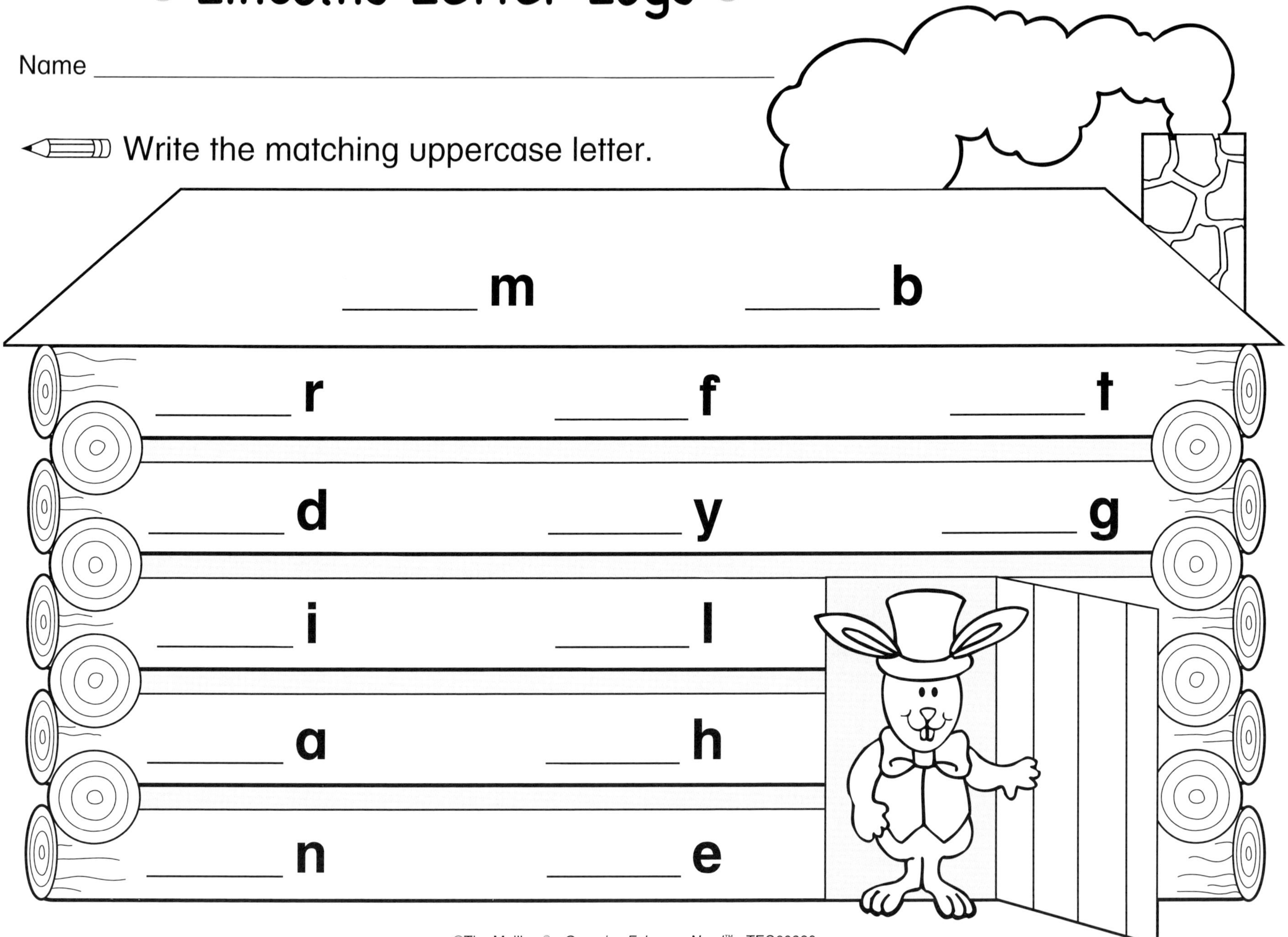

Presidential Celebration

Name ____________________

Subtract.

Color by the code.

Color Code

4 or 5—blue 6 or 7—red

$8 - 4$	$12 - 6$	$10 - 5$	$12 - 5$
$9 - 3$	$10 - 3$	$12 - 8$	$9 - 4$
$12 - 7$	$11 - 7$	$9 - 2$	$11 - 5$

Dental Health

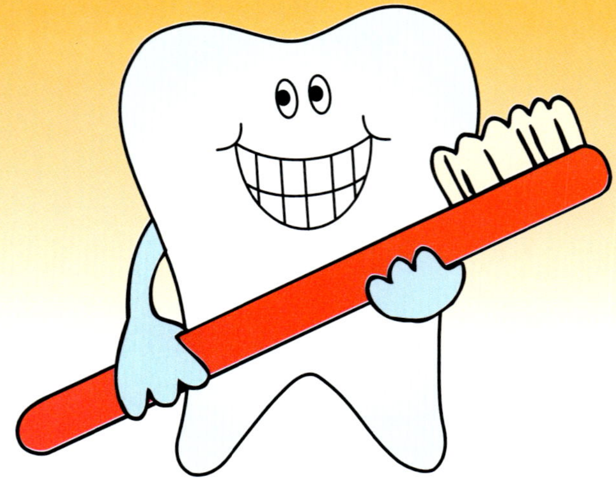

Literacy · Beginning sounds

Under the Pillow

At this center, it's the children who get to be the tooth fairies! Cut a few large pillow shapes from white paper. Program each one with a different letter; then tape the top edge of each pillow (so it can be lifted) to a length of colorful bulletin board paper. Also cut from magazines pictures of items that begin with the chosen letters. Place the pictures and the prepared paper at a center. A child sorts the pictures and places each one under the corresponding pillow. She continues in this manner as time allows.

Health · Healthy dental habits

The Dentist Says...

This little ditty is sure to remind students of good dental care. Sing the song several times, spotlighting a different positive dental health habit in each rendition (see suggestions below).

(sung to the tune of "The Mulberry Bush")

The dentist says, "Please [brush your teeth],
[Brush your teeth, brush your teeth].
The dentist says, "Please [brush your teeth]
Each and every day!"

Other suggestions: *floss your teeth, eat good foods*

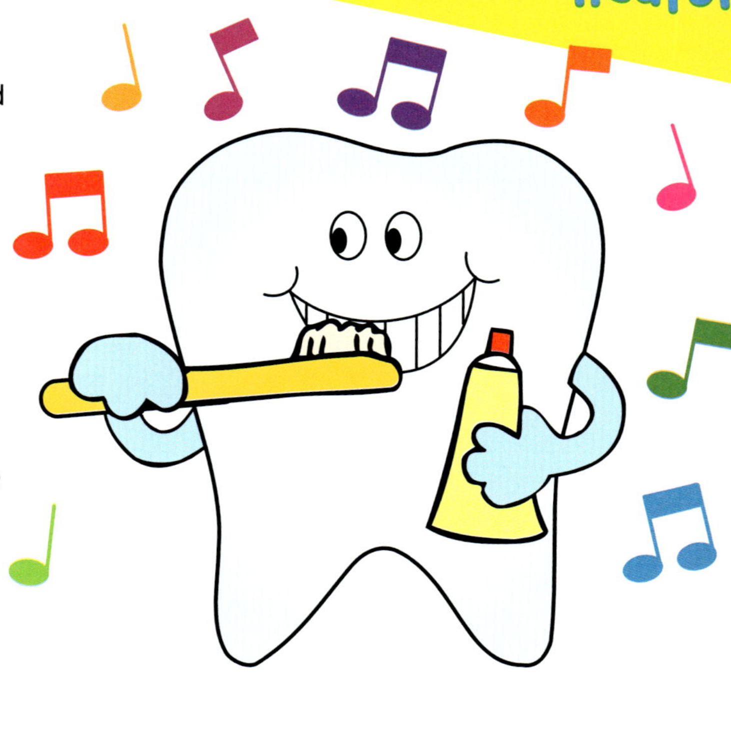

Sink your teeth into ideas that allow students to brush up on literacy and math skills!

Math

Comparing lengths

Brushing Up!

For this small-group activity, obtain five identical toothbrushes. (Consider asking a local dentist for donations.) Also gather a few objects that are longer than the toothbrushes and a few objects that are shorter. Model for youngsters how to use the toothbrushes to measure an item in the collection. Then, as a group, divide the objects into two categories: longer than or shorter than the brushes. Next, give each child a toothbrush and have her search the room for two objects: one longer and one shorter than her toothbrush. Encourage youngsters to share their findings with the group; then write their responses on a chart similar to the one shown.

Toothbrush Measurement	
longer than	shorter than
book	pencil
shoe	crayon
ruler	block
water bottle	sticker
lunchbox	scissors

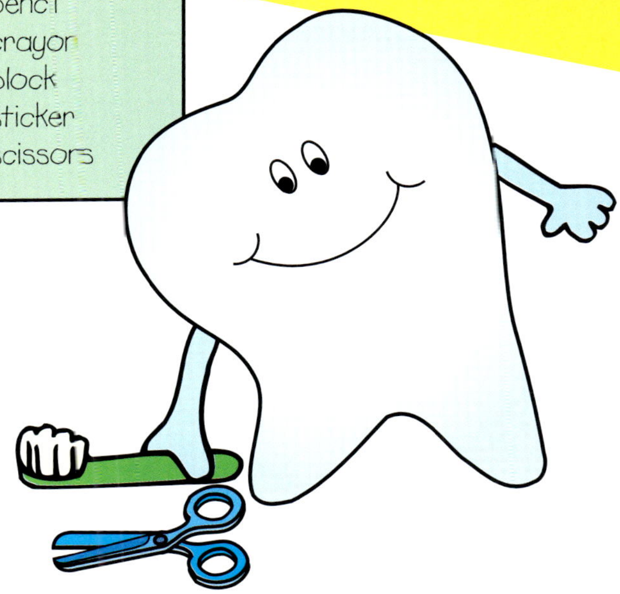

Literacy

Syllables

Brush to the Beat

Use dental-related words to help students brush up on phonological awareness. Color and cut out ten copies of the toothbrush pattern on page 46 and program each one with a word from the list shown. Also cut out two toothpaste swirls from construction paper and label them as shown. Place the toothpaste swirls in a pocket chart.

To begin, invite a student to choose a toothbrush and read the word aloud. Provide assistance as needed. Lead his classmates in repeating the word as they clap once for each part (syllable). Then ask the youngster to place the toothbrush in the corresponding column. Continue in this manner for each remaining toothbrush.

Word List
- tooth
- smile
- floss
- loose
- rinse
- toothbrush
- dentist
- filling
- fluoride
- mouthwash

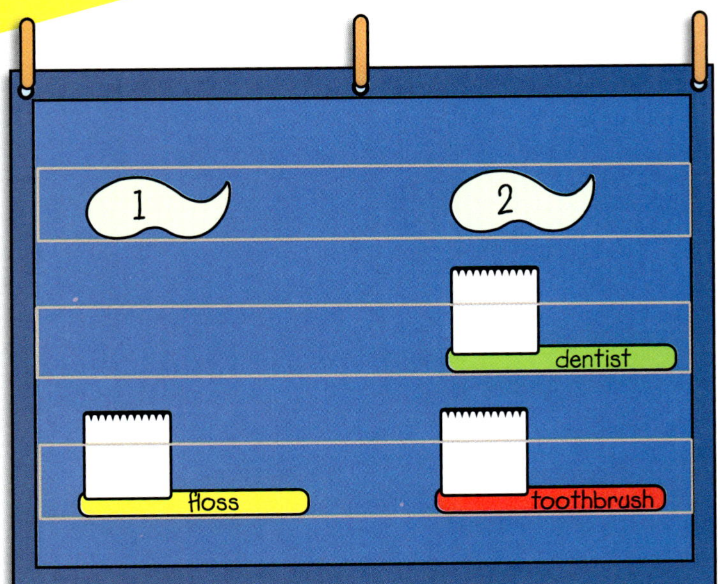

Literacy • • • Spelling

Cavity Capers

Youngsters help fix less-than-perfect teeth with this center activity! Cut out several white construction paper copies of the tooth patterns on page 46. Write a different spelling word on half of the teeth. On each of the remaining teeth, write a different misspelled word. Then flip over each tooth with a misspelled word and draw a black spot to indicate a cavity. Place the teeth at a center along with writing paper and pencils. A child reads the word on each tooth and then sorts the teeth into piles for correctly spelled words and misspelled words. He flips each tooth to check his work. Then, for each tooth that has a cavity, he writes the word correctly on a sheet of paper.

Building numbers • • • Math

And the Number Is…

For this small-group activity, cut out ten copies of the tooth patterns on page 46. Program each tooth with a different number from 0 to 9. Gather a small group of students and give each child two teeth. To begin the activity, have each student use her tooth cutouts to make the smallest (or largest) number possible. After each child has made a number, ask her to announce it to the group. If desired, challenge students to determine who in the group has the smallest (or largest) number. Then collect the teeth, mix them up, and redistribute them to play additional rounds.

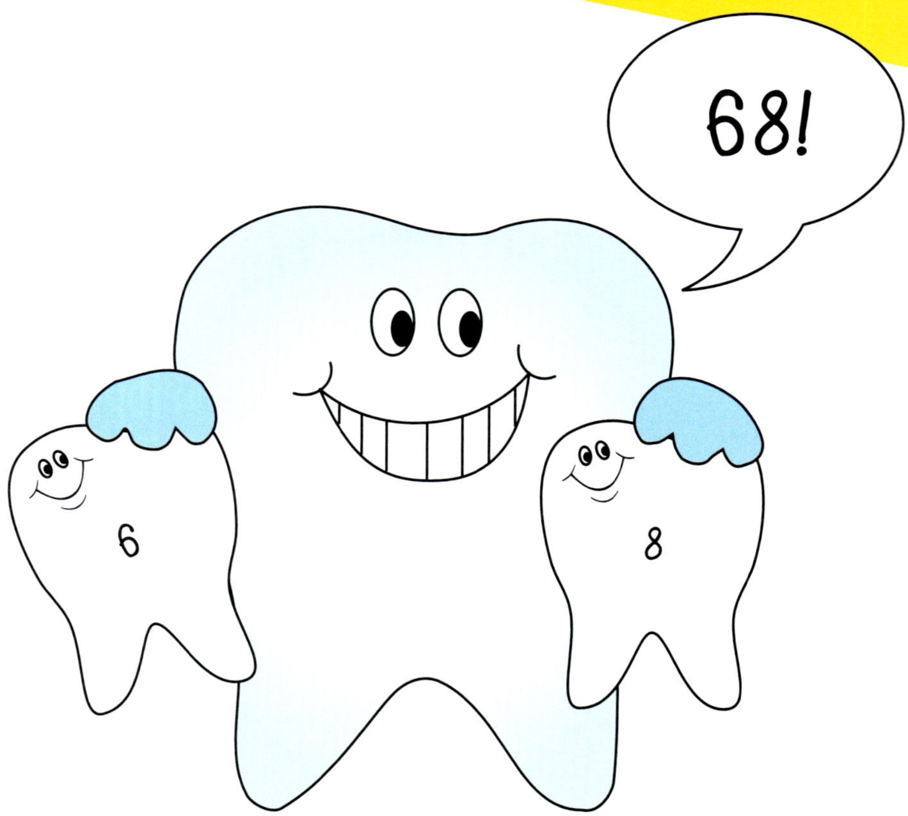

Word problems · · · · · · · · · · · · · · · **Math**

Mouthful of Math

Youngsters become little dentists when they solve the word problems in this small-group activity. For each child in the group, draw on a paper plate a smiley face with a large open mouth. Give each child a prepared plate and a supply of white ¾-inch paper strips to resemble teeth. Announce a word problem related to teeth, such as "Ethan has four teeth on top and three teeth on the bottom. How many teeth does he have in all?" or "Kaleigh had nine teeth. She lost two teeth. How many teeth does she have left?" Encourage each youngster to use her manipulatives to solve the problem. After several rounds, invite students to create dental health word problems for their group members to solve.

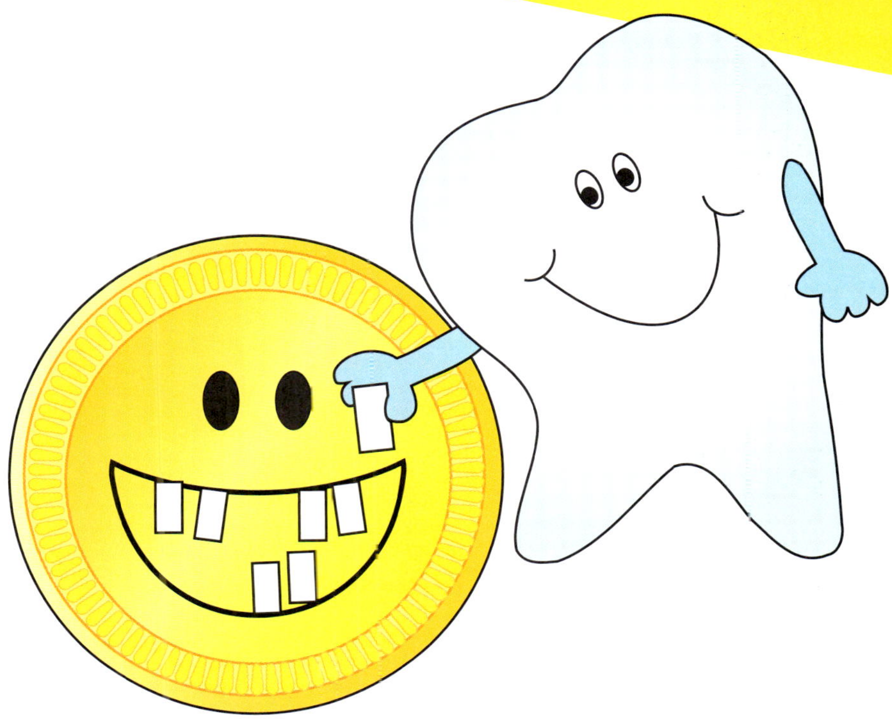

Health · · · · · · · · · · · · · · Healthy dental habits

Pearly Whites

Give each child a copy of the toothbrush pattern on page 46 and a copy of the booklet cover and pages on page 47. To make a booklet, a child colors the toothbrush and cuts it out. After writing his name on the booklet cover, he colors and cuts out each page. Next, he glues a short length of dental floss to page 2 and adds glue and glitter to the teeth on page 3. After the glue dries, help the child sequence the pages and staple them atop his toothbrush. Then read aloud the text as students follow along in their booklets.

Find reproducible activities on pages 48–49.

Toothbrush Pattern

Use with "Brush to the Beat" on page 43 and "Pearly Whites" on page 45.

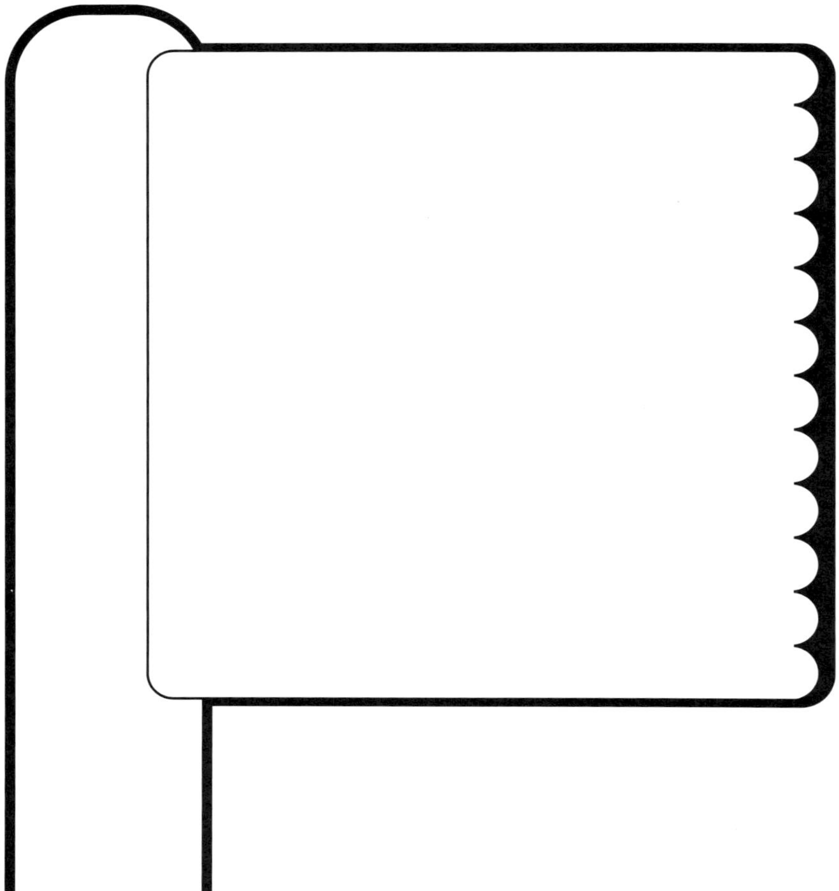

Tooth Patterns

Use with "Cavity Capers" and "And the Number Is…" on page 44.

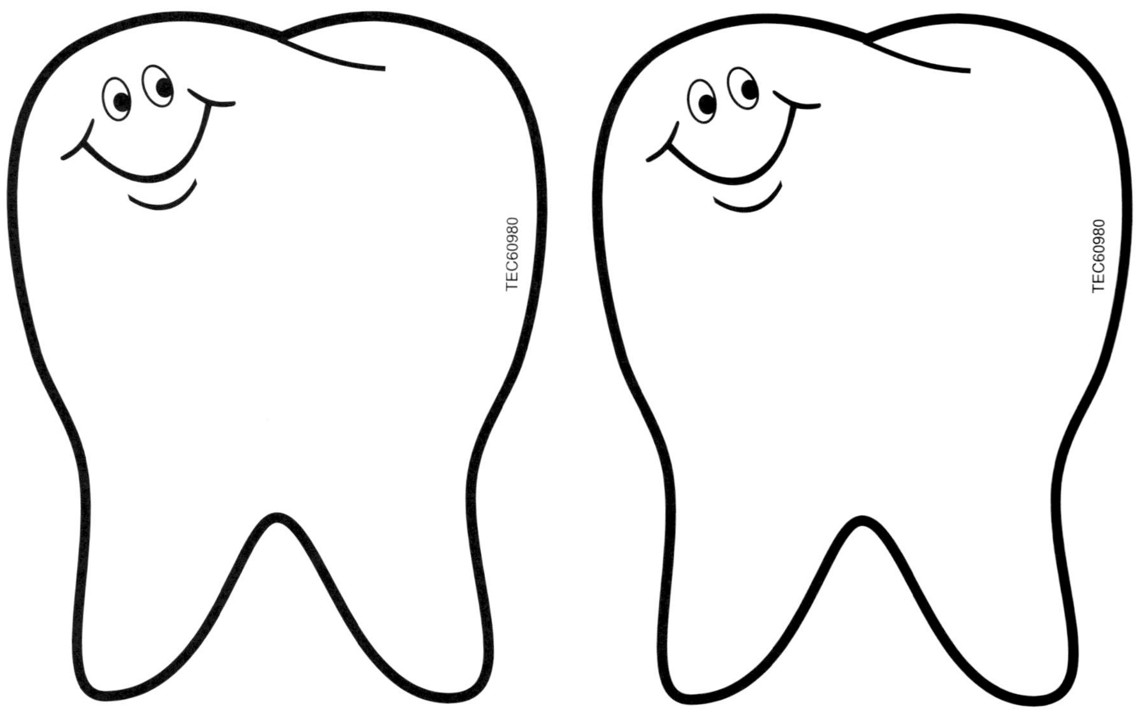

Use with “Pearly Whites” on page 45.

My Tooth Book

Name ____________________

Brush your teeth two times a day;

1

then rinse and floss

2

to keep cavities away!

3

Terrific Teeth

Name ____________________________________

Add or subtract.

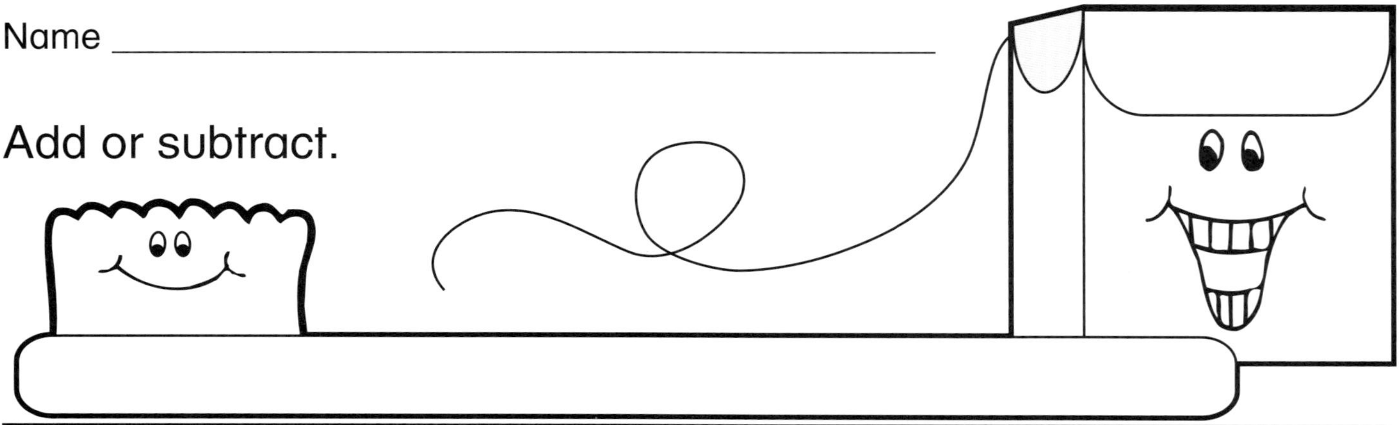

a.

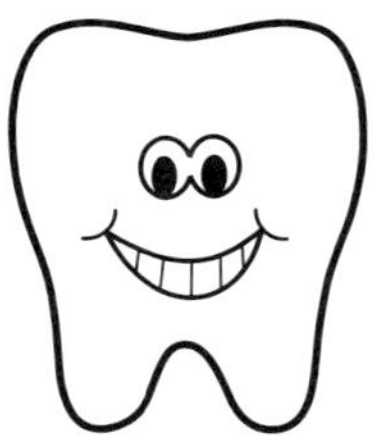

7 + 2 = ____

2 + 7 = ____

9 – 7 = ____

9 – 2 = ____

b.

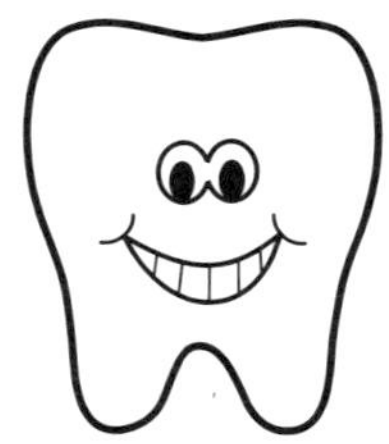

8 + 4 = ____

4 + 8 = ____

12 – 4 = ____

12 – 8 = ____

c.

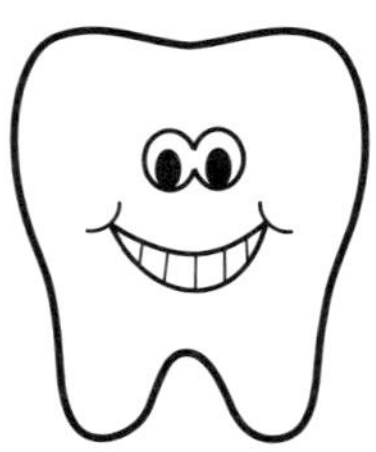

7 + 3 = ____

3 + 7 = ____

10 – 3 = ____

10 – 7 = ____

d.

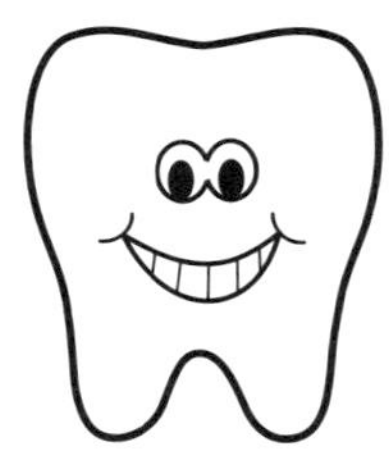

5 + 4 = ____

4 + 5 = ____

9 – 4 = ____

9 – 5 = ____

e.

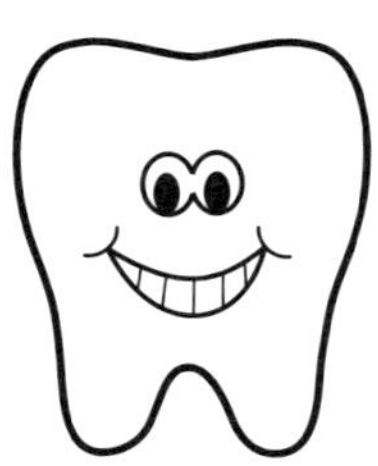

6 + 5 = ____

5 + 6 = ____

11 – 6 = ____

11 – 5 = ____

f.

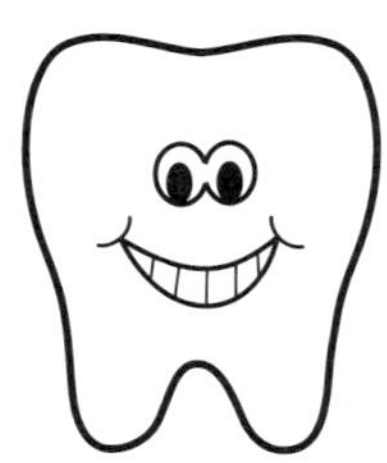

3 + 5 = ____

5 + 3 = ____

8 – 5 = ____

8 – 3 = ____

A Grinning Gator

Name ______________________________

Write the missing numbers.

8, 9, ___, 11, 12, 13, ___

2, ___, 4, 5, ___, ___, 8

15, ___, ___, 18, ___, 20

10, 11, ___, 13, ___, ___

5, ___, 7, ___, 9, ___, 11

Weather Forecast

After the groundhog has made its weather prediction on February 2, use this idea to create a unique groundhog project.

Materials for one project:
copy of page 52
4" cardboard tube
brown paper lunch bag
9" x 12" white construction paper
tape
scissors
glue
crayons
cotton ball (optional)

Steps:
1. Color and cut out the groundhog pattern and either the sun or cloud pattern (depending on the groundhog's prediction).
2. Position the white paper vertically and fold it in half from top to bottom. Unfold it.
3. Roll down the paper lunch bag and glue it to the bottom half of the paper to resemble a groundhog hole.
4. Fold the groundhog cutout where indicated, and glue the tab inside the bag.
5. If the groundhog saw its shadow, draw a wintry scene on the upper half of the paper. Glue the sun cutout to the scene; then draw the groundhog's shadow. If the groundhog did not see his shadow, draw a spring scene and glue the cloud cutout to it. (If desired, glue a cotton ball to the cloud.)
6. Tape the tube to the back of the top section of the paper to help it stand upright.

A Special Valentine

To make a valentine, twist two different-colored pipe cleaner halves together and then secure the ends to make a circle. Form the resulting ring into a heart shape. Write a valentine message on a half sheet of light-colored paper and then roll the paper into a scroll. Slip the scroll into the heart. This valentine is ready for delivery!

Handfuls of Love

This pretty pouch comes in handy for carrying valentines! To make one, cut out two identical hearts from 9" x 12" sheets of construction paper. Staple the hearts together along the sides. Then press your hands in red paint and print them on the pouch as shown. After the paint is dry, sign your name. Then hole-punch each side of the pouch and tie one end of a 24-inch length of yarn to each hole to make a hanger.

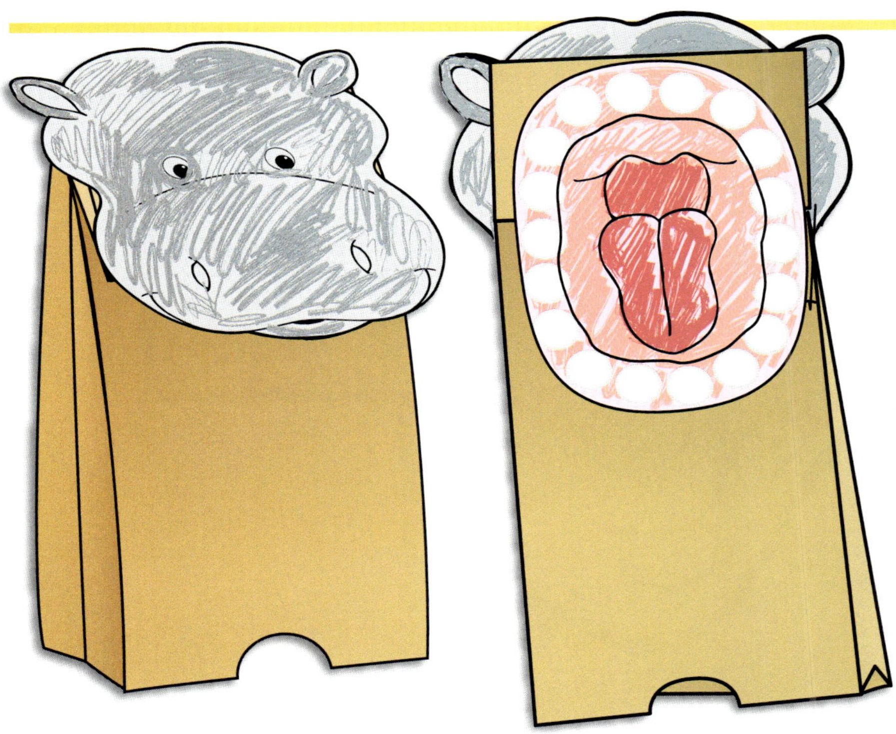

Open Wide!

This friendly hippo puppet is ready for a dental checkup! Color and cut out a copy of the hippo head and mouth patterns on page 53. Glue the head cutout to just the base of a folded paper lunch bag. Fold back the bottom half of the head and glue the mouth in place. Attach white sticky dots to the mouth to resemble teeth.

Groundhog, Sun, and Cloud Patterns

Use with “Weather Forecast” on page 50.

Use with "Open Wide!" on page 51.

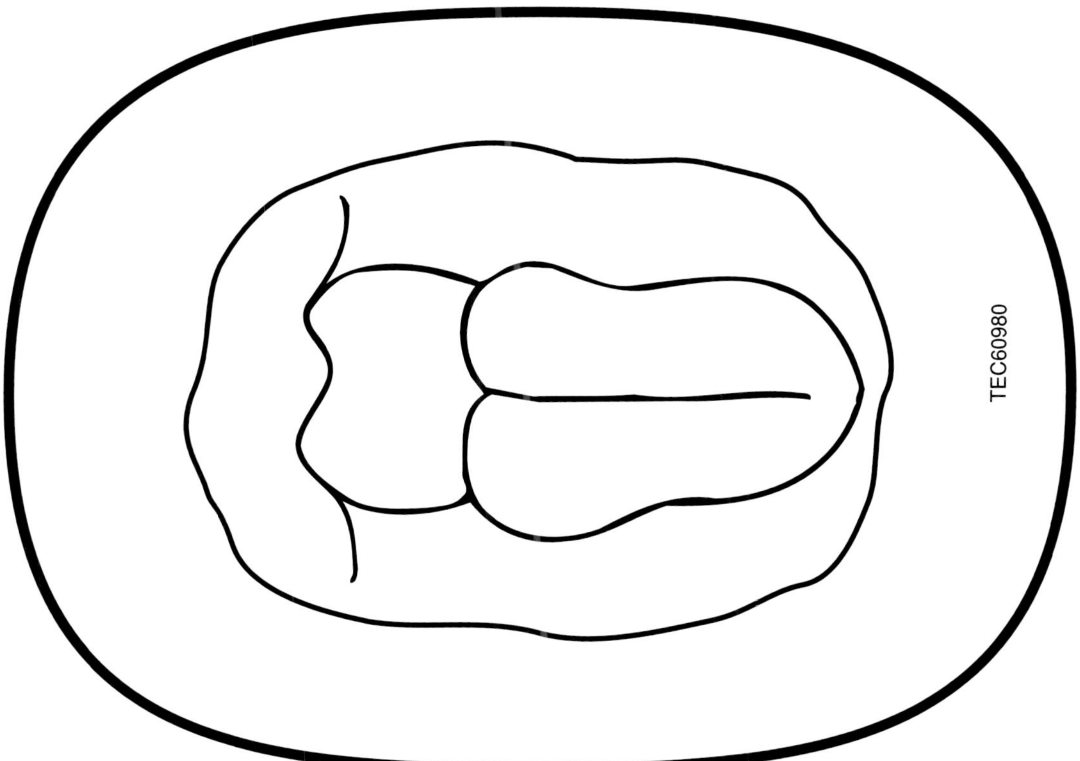

Bulletin Boards &

Mount on a bulletin board a large, animated cloud and a sunshine shape along with the title shown. Have each child personalize and cut out a copy of the groundhog pattern on page 56. Ask each student to predict whether the groundhog will see its shadow on Groundhog Day. Then help her complete the speech bubble (page 56) according to her prediction. Post each groundhog with its speech bubble under the appropriate weather symbol.

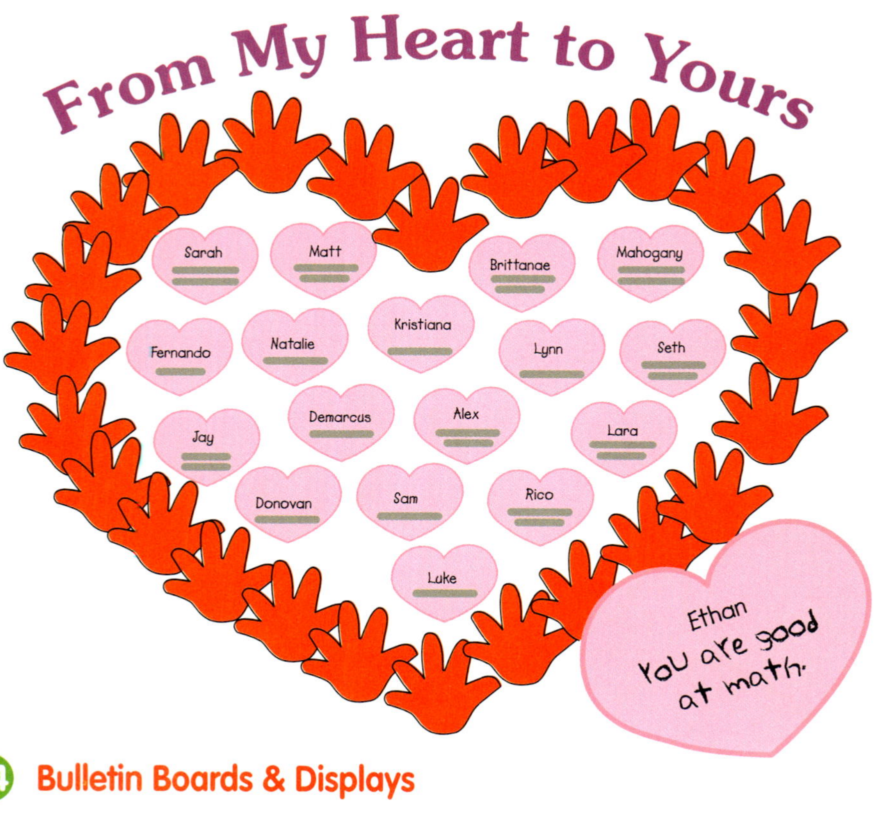

For each child, cut a heart from a four-inch pink construction paper square. Write each child's name on a different heart cutout. Randomly distribute the hearts and have each child write (or dictate) a heartfelt message to the named student. Display the hearts within a large heart formed from hand cutouts. Then help youngsters find their names and read their messages!

Displays

Have each child draw on a white construction paper oval a portrait of herself as president. If desired, show youngsters pictures of past presidents for inspiration. Then have her write on a paper strip her last name following the word *President*. Display the student portraits, name strips, and title shown.

To make a personalized candy cutout, have each child cut out a tagboard copy of the candy pattern on page 57, glue it to a sheet of aluminum foil, and trim off the excess foil. Next, direct him to glue on a paper strip programmed with "My Best Work!" and then write her name in glitter glue in the center of the candy. After the glue is dry, ask each student to choose a sample of her best work; then display each work sample with its matching candy and the title shown.

Use with “Groundhog Day Forecast” on page 54.

Candy Patterns

Use with "Sweet Success!" on page 55.

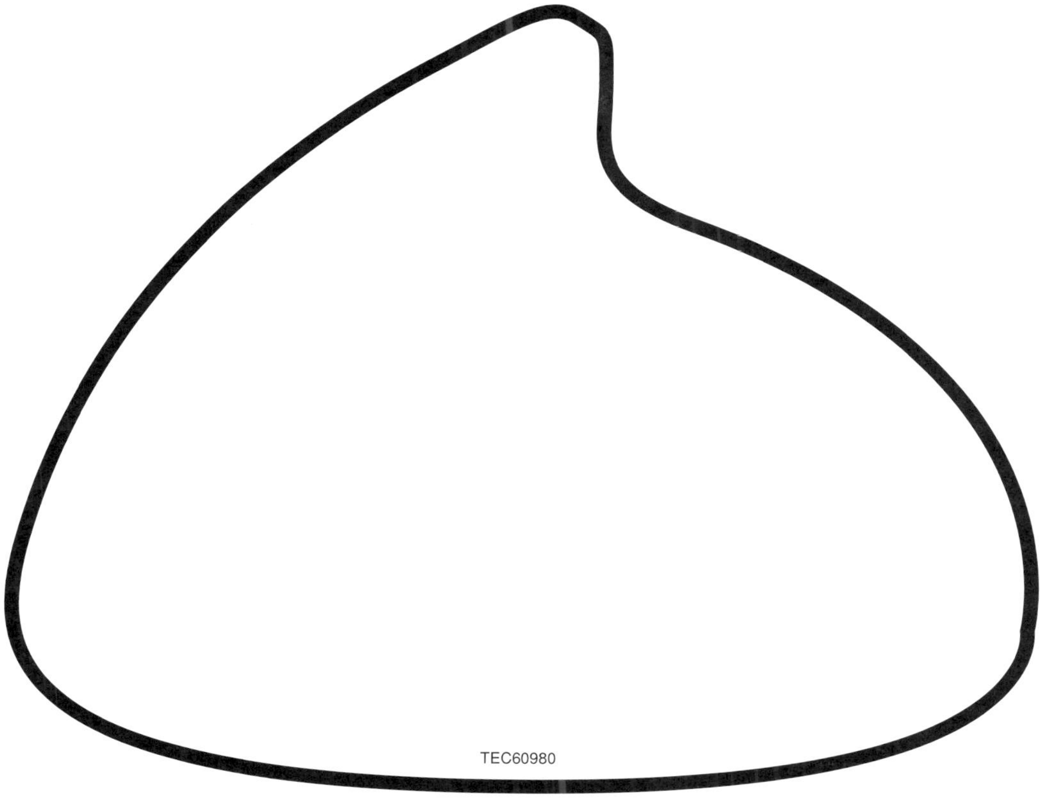

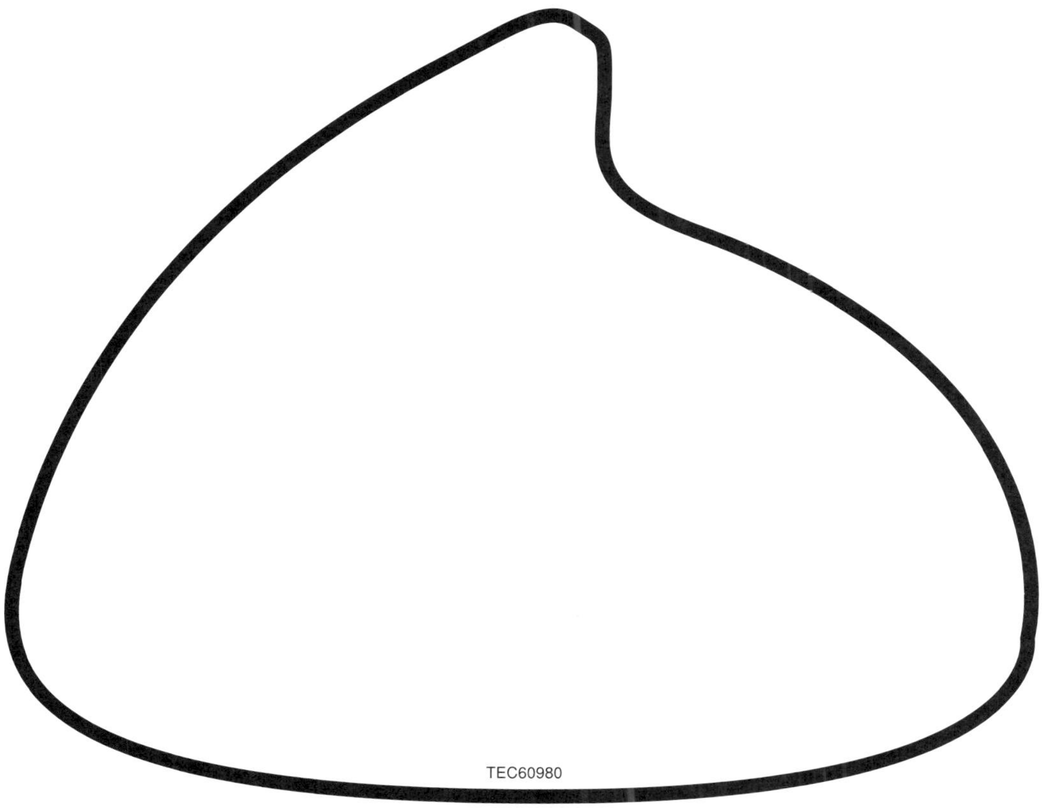

Centers

Math

Counting pennies

Toothy Treasures

To prepare, seal legal-size envelopes and cut them in half, forming pockets. On each envelope half, write a different value of up to 15¢ and add details to make the pocket resemble a pillow. For each pillow, program a tooth cutout (pattern on page 60) with a corresponding number of penny stamps or penny cutouts. Place the teeth and pillows at a center. A child chooses a tooth, counts the pennies on it, and places it in the pillow with the matching value. For more advanced students, program the pillows and teeth with values that include a variety of coins.

Literacy

Sight words

Roll and Read

For this partner center, draw a large heart on a sheet of paper and program it with ten grade-appropriate sight words. Then copy and cut out a heart gameboard for each child. Place at a center the gameboards, a die, and a supply of candy hearts or small heart cutouts to be used as game markers.

To play, a child rolls the die and reads the corresponding number of words on her gameboard. After her partner checks her reading, she places a game marker over each word read correctly. Play continues until each child has all of her words covered.

Literacy

Short and long vowels

Hearts in a Row

This heartfelt variation of tic-tac-toe allows for up to four students to play at a time! Program a 3" x 12" paper strip with one word for each short and long vowel (for a total of ten words). Make three more strips with the same words in a different order. Also, cut out a tagboard copy of the vowel cards on page 60. Stack the cards facedown at a center along with the word strips and a supply of small heart cutouts to be used as game markers.

To play, each center visitor takes a word strip. One player draws a vowel card and reads it aloud. Each player uses a game marker to cover the corresponding word on his word strip. Students take turns drawing cards and continue until a player covers three words in a row. Players then clear their boards and play again.

Math

Addition

Lovely Sums

Love is in the air at this partner center! To prepare, make a class supply of the gameboards on page 61 and place them at a center along with two large dice and crayons. When a twosome visits the center, Player 1 rolls the dice and determines the sum. Player 2 counts the total number of dots to verify the answer. Then Player 1 colors the corresponding heart on her gameboard. (If the sum rolled is already colored, then her turn is over.) Play continues in this manner until both players have all of their hearts colored.

Tooth Patterns

Use with “Toothy Treasures” on page 58.

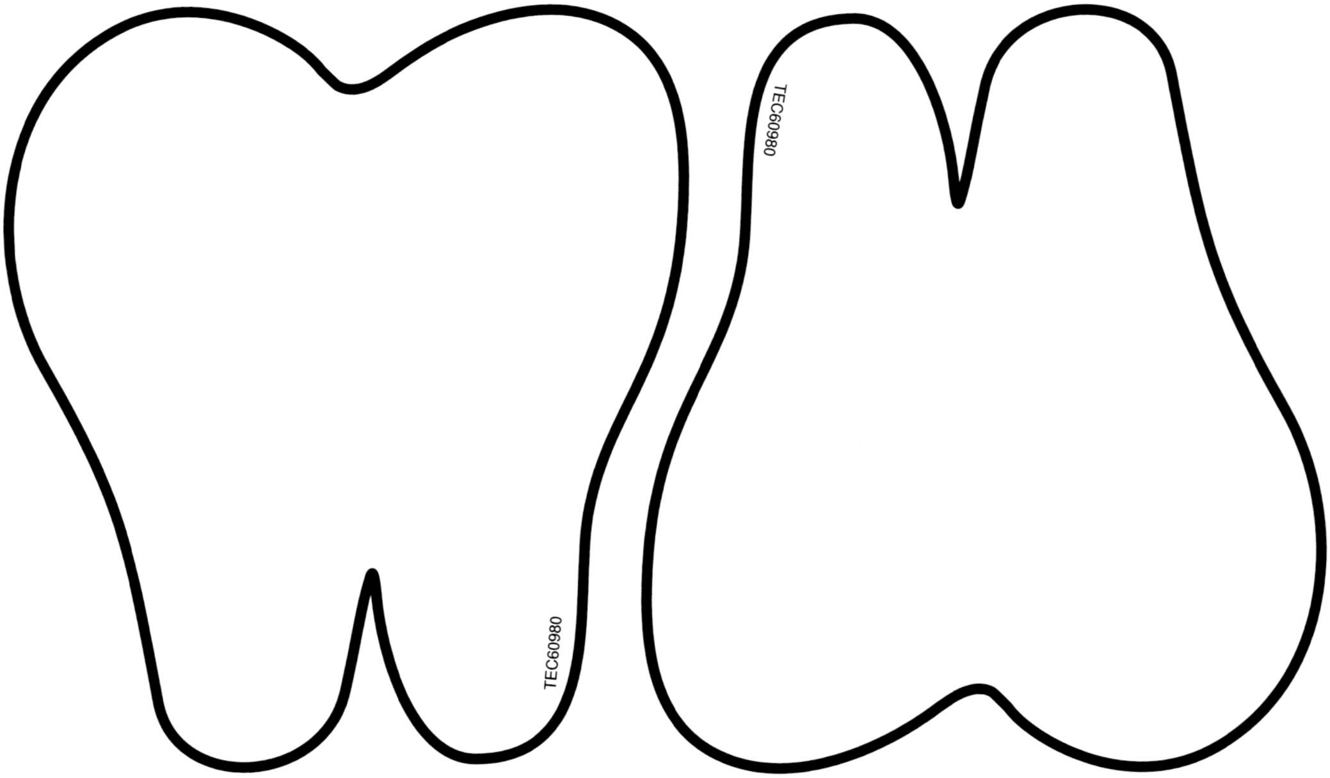

Vowel Cards

Use with “Hearts in a Row” on page 59.

short *a* TEC60980	short *e* TEC60980	short *i* TEC60980	short *o* TEC60980	short *u* TEC60980
long *a* TEC60980	long *e* TEC60980	long *i* TEC60980	long *o* TEC60980	long *u* TEC60980

Use with "Lovely Sums" on page 59.

Name ______________________________________

Name ______________________________________

©The Mailbox® • *Organize February Now!*™ • TEC60980

Games

Math

Compare sets

Pop Up!

To prepare, make enough copies of the groundhog cards on page 64 so that each child will have one card. Gather youngsters in a circle and randomly pass out the cards. Choose two students to pretend to be groundhogs. Have them squat in the center of the circle. On your cue, have each child name the number on his card. The student with the greatest number of groundhogs on his card pops up to a standing position. (If the cards have the same number, both youngsters pop up.) Then invite a volunteer from the circle to compare the two sets. For example, he might say, "Five groundhogs are greater than three groundhogs." After several rounds, change the rules and allow the student with the least number of groundhogs to pop up.

Literacy

Onsets and rimes

Heart Makers

Youngsters mend broken hearts while making new words with this class game. Make enough copies of the heart cards on page 65 so that there is one card for every two students. (Plan to participate if there is an odd number of students.) Program the left side of each heart with a chosen onset. Cut apart the cards and then cut each one in half.

To begin, divide students into two equal groups, giving one group the right half of the hearts and the other group the left half. One group stands in an inner circle, facing outward. The other group stands in an outer circle with each person facing a partner from the inner circle. Each twosome puts its cards together to form a heart. In turn, each pair reads the word on the heart and announces whether it is a real word. Then, at your signal, members of the inner circle take one step to the right, and the new pairs repeat the activity. Continue for a desired number of rotations.

Healthy dental habits

Health

Terrific Teeth

Check up on students' knowledge of healthy dental habits with this group game. To prepare, ask students to cut out from magazines and newspapers pictures of a variety of healthy and unhealthy foods. Glue each picture to a separate blank card. Randomly distribute the cards, and ask a child to name her food. If the food is healthy and good for teeth, she remains standing. If the food is unhealthy, she sits down to represent a tooth that has a cavity. Confirm her response and then continue in this manner until each child has had a turn. After the round, pretend to be a dentist and tap each tooth (child) to repair it. Collect the cards and redistribute them for another round of play.

Math

Counting

Leap Year Lineup

A leap year may occur only once every four years, but this quick game can be used any year! After a short explanation of leap year, have youngsters form a line. Designate the first child in line to call out "One." The counting continues with the next two children, who say "Two" and "Three." Instead of saying "Four," the fourth youngster leaps in the air, yells "Leap year!" and then squats down. Have students continue counting from one to four until everyone is squatting.

Groundhog Cards

Use with "Pop Up!" on page 62.

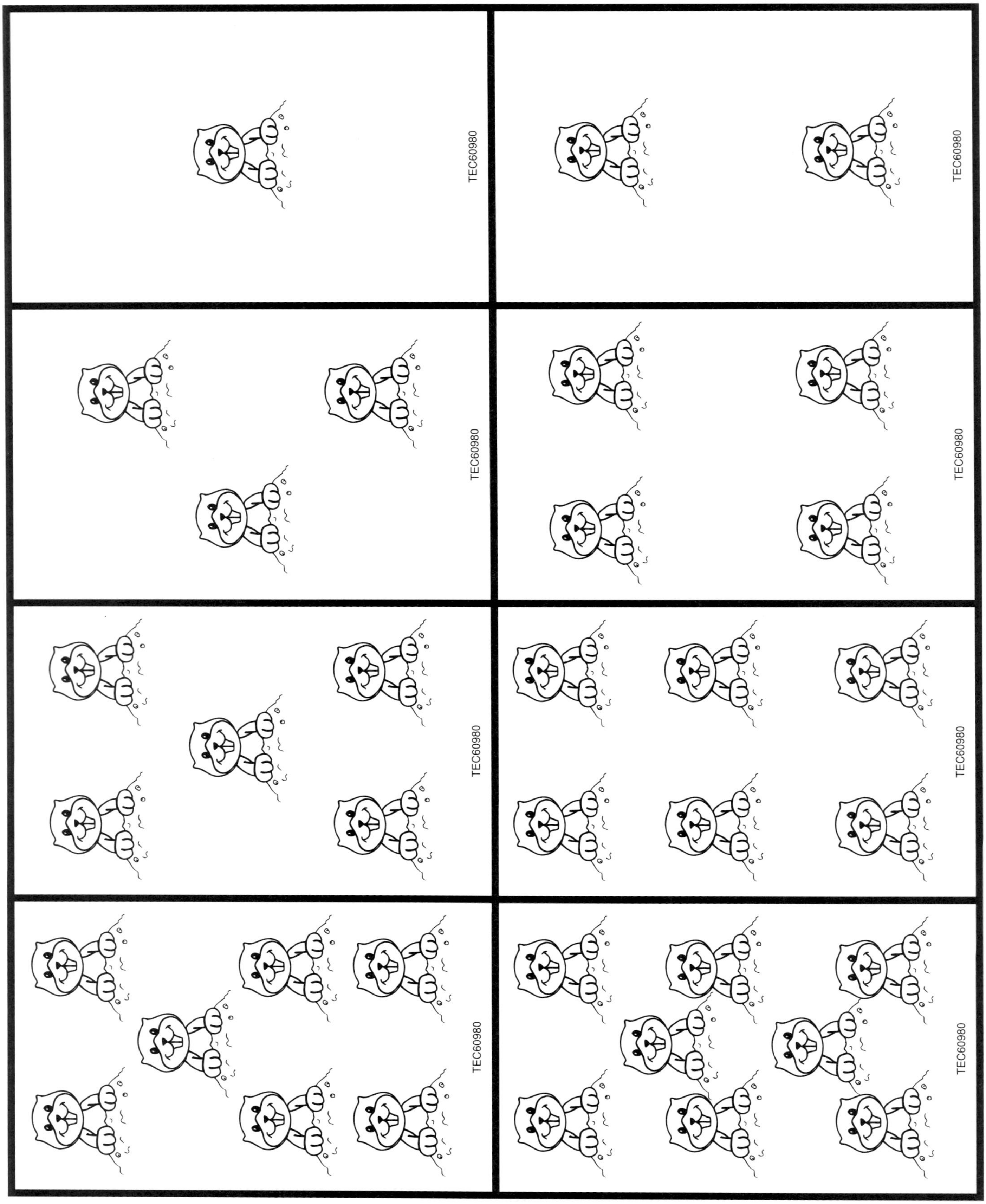

Use with “Heart Makers” on page 62.

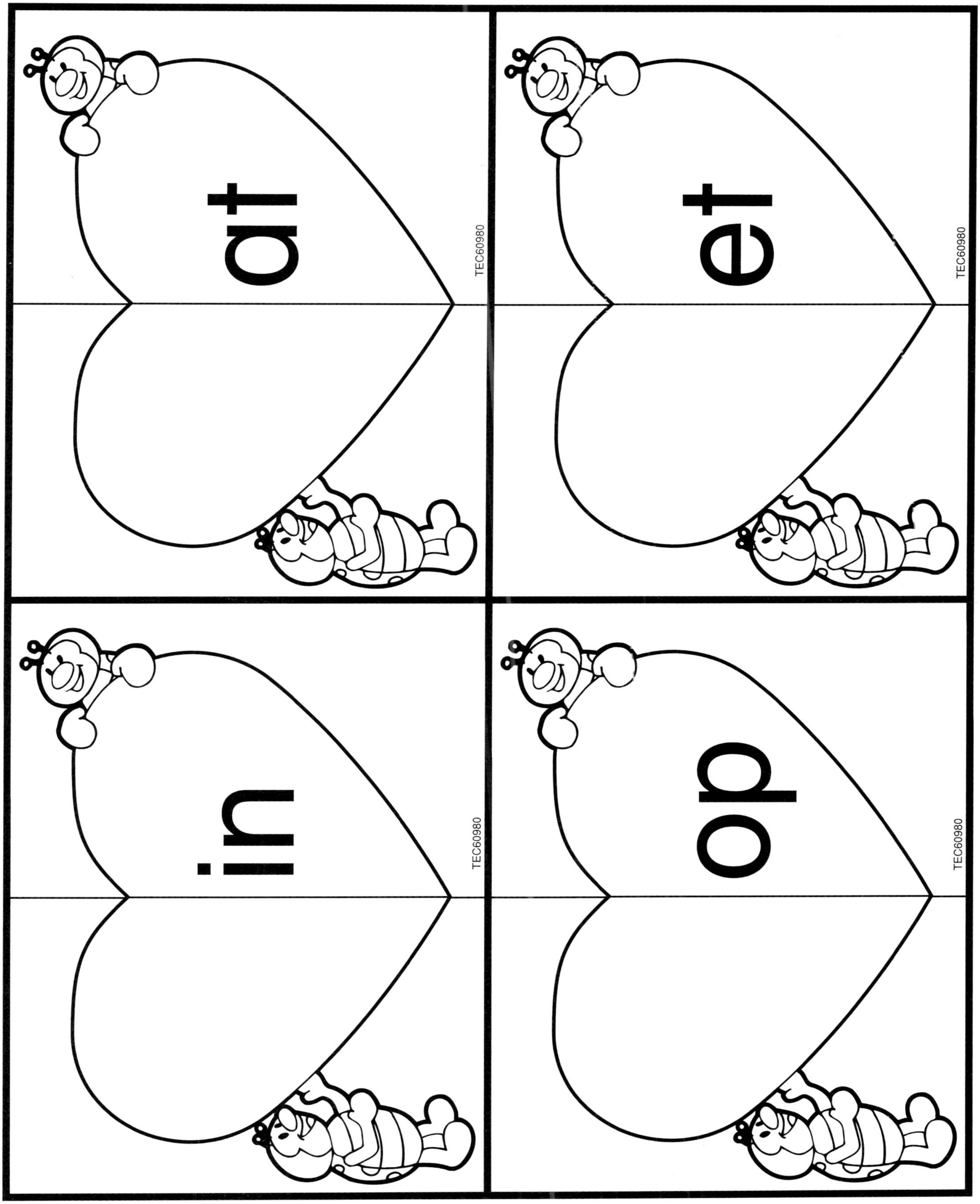

Management Tips

Clean-Desk Fairy

Many youngsters may believe that the tooth fairy leaves a treat when she finds a tooth, but do they know about the fairy who likes to find clean desks? Introduce your class to the "desk fairy." Explain that this fairy occasionally comes by after school to check on the cleanliness of the classroom, especially students' desks (or other work areas). Tell students that she rewards youngsters who have neat and orderly desks with a small treat or special privilege.

A Name Reminder

No-name papers are a thing of the past with this whole-hearted strategy! Before students turn in an assignment, have each child draw and color a heart (or another simple seasonal picture) next to his name. If a name was forgotten, it's sure to be added!

Love Notes

Use this noteworthy idea to encourage positive behavior. Reserve a corner near the bottom of your board and title it "Love Notes." At the end of each school day, choose four students whom you'd like to recognize for their efforts or behaviors. Personalize a copy of an incentive note on page 67 for each child and program it with an appropriate message; then tape it to the display. When students arrive the next day, have them check the board and remove any love notes addressed to them.

Use with "Love Notes" on page 66.

A Love Note for

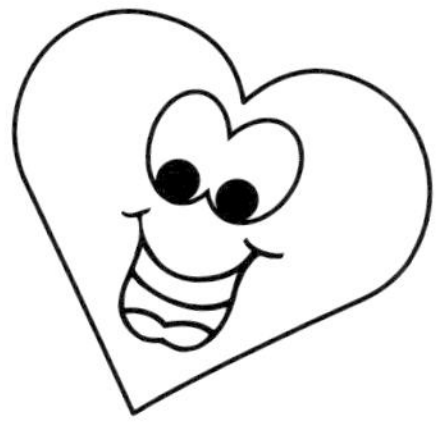

____

I love the way you__________

____________________________.

Thanks!

____

TEC60980

Love Note

for __________________________

I love the way you ________

____________________________.

Thanks!

____

TEC60980

Love Note

To: _______________________

From: ____________________

I love the way you ________

____________________________.

Thanks!

____

TEC60980

Love Note

To: _______________________

From: ___________________

I love the way you ______

____________________________.

Thanks!

____

TEC60980

Cupid Says

When you have a few minutes to spare, put a seasonal twist on the traditional game Simon Says by putting Cupid in charge! Change the game to Cupid Says and give commands for valentine-related movements, such as blowing kisses, hugging a friend, shaking a classmate's hand, dancing like Cupid, or saying "I love you." If one of your youngsters forgets to move only when Cupid says to, give him a reminder to wait for Cupid's command before starting. Once youngsters are familiar with the game, invite them to take turns playing the role of Cupid!

Very Cherry

This spur-of-the-moment listing activity is inspired by the legend of George Washington chopping down a cherry tree. Draw a large cherry on the board or cut one from bulletin board paper. Then have students name food that includes cherries as you record their responses on the cherry. For added fun, invite students to suggest new cherry-type foods, such as cherry tacos or pizza with cherry toppings.

Don't Forget the Floss!

This time filler is perfect for February, which is National Dental Health Month. Present to youngsters a length of dental floss or white string. On the board, draw a large tooth labeled as shown. Have youngsters name items that are shorter, longer, or about the same length as the floss as you record their responses on the tooth.

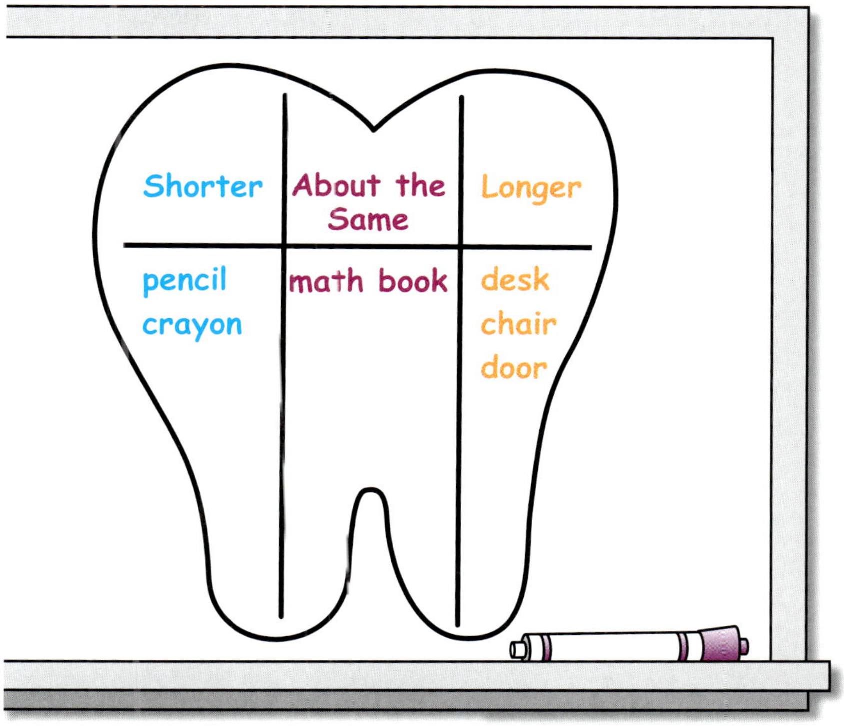

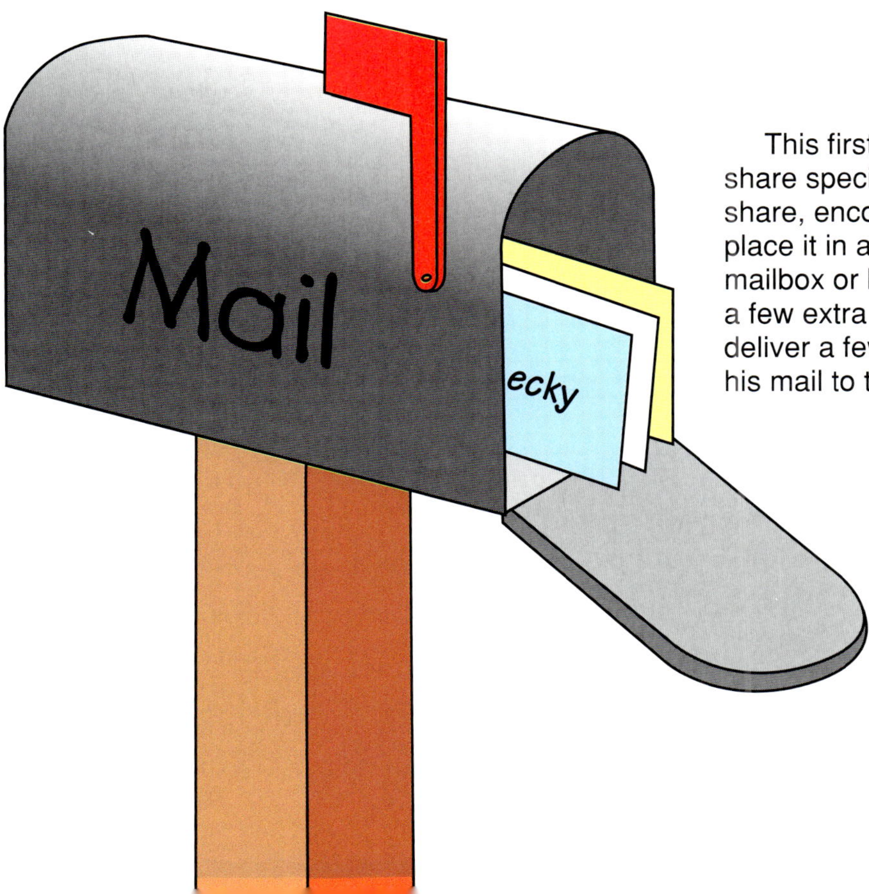

Mail to Share

This first-class time filler encourages students to share special news. When a youngster has news to share, encourage him to write it on a sheet of paper, place it in a personalized envelope, and put it in a mailbox or basket labeled "Mail." Whenever you have a few extra minutes, announce "Mail call!" as you deliver a few pieces of mail. Invite each writer to read his mail to the class.

Writing Ideas &

Journal Prompts

- Folklore says that when a groundhog sees its shadow, six more weeks of winter weather are predicted. What other animal do you think could do a good job of predicting the weather? Why?
- Would you rather grow up to be a dentist, a mail carrier, or a weather forecaster? Why?
- What makes a person a good friend?
- George Washington Carver was a Black American scientist who made over 300 items using peanuts, such as shampoo, cheese, and glue. If you were a scientist, what would you invent?
- Imagine you were elected president for a day. What would you do?
- What do you think would make the perfect Valentine's Day gift? What makes this gift better than others?
- Write a special message to someone you love. Include the things that make this person so great!
- February 29 occurs once every four years. Does this make the day more or less special? Why?

Use one or more of the following ideas and the heart pattern on page 72 to create a love of writing in your classroom!

- Make three copies of the heart pattern, each on a different color of paper. Program one with the adjectives shown, one with nouns (animals or people), and one with action verbs. Ask each child to choose one word from each list. Then, on another copy of the heart pattern, have her write a sentence with the words and illustrate her work.
- Use the heart pattern for journal writing. Write one of the valentine-related prompts from above on a copy of the heart pattern and add writing lines if desired; then make a class supply.

Prompts

Toothy Tales

Brush up on students' creative-writing skills with this activity! Ask youngsters to decide what they think the tooth fairy does with the teeth she collects. Have each child write his thoughts on a copy of the tooth pattern on page 73 and then cut out the pattern. After students finish, ask each child to share his work. Group the teeth based on similar scenarios and bind them between two tooth-shaped covers titled "What Does She Do With All Those Teeth?"

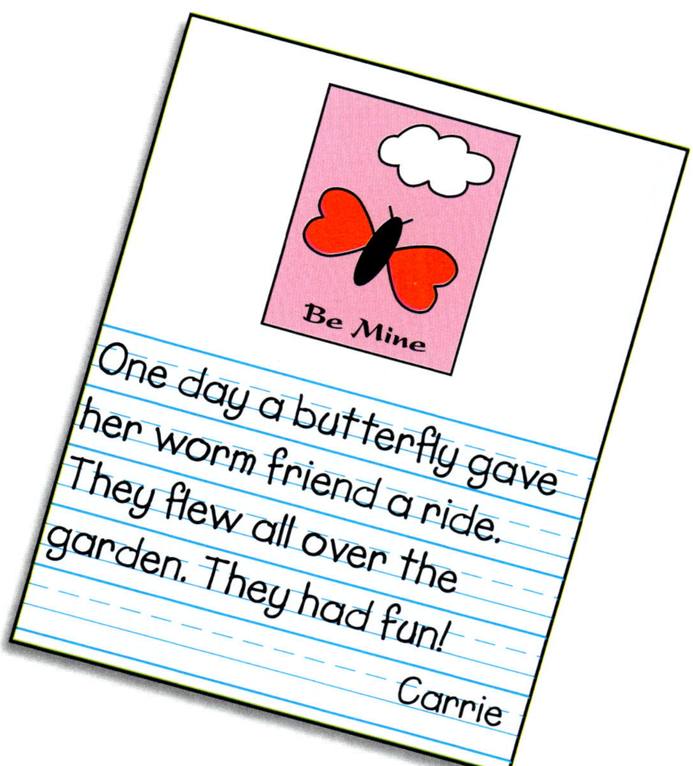

Valentine Story Starters

Youngsters will fall in love with writing stories using valentines as inspiration! At your writing center, place in a mailbox (or another similar container) a large supply of various valentines. Encourage students to choose a valentine and glue it to the top of a sheet of story paper. Have her use the picture on the card as inspiration to write a story. After her writing is complete, invite each child to read her story to the class; then bind the pages between construction paper covers and title the class book "Valentine Stories."

Heart Pattern

Use with the ideas at the bottom of page 70.

Use with "Toothy Tales" on page 71.

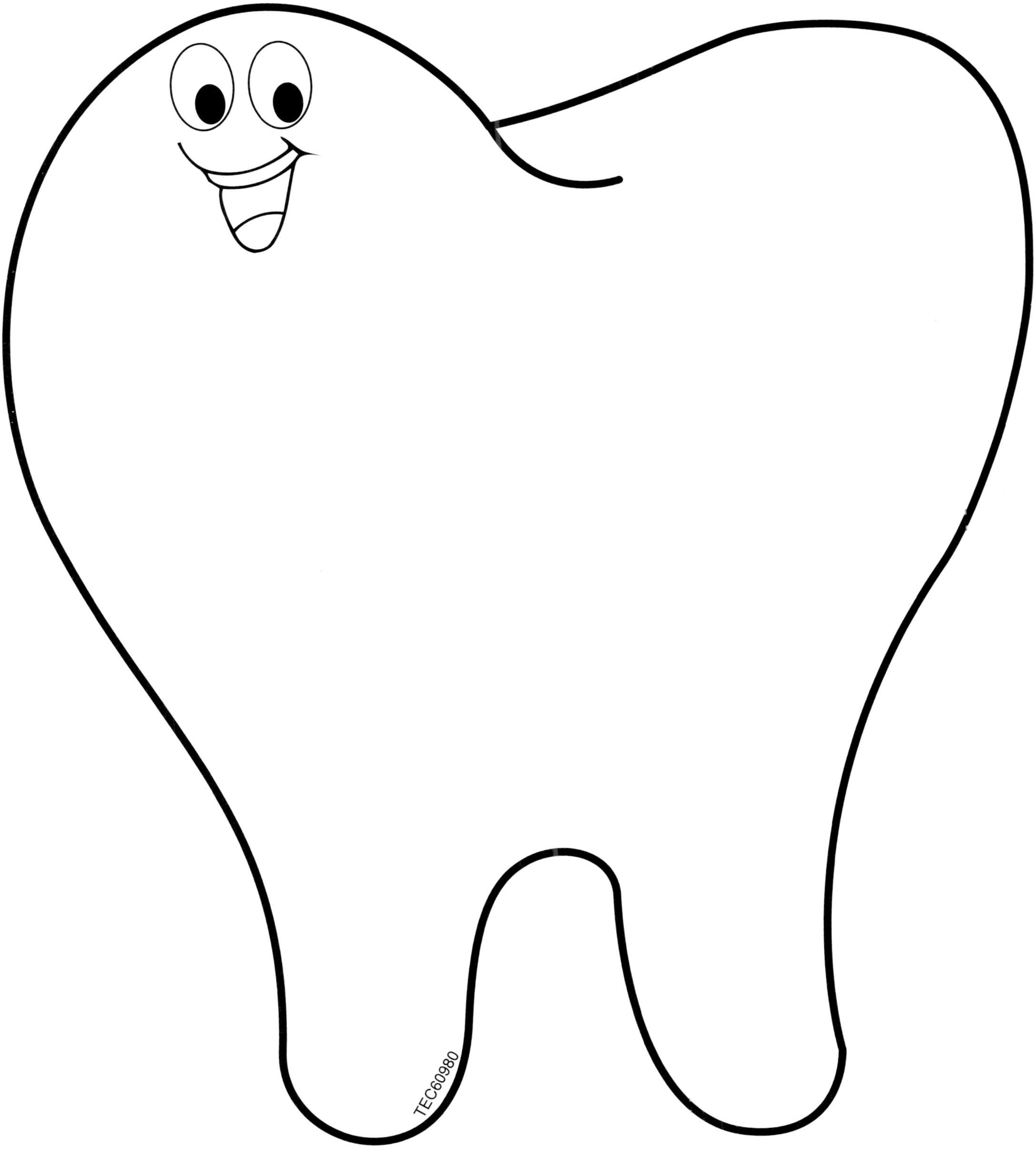

Suppertime Serenade

A ready-to-use center mat and cards for two different learning levels

Ending sounds: /g/, /l/, /t/

Materials:

center mat to the right
center cards on page 77 (two different ending sounds)
center cards on page 79 (three different ending sounds)
2 resealable plastic bags

Preparing the center:

Cut out the cards and place each set in a separate bag.

Using the center:

1. A child removes the cards from a bag and places them picture side up in the center area.
2. She puts each tray card above a different table.
3. She chooses a picture card and says the name of the picture.
4. She identifies the ending sound and then places the picture card below the corresponding tray card.
5. She repeats Steps 3 and 4 for each remaining picture card.
6. To check her work, she turns over all of the picture cards on the mat. If the letter on the back of each card matches the letter on the corresponding tray, she is finished. If not, she rearranges the cards until they are sorted correctly.

Follow-Up

After a child completes the center activity for sorting three different ending sounds, use the skill sheet on page 81 for more practice.

Suppertime Serenade

Put [cloche icon] on separate tables.

Say and sort [pink card icon] .

Check.

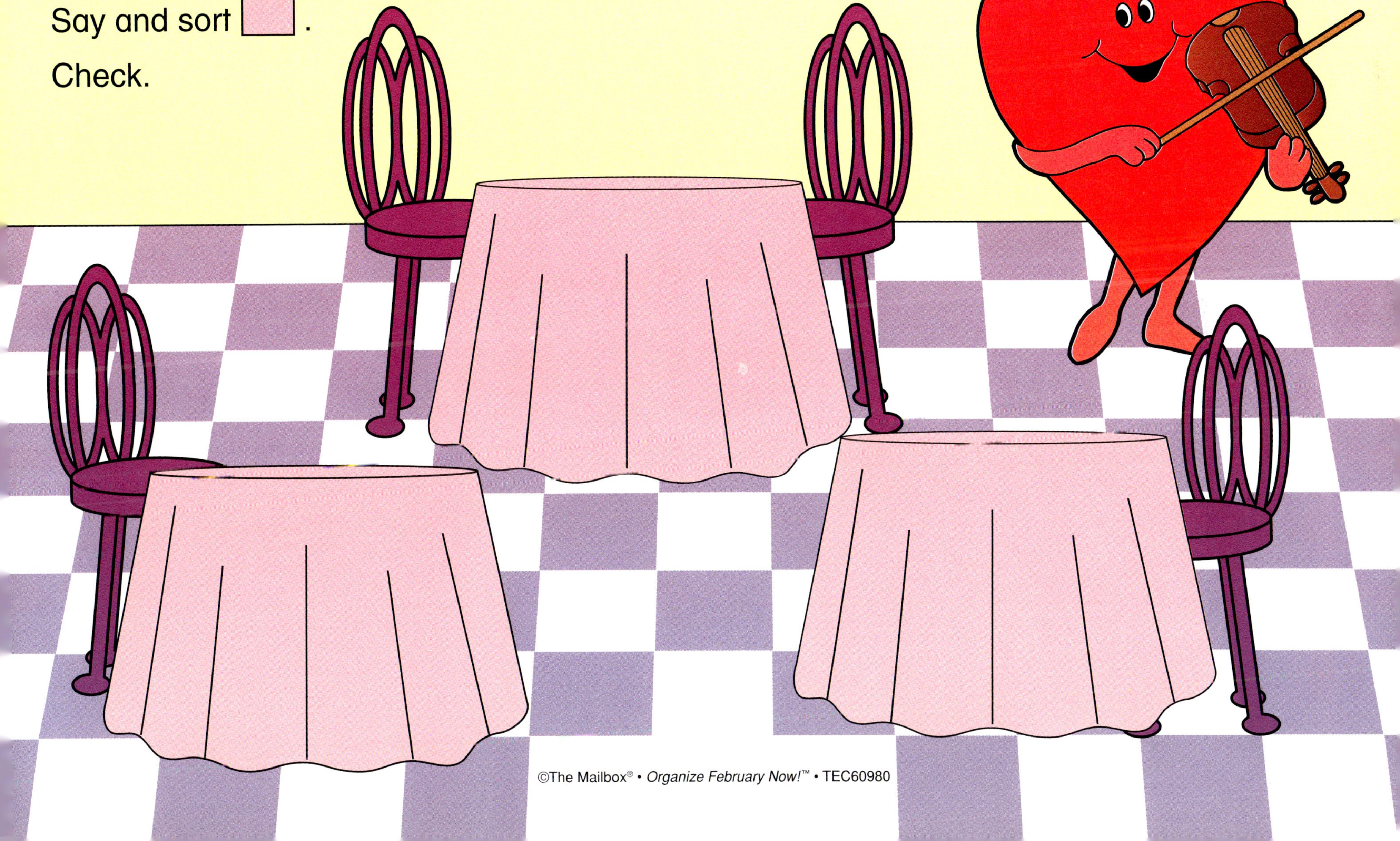

Center Cards

Use with the directions on page 74.

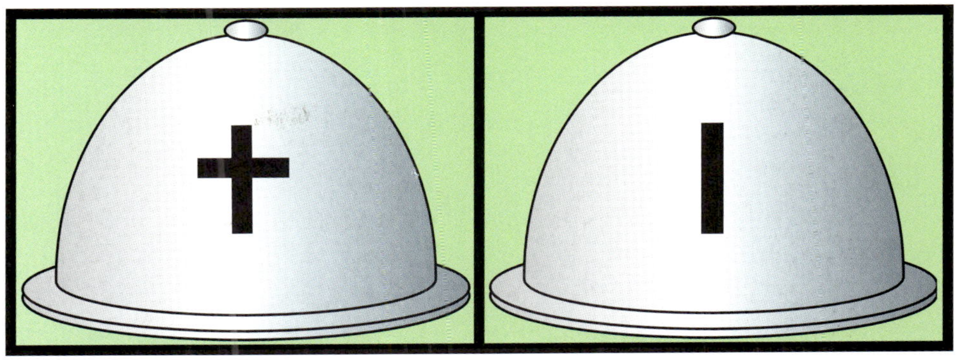

Suppertime Serenade
TEC60980

Suppertime Serenade
TEC60980

Suppertime Serenade
TEC60980

Suppertime Serenade
TEC60980

Suppertime Serenade
TEC60980

Suppertime Serenade
TEC60980

Suppertime Serenade
TEC60980

Suppertime Serenade
TEC60980

Suppertime Serenade
TEC60980

Suppertime Serenade
TEC60980

Suppertime Serenade
TEC60980

Center Cards

Use with the directions on page 74.

Suppertime Serenade
TEC60980

Suppertime Serenade
TEC60980

Suppertime Serenade
TEC60980

t t t

Suppertime Serenade
TEC60980

Suppertime Serenade
TEC60980

Suppertime Serenade
TEC60980

g g g

Suppertime Serenade
TEC60980

Suppertime Serenade
TEC60980

Suppertime Serenade
TEC60980

l l l

Suppertime Serenade
TEC60980

Suppertime Serenade
TEC60980

Suppertime Serenade
TEC60980

A Sweet Treat

Name ______________________________

Color by the code to show the ending sounds.

Color Code

t—red

g—yellow

l—blue

The Sugar Shop

A ready-to-use center mat and cards for two different learning levels

Coins

Materials:

center mat to the right
center cards on page 85 (coin values)
center cards on page 87 (coin combinations)
2 resealable plastic bags

Preparing the center:

Cut out the cards and place each color-coded set in a separate bag.

Using the center:

1. A child removes the cards from a bag and lays them coin side up in the center area.
2. He chooses a card. If he's using the first set of cards, he identifies the coin and its value and then places it on the appropriate jar. If he's using the second set of cards, he determines the value of the coins and then places the card on the appropriate jar.
3. He repeats Step 2 for each remaining card.
4. To check his work, he turns over all the cards on the mat. If the amounts on the cards from each jar match, he is finished. If the amounts do not match, he rearranges the cards until they are sorted correctly.

Follow-Up

After a child completes the center activity for coin values, use the skill sheet on page 89 for more practice.

The Sugar Shop

Choose.

Put.

Check.

EZ 2 LOVE
HEY THERE
EZ 2 LOVE
BE MINE
CUTIE PIE
LOVE YOU
NEAT
TRUE LOVE
COOL FOOL
GUESS WHO?
COOL FOOL
R U SHY?
BE TRUE
LOVE YOU
LOVE YOU
TRUE LOVE
HEY THERE
CUTIE PIE
TRUE LOVE
NEAT
COOL FOOL
BE MINE
COOL FOOL
GUESS WHO?
LOVE YOU
BE TRUE
EZ 2 LOVE
TRUE LOVE
HEY THERE
R U SHY?

Use with the directions on page 82.

1¢ The Sugar Shop TEC60980	**1¢** The Sugar Shop TEC60980	**1¢** The Sugar Shop TEC60980
5¢ The Sugar Shop TEC60980	**5¢** The Sugar Shop TEC60980	**5¢** The Sugar Shop TEC60980
10¢ The Sugar Shop TEC60980	**10¢** The Sugar Shop TEC60980	**10¢** The Sugar Shop TEC60980
25¢ The Sugar Shop TEC60980	**25¢** The Sugar Shop TEC60980	**25¢** The Sugar Shop TEC60980

Use with the directions on page 82.

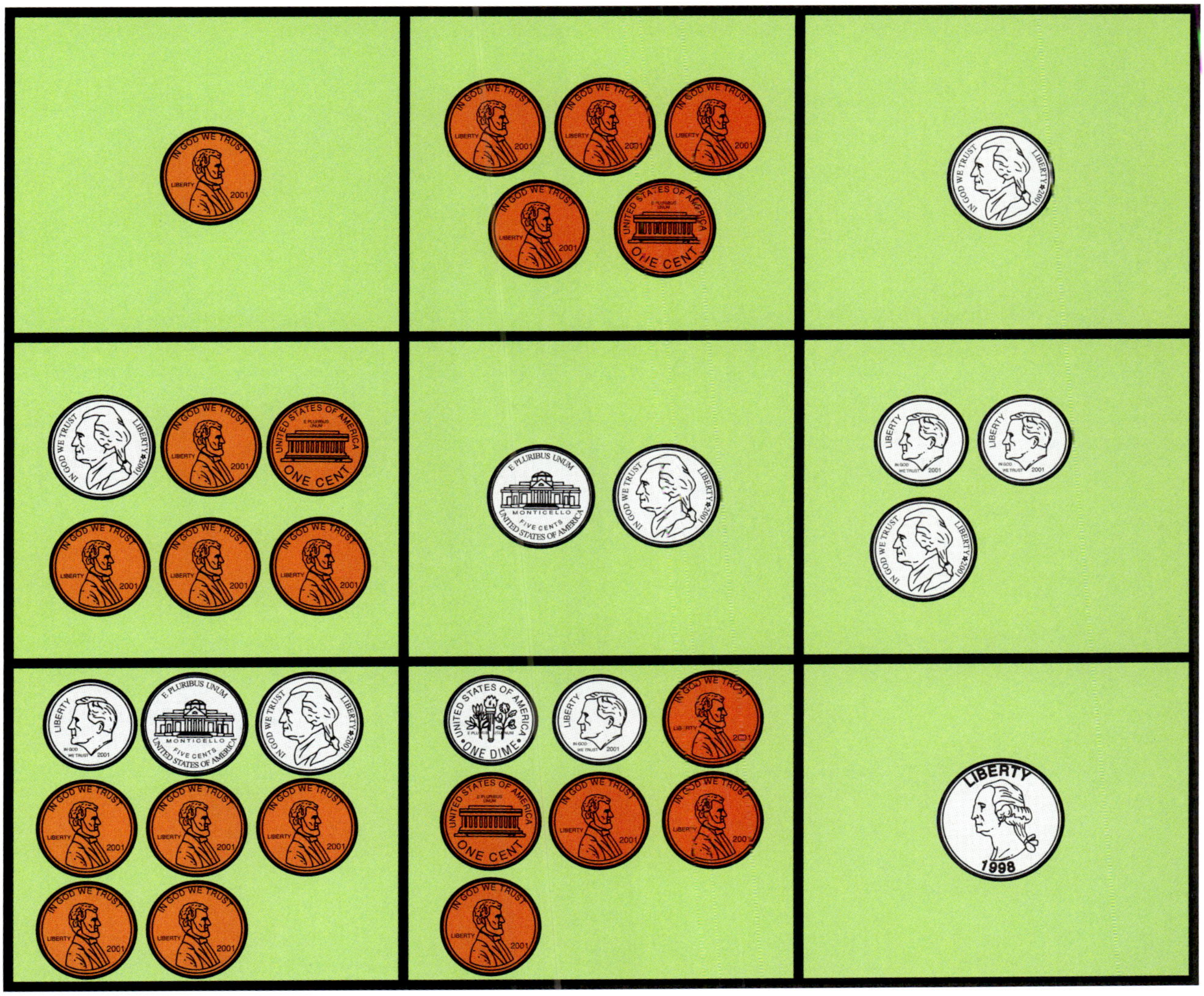

5¢ The Sugar Shop TEC60980	**5¢** The Sugar Shop TEC60980	**1¢** The Sugar Shop TEC60980
25¢ The Sugar Shop TEC60980	**10¢** The Sugar Shop TEC60980	**10¢** The Sugar Shop TEC60980
25¢ The Sugar Shop TEC60980	**25¢** The Sugar Shop TEC60980	**25¢** The Sugar Shop TEC60980

Money Match

Name ____________________

Cut. Match. Glue.

5¢ | 1¢ | 10¢ | 25¢

10¢ | 5¢ | 1¢

Hippo's Hearts

Name ____

Cut.

Glue the pictures that begin with **h.**

Mail Call

Name ______________________________

Cut.

Glue to match the ending sounds.

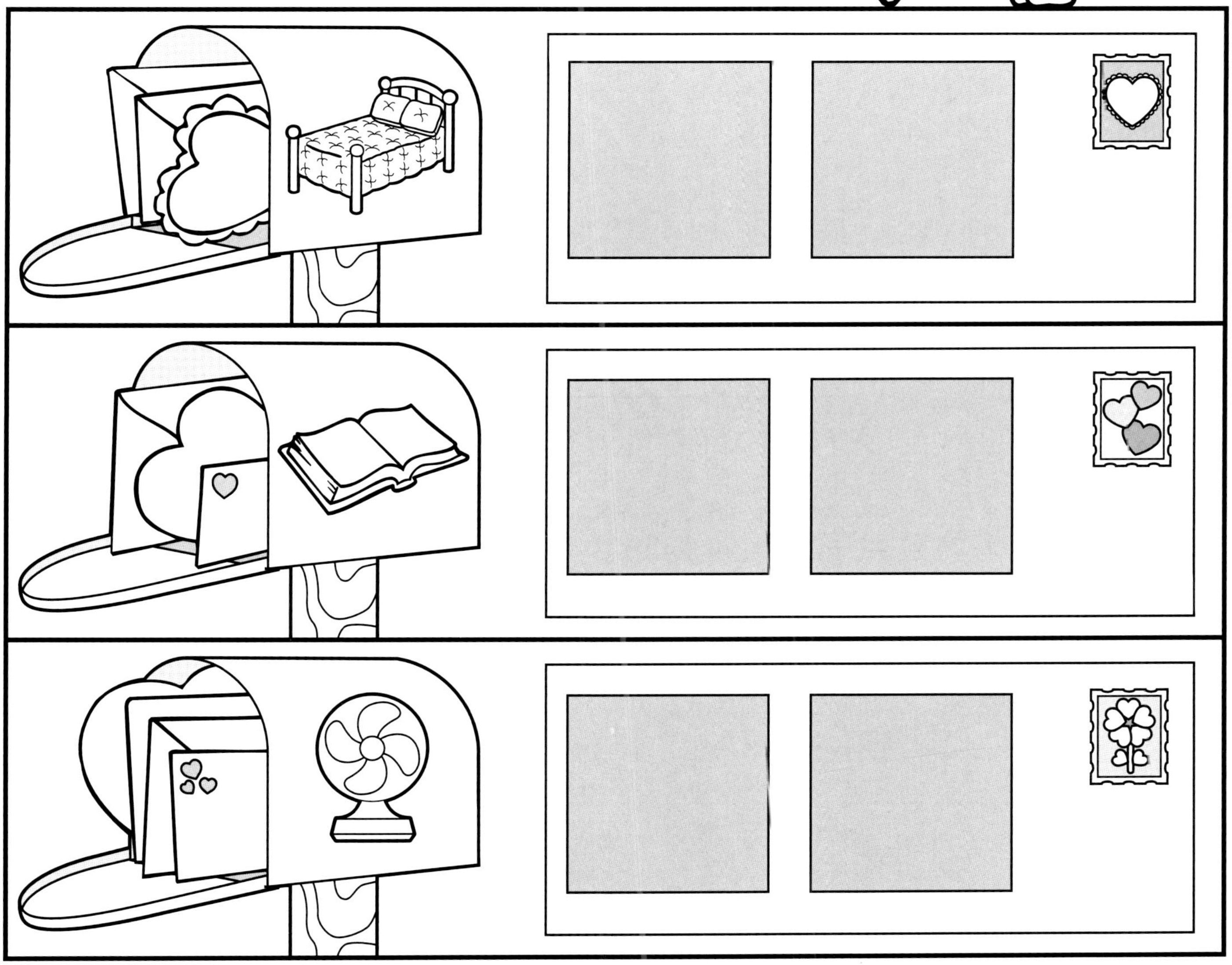

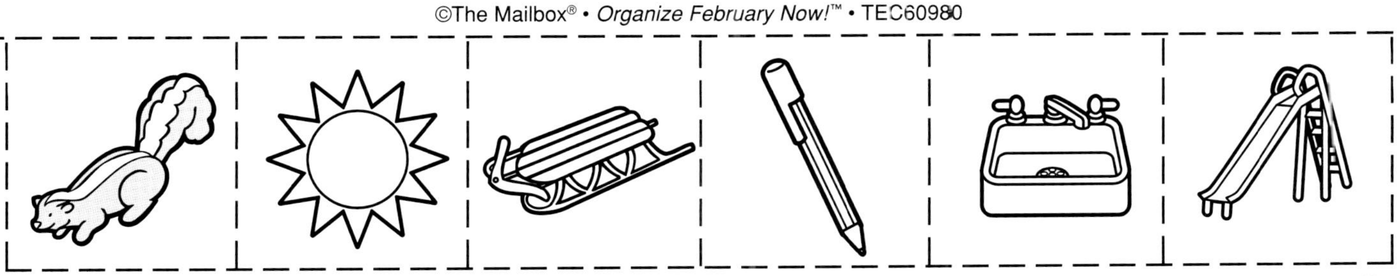

Good Morning, Groundhog!

Name ______________________________

Cut.

Glue to match the vowel sounds.

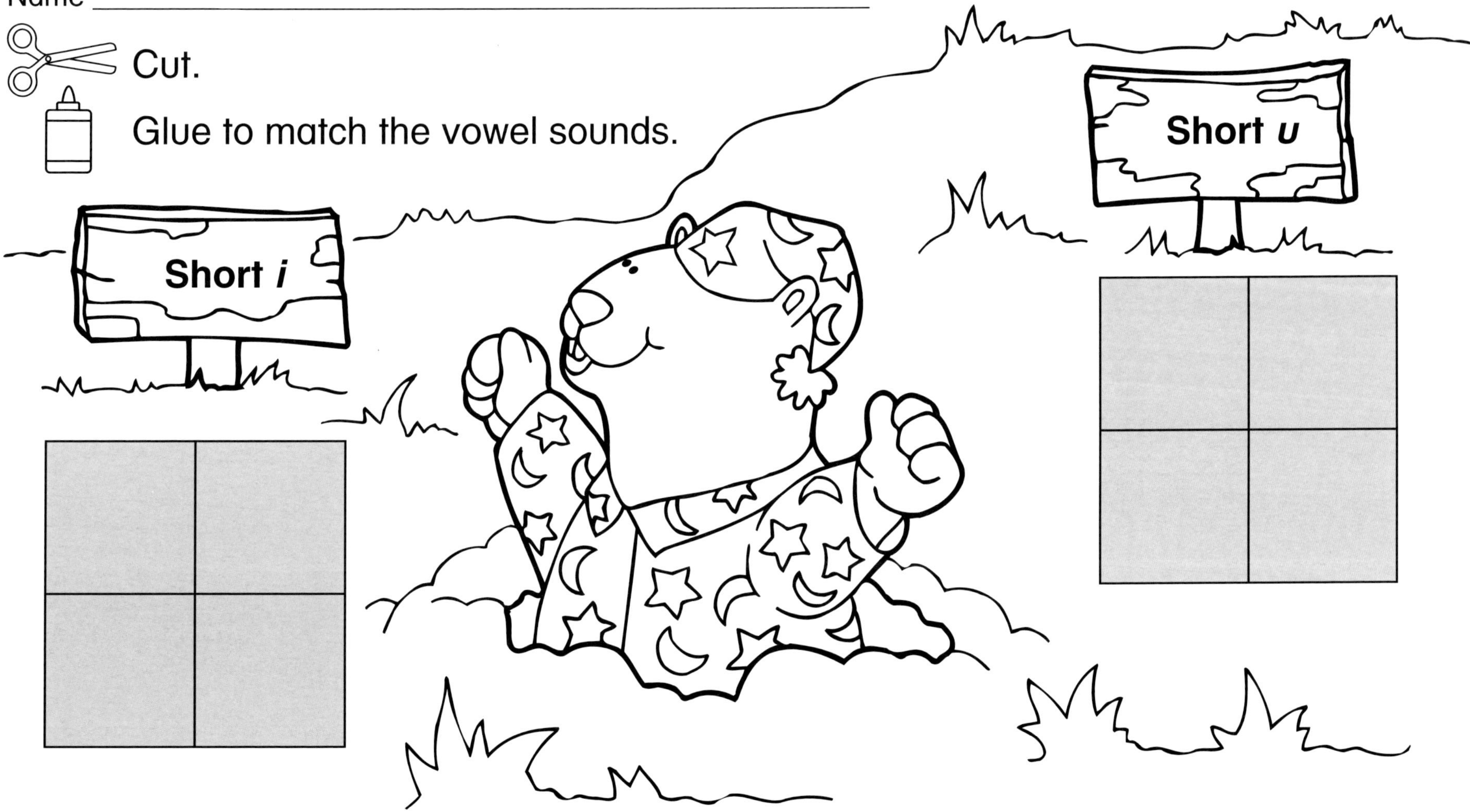

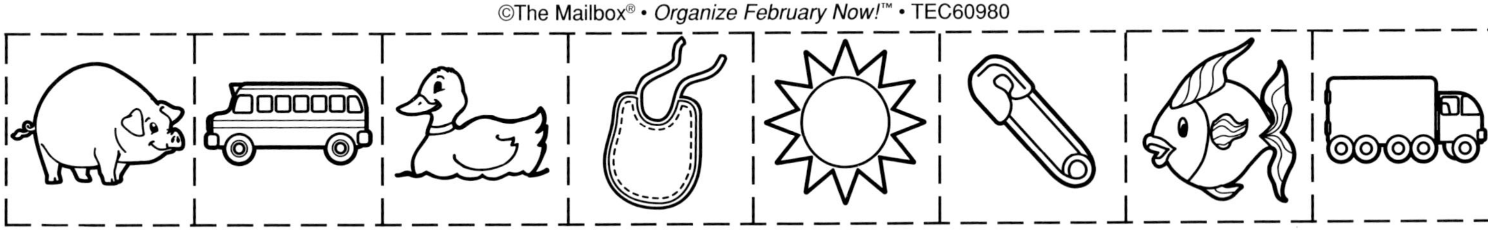

Party Time!

Name ______________________________

Read.

Circle each word that needs a capital letter.

Dear pam,
will you come to my Valentine's Day party? it will be fun. i am making cookies. we will drink juice. kim, dan, and ted will be there. i hope you can come.

Love,
bill

Puppy Love

Name ______________________________

Write the missing numbers.

Flower Shopping

Name ______________________________

Count the pennies.

Write the amount in each box.

¢

¢

¢

¢

¢

¢

¢

¢

Crazy for Chocolates

Name ________________________________

Circle each set of ten.

Count and write how many tens and ones.

Write the number in the box.

1.

____ ten ____ ones ☐

2.

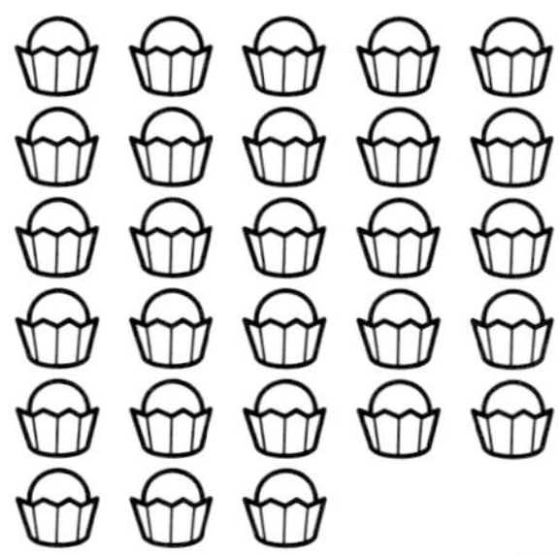

____ tens ____ ones ☐

3.

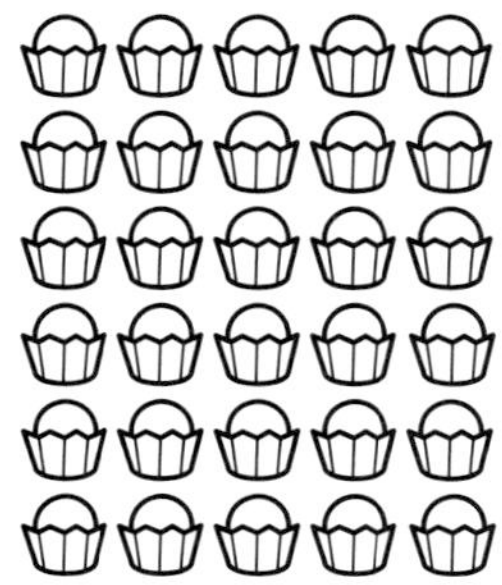

____ tens ____ ones ☐

4.

____ tens ____ one ☐

5.

____ ten ____ ones ☐

6.

____ tens ____ ones ☐

7.

____ ten ____ ones ☐

8.

____ tens ____ ones ☐

9.

____ ten ____ ones ☐

Science for First-Timers

By Q. L. Pearce, Francesca Rusackas, and Natalie Goldstein

Illustrated by Kerry Manwaring and Janise Gates

BARNES & NOBLE BOOKS
NEW YORK

Managing Director and Publisher: Jack Artenstein
Director of Publishing Services: Rena Copperman
Editorial Director: Brenda Pope-Ostrow
Director of Art Production: Bret Perry
Project Editor: Amy Downing

This edition published by Barnes & Noble, Inc.,
by arrangement with Lowell House Juvenile,
a division of NTC/Contemporary Publishing Group, Inc.

2000 Barnes & Noble Books

ISBN 0-7607-2031-2

Printed and bound in the United States of America

RCP 99 00 01 02 M 9 8 7 6 5 4 3 2 1

Part One:
Science Fair Projects

Reviewed and endorsed by Anthony Fredericks, Ed.D., Associate Professor of Education, York College, York, PA, and author of The Complete Science Fair Handbook

Contents

To Parents and Teachers

A science fair is a fun and memorable experience. Your child (or student) will gain self-confidence through sharing with others what he or she has discovered. *Part One: Science Fair Projects* takes your young scientist step by step through the thrill of developing and presenting a science fair project.

Each project in this section is safe and simple. The required materials are inexpensive and easy to obtain. Each project includes suggestions for research, complete with a list of key words that give a child direction when he or she begins to look up information. "How They Work" at the back of this section gives simple explanations of project results.

Help your child to find a project that interests him or her. With the Timetable on page 80, encourage your child to schedule plenty of time to do research, organize materials, and create an eye-catching and complete presentation. Promote creativity and organization. Resist directing your child's project but give plenty of support. With planning and patience, a science fair can be a marvelous way to uncover your youngster's gifts and talents.

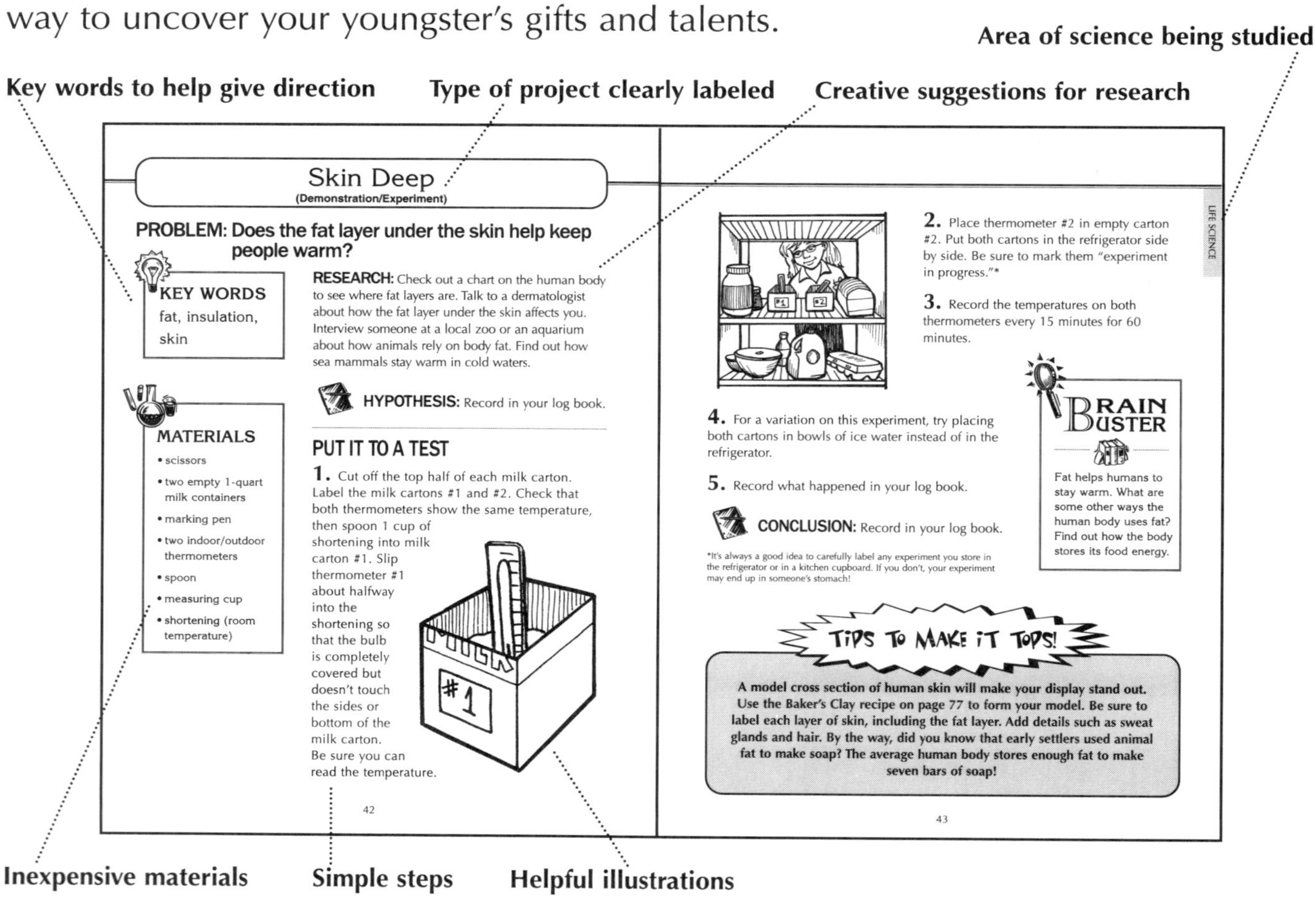

Skin Deep
(Demonstration/Experiment)

PROBLEM: Does the fat layer under the skin help keep people warm?

KEY WORDS
fat, insulation, skin

RESEARCH: Check out a chart on the human body to see where fat layers are. Talk to a dermatologist about how the fat layer under the skin affects you. Interview someone at a local zoo or an aquarium about how animals rely on body fat. Find out how sea mammals stay warm in cold waters.

HYPOTHESIS: Record in your log book.

MATERIALS
- scissors
- two empty 1-quart milk containers
- marking pen
- two indoor/outdoor thermometers
- spoon
- measuring cup
- shortening (room temperature)

PUT IT TO A TEST

1. Cut off the top half of each milk carton. Label the milk cartons #1 and #2. Check that both thermometers show the same temperature, then spoon 1 cup of shortening into milk carton #1. Slip thermometer #1 about halfway into the shortening so that the bulb is completely covered but doesn't touch the sides or bottom of the milk carton. Be sure you can read the temperature.

2. Place thermometer #2 in empty carton #2. Put both cartons in the refrigerator side by side. Be sure to mark them "experiment in progress."*

3. Record the temperatures on both thermometers every 15 minutes for 60 minutes.

4. For a variation on this experiment, try placing both cartons in bowls of ice water instead of in the refrigerator.

5. Record what happened in your log book.

CONCLUSION: Record in your log book.

*It's always a good idea to carefully label any experiment you store in the refrigerator or in a kitchen cupboard. If you don't, your experiment may end up in someone's stomach!

BRAIN BUSTER
Fat helps humans to stay warm. What are some other ways the human body uses fat? Find out how the body stores its food energy.

TIPS TO MAKE IT TOPS!
A model cross section of human skin will make your display stand out. Use the Baker's Clay recipe on page 77 to form your model. Be sure to label each layer of skin, including the fat layer. Add details such as sweat glands and hair. By the way, did you know that early settlers used animal fat to make soap? The average human body stores enough fat to make seven bars of soap!

42 43

Introduction

Your School Is Having a Science Fair!

So, now what? And what exactly is a science fair, anyway? A science fair is simply an event where you and your classmates display your latest science projects. In many fairs, teachers judge the projects and award prizes to winners. But even if you don't get a prize, you're a winner because you learn and have lots of fun taking part in the fair.

A science fair may be sponsored by a single class, or a whole city, county, or state. One of the first science fairs was the Children's Science Fair held in New York nearly sixty years ago. Now the National Science Fair is held every year to judge the best science projects in the country.

Do you like to do experiments? There are different categories of science fair projects, but most projects are experiments. In an experiment, you ask a scientific question, then design a test to find the answer. You can put together a project in other ways, too. You can demonstrate a scientific idea, present research, or show off a cool collection.

Every day, adventurous people make new scientific discoveries that affect your life. You can be a part of the adventure. By participating in a science fair, you get to think and work like a real scientist. The ideas in this section will help you get started. Change them, add details, make them your own. GOOD LUCK and HAVE FUN!

Choosing a Project

Two very important steps must take place when you begin planning for a science fair. The first is to ask your teacher for a copy of the fair guidelines, so you know what rules and regulations to follow, and what restrictions there may be. The next step on your science fair adventure is choosing the right project. This is one of the most important steps you'll make, because you'll be working on your project for days, maybe even weeks. Begin by asking yourself these questions:

- What kind of science interests me?
- What would I like to learn about?
- What special hobbies or talents do I have that I could use to put together my project? (Examples are stargazing, bird-watching, or gardening.)

Write down several ideas that come to mind, and list the materials and equipment you will need for each. Then, to narrow down your choices, consider the following:

- Is the idea something you can easily study? (An investigation of the surface of Pluto might be cool, but it's not exactly practical!)
- Will you have to order some things through the mail?
- Do you have, or can you get, the money needed to buy supplies?
- Will you need any help with the project idea? From whom?
- Can you get the project ready by the due date?

If you're having trouble choosing an idea from your list, ask a parent or a teacher to help you select the best one. Once you have chosen the topic you'd like to work on, decide how you'll show it. Generally, you can do four things:

1. Present research.
2. Demonstrate a scientific idea or an apparatus.
3. Show a collection.
4. Perform an experiment.

PRESENTING RESEARCH

Would you like to be a science detective? Then research is for you. For a research project, you ask a question, make observations, do plenty of reading, conduct interviews with experts, and use what you learn to discover a pattern or a trend.

For example, a good research question might be: "What type of seeds do wild sparrows like to eat best?" To find the answer, you could start by reading about sparrows at the library, then interview bird-watchers. You could also put out a variety of seeds and observe which birds come to the feeder (hopefully sparrows) and what type of seed they eat.

Another example of a research project is to test a product to find out if the manufacturer's claims are true (for instance, ask the question, "Which cereal really stays crispy in milk?").

DOING A DEMONSTRATION

Would you like to demonstrate a scientific principle or fact, or show how a tool or a device works? Start by coming up with an interesting question, such as "How does rain form?" or "How is Gak® made?" or "How does a microscope work?" Then find a way to show the process. If you're demonstrating an apparatus, it's also fun to uncover the history of the equipment, how it is used, and why it is important.

Models and cross sections (objects cut in half to see inside) also make good demonstrations. For instance, you could show a model of the human eye or a cross section of a pair of in-line skates.

WHAT'S THE POINT?

For any science fair project you do, you need to explain the point, or *purpose,* of the project. For example, if you make a model of the human eye, your purpose needs to be clear. Is it to show how we see white light, or how we see color, or perhaps something else?

SHOWING A COLLECTION

If you are a collector, this is your chance to shine. A display of a well-organized collection of rocks, shells, fossils, pressed leaves or flowers, insects, or anything else can be a great science fair project. To make your collection spectacular, show plenty of variety, and label everything clearly. Interesting pictures and maps of your discovery sites will jazz up your display. Also, if you've kept a log book detailing your discoveries, show that, too. (If you plan to come up with a collection in time for the science fair, keep a log book from the beginning. Read more about log books on page 15.)

PERFORMING AN EXPERIMENT

The type of project most often presented at a science fair is an experiment. An experiment is a test that's designed to find the answer to a problem.

Exploring the universe through science is exciting, but there are rules to the game. To gather and present information in an orderly manner, scientists use the scientific method, a step-by-step approach to discovering answers and solving problems. In general, the steps are:

1. Find a problem. (Ask a scientific question that you are *able to test.*)
2. Do the research. (Gather as much information as possible.)
3. Make a hypothesis—that is, a guess. (Predict what the answer to the question will be. Be confident. Write your hypothesis in the form of a statement. Don't begin your statement with "I think.")
4. Experiment! (Think of a way to test your hypothesis. The test is the experiment.)
5. Record the results. (Collect data from the experiment.)
6. Draw a conclusion. (Figure out what the experimental data tell you by asking the questions below.)
    - Do the results of your experiment tell you your hypothesis is on the right track or the wrong track? How?
    - Is it possible to repeat the experiment? Should you change the experiment in any way?
    - Did the experiment make you think of new questions that need answers?
    - How can the information you found be useful? How does it relate to the world in which you live?

"E" IS FOR EXCELLENT

Here are a few tips for doing a prize-winning experiment.

- Perform your test more than once to be sure your results are accurate. Repeat the first test exactly. (Each repeat is called a trial.) Record the results of each trial separately.
- Keep a log. For each trial, record the date and time, any measurements, observations, or results, as well as any comments you have.
- Be precise in taking and recording measurements and results.
- If possible, take photographs of noticeable changes that take place during the experiment.
- Be sure you don't gather only those results that say your hypothesis is correct. Finding the real answer is more important than proving your hypothesis is true.

IMPORTANT FACTORS: VARIABLES AND CONTROLS

Your experiment should be carefully planned (that is, designed) to test one idea only. To do this, you will need a test *variable* and a *control* subject. A variable is a part (the one and only part) of the experiment that you change to test your idea. For example, to test whether plants need light, light should be the only variable.

Say you use four plants in your experiment. You begin by setting plant #1 aside, giving it enough light and water to keep it healthy and lush. Plant #1 is your control.

For the other three plants, the only thing you change is the amount of light each gets (more or less than the standard set for your control plant). The amount of light is your variable. Everything else, such as soil, water, air, type of plant, type of pot, and temperature, should be the same for all four test subjects.

SAFETY FIRST

No matter what kind of experiment you do, it's very important to always follow a few safety rules:

- *Before* performing an experiment, plan it carefully with an adult. Decide together whether the adult should be there *during* the experiment. If the experiment calls for something electrical, hot, or sharp, an adult must be present.

- Know your tools and ingredients. Have each ready before you begin.
- Tie back long hair in a ponytail or pin it up.
- Keep your work area clean and dry. If necessary, cover surfaces with newspaper.
- Never put an unknown material in your mouth or eyes.
- Never use electrical appliances near water.
- Ask for help if something unexpected happens.
- Clean your work area when you're finished.
- Wash your hands after the experiment.
- Do no harm to a living thing.

Doing the Project

Once you've decided on your project, it's time to make it a reality. A science project can be lots of fun, but there's plenty of work involved, too. That includes doing research, completing your experiment (or demonstration, collection, or research), writing your report, and building your display. Before you begin, find a calendar and clearly mark the due date of the project in red. Count how many days you have until that date, and use the Timetable on page 80 to plan each step.

THE RESEARCH

No matter what kind of project you do, you need to gather as much information about your topic as possible. When doing your research, use a wide variety of resources, including:

- Libraries (for books, magazines, cassette tapes, videotapes, and maps)
- Government agencies
- Local colleges and universities
- Museums
- Local science laboratories
- Historical societies
- National parks
- Hospitals
- Planetariums
- Zoos

You can get addresses and phone numbers for government agencies, historical societies, and national parks at your local library. Colleges, museums, hospitals, planetariums, and zoos are likely to be listed in the telephone book. When you call or write to these sources, ask if they have a public education department. They might have useful written materials they can send you. Call or write first to find out if they require a self-addressed envelope or, in some cases, a small fee.

Another way to do research (perhaps the most exciting way) is to contact an expert in the field you are studying and set up an interview.

Don't forget to keep a careful list of all your sources, no matter what they are. Make an index card for each source. You may need several cards for one source, depending on how much information you find. Here are some sample source cards to make:

FOR BOOKS AND TAPES (include which it is on card)

Title:
Author:
Publisher:
Where published:
When published:
Page #:
Notes:

FOR MAGAZINES AND PAMPHLETS (include which it is on card)

Name of magazine/pamphlet:
Title of article:
Author:
Date:
Volume:
Page #:
Notes:

FOR INTERVIEWS

Person's name:
Person's title:
Person's workplace:
Telephone #:
Date of interview:
Notes:

THE LOG BOOK

You will need to create a log book—an informal record you keep while your work is in progress. Your log book is the "story" of your project, containing your daily notes and thoughts. Judges often like to review log books to see how a student's work progressed.

The log book is an exception to the "neatness rule." It doesn't have to be retyped or rewritten. Drawings, smudges, and scribbled notes are okay.

THE DISPLAY

The purpose of the display is to give a "project summary" at a glance. It is the first part of your science project that people will notice, so make it stand out. The display is made of tall boards. It should be easy to assemble and take apart, and sturdy enough to stand on its own for several days. The display board is usually two or three sections of strong material, sometimes held together with hinges. It can be made from pegboard, plywood, cork, particleboard, or foam board (cardboard and poster board are too flimsy to hold up over time). Many stationery supply stores carry lightweight, three-sectioned foam board, perfect for a science fair display. You'll have to check the rules to find out what size you'll need, but the average is about 3 feet by 5 feet.

You can cover your display board with fabric, burlap, or wallpaper to make it interesting. Over this board covering, you can put bright posters with clear, crisp lettering on them. You can also use snappy visual effects. For example, if your experiment is about plants, cut your display boards into large leaf or tree shapes. Use three-dimensional or exaggerated designs where possible. But be careful not to make your display so busy that people look only at it and not at your work!

Your display must include several things, each typed or lettered neatly on a separate poster (or on heavy paper).

1. A descriptive title of ten words or less
2. The purpose of your project (whether it's research, a collection, a demonstration, or an experiment)
3. Your hypothesis
4. A short summary of your procedures
5. A short summary of your results
6. A short summary of your conclusions

A clever title grabs attention. For example, "This Experiment Stinks!" would be a great title for your project if you did an experiment involving something smelly (see the project idea on page 40). The lettering should be easy to read and your title should be clear from a distance.

Use your space wisely. Fill the display board, but don't crowd things. Your presentation will be more spectacular if you use graphs, photographs, charts, drawings, diagrams, or samples. Triple-check your spelling and grammar, and remember that neatness counts.

EXHIBIT MATERIALS

Think of the space in front of your display board as a scientific fun park. Show off experiment samples, cross sections, models, or tools. Remember, you won't always be standing at your project, so make it safe. If electricity is involved, nothing should get hot enough to burn someone or something. Place liquid or smelly samples in sealed, unbreakable containers. If any spillable material is unsafe, it is smarter to simply show photographs of it rather than have a sample. Be sure that electrical cords and small or sharp objects are out of reach of little children.

Most science fairs do not allow the use of live animals. However, that doesn't mean you can't study animals for your project. For example, if your project is a study of ant behavior, leave the critters at home and display photos only.

THE WRITTEN REPORT

Your written report is a summary of your project. The judges will want to see a report that shows you understand the material you are presenting. Type it neatly and place it in a folder or binder. Decorate the cover of your binder or folder so that it goes with your display. Be sure to make it handy so anyone visiting the science fair can read it.

Your report needs to include:

- Title page (the title of your project, your name, your grade, and your school)
- Table of contents (a list of items included in the written report, with page numbers)
- The purpose of your project
- The problem being examined (if you do an experiment), as well as your hypothesis
- Research references
- List of materials used
- Procedures and observations
- Results
- Conclusion
- Acknowledgments (thanks to those who helped you)
- Any required forms
- Bibliography (a list of the resources you used to find information)

> **HANDS OFF!**
>
> The following items are not allowed in science fairs:
>
> - any body parts (except for teeth, hair, nails, or animal bone)
> - hypodermic needles
> - drugs
> - dangerous chemicals
> - materials that explode or catch on fire

You need to give proper credit to each kind of resource you use. In your bibliography, credit your resources as follows:

For encyclopedias: Name of encyclopedia, copyright date, topic, page number

For books and videos: Last name of author, first name of author, title of book or video, where published, publisher, when published

For magazines: Last name of author, first name of author, title of article, name of magazine, date of magazine, volume number, page number

For interviews: Person's name, person's job or position, person's workplace, address, phone number

IN CASE OF EMERGENCY

It's helpful to bring along an emergency "fix-it" kit in case your project needs any last-minute repairing. Your kit should include tape, glue, scissors, a stapler, markers, and anything else you think you might need.

THE JUDGE

A science fair judge looks for certain things. Originality is very important. Although it's okay to ask someone's opinion about your project, or to get adult help for your own safety, the judge wants to see that you did the project by yourself. Also, it's fine to follow a plan, but don't just copy an experiment from a book. Find a way to make the project uniquely yours. The following are some of the other things a judge looks for:

- Is the project complete?
- Is its purpose stated clearly?
- Is the information displayed creatively? Does it look good?
- Is the display safe?
- Is the display well-organized and clearly labeled?
- Is the written report neat and clear?
- Is the hypothesis stated clearly?
- Is the procedure explained clearly?
- Are the data easy to understand and do they support the conclusion?
- Have any variables been identified?

YOUR TALK

In many science fairs, each student is given an opportunity to explain his or her project to the judge, and then answer questions about it. Don't worry! Judges are friendly and supportive, and they love science. You can use your display to guide them through the details of your work. If you don't know the answer to a question, it's okay. *A good project always raises new questions to be explored.*

On the day of your talk, dress neatly, be pleasant, and speak clearly. Finally, remember that your enthusiasm for your work can be contagious!

Ideas for Science Fair Projects

In this section, you'll find many ideas for projects in the areas of physical science, life science, and earth science. The ideas cover the four major project types:

1. Research
2. Demonstration
3. Collection
4. Experiment

For any idea you choose, you'll want to mold and change it into something you can call your own. Also, be sure you understand the project fully. Look at the Key Words and Research sections to learn more about the subject.

You'll find that these projects are so much fun, you'll want to work on them whether or not you have a science fair in the near future!

Balancing Act
(Experiment)

PROBLEM: How is the fulcrum important when using a lever?

KEY WORDS
fulcrum, force, lever, load, simple machines

RESEARCH: At the library, research simple machines. Ask a parent to take you to a hardware store where you can look at a few different kinds of levers. With an adult, check out a construction site. Take pictures for your display.

HYPOTHESIS: Record in your log book.

MATERIALS
- marking pen
- tongue depressor (or craft stick)
- ruler
- pencil
- six or seven quarters

PUT IT TO A TEST

1. With a marking pen, label one end of the tongue depressor F for *force*. Label the other end L for *load*. Using the ruler, mark the center of the stick and label it B. Measure and mark the point halfway between F and B. Label that point A. Then measure and mark the point halfway between B and L. Label that C.

F A B C L

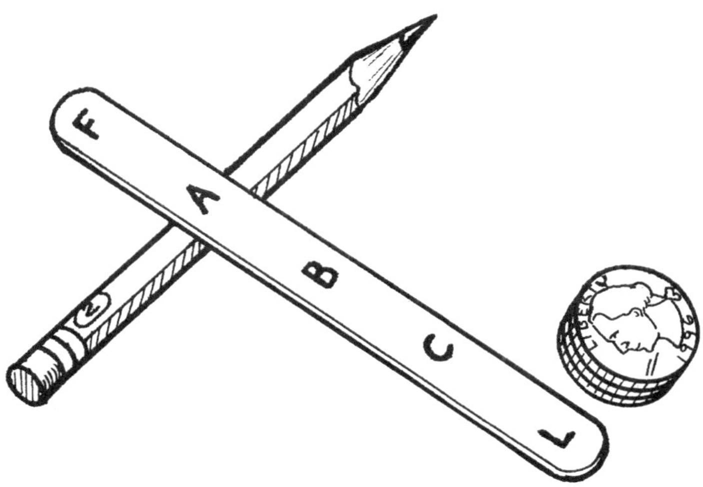

2. Place the pencil (your fulcrum) under the part of the stick labeled A. Place one quarter (your load) on top of the part labeled L. Place one quarter (your force) on top of the part labeled F. Does the force lift the load?

3. Place more quarters, one at a time, on top of the spot labeled F. How many does it take to lift the load? Carefully record your observations in your log book.

4. Remove all of the coins, move the fulcrum under point B, and repeat the process. Now how many quarters does it take to lift the load?

5. Remove all of the coins, move the fulcrum under point C, and repeat the process. Does it take more or fewer quarters to lift the load than it did in step 4? Does moving the fulcrum closer to the load make it easier to lift, or harder?

6. Record what happened in your log book.

CONCLUSION: Record in your log book.

BRAIN BUSTER

Using your model of a lever, find the point at which the force and the load are equally balanced. Where is that point? Record it in your log book.

TIPS TO MAKE IT TOPS!

For your presentation, collect and display pictures of levers used in everyday life. For example, a car jack, a teeter-totter, a crowbar, a wheelbarrow, a can opener, and scissors all use a lever in order to do their job. Even the human forearm acts as a type of lever. Label the lever and fulcrum in each example. Can you come up with a few more?

Run It Up the Flagpole

(Demonstration)

PURPOSE: To show how a fixed pulley works.

KEY WORDS

force, pulley, simple machines, work

MATERIALS

- drill
- two wooden yardsticks
- one unsharpened pencil (thin enough to slip through the holes in the thread spools)
- small saw
- sandpaper
- two empty thread spools
- scissors
- construction paper
- marking pens
- 6 feet of light string
- adhesive tape

RESEARCH: Go to the library and research simple machines. Ask your school principal if you can help to raise or lower your school flag. Ask an adult to take you to an auto repair shop. While there, ask a mechanic how pulleys are used to help lift a heavy load.

PUT IT TO A TEST

1. Have an adult drill a hole at each end of the two yardsticks. The holes should be ½ inch from the ends and big enough for a pencil to fit through snugly.

2. Ask your adult helper to saw the pencil in half. Sand down the jagged ends on each piece until they are smooth.
Slip a pencil half through each thread spool. Make sure you can turn the spools easily.

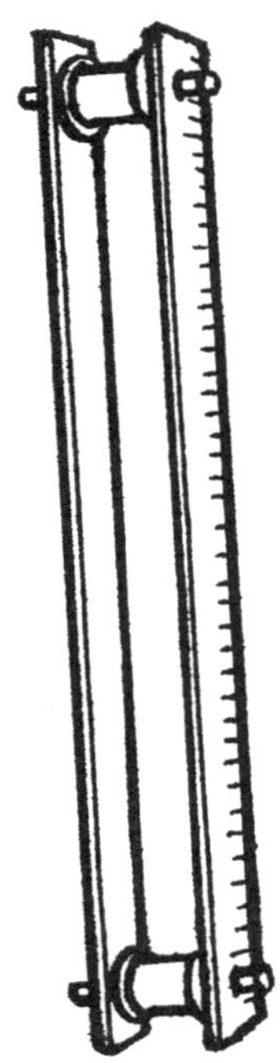

3. Place the yardsticks side by side, so that the holes at their tops and bottoms line up. Keeping the spools on the pencils, slip the pencil ends through the holes in the yardsticks, creating a sandwich effect.

4. Cut out a small flag (about 4 inches by 6 inches) from construction paper and decorate it as you choose. Punch a *tiny* hole near the top and bottom corner of your flag. Thread the string through the holes. If the flag slips easily on the string, tape it in place.

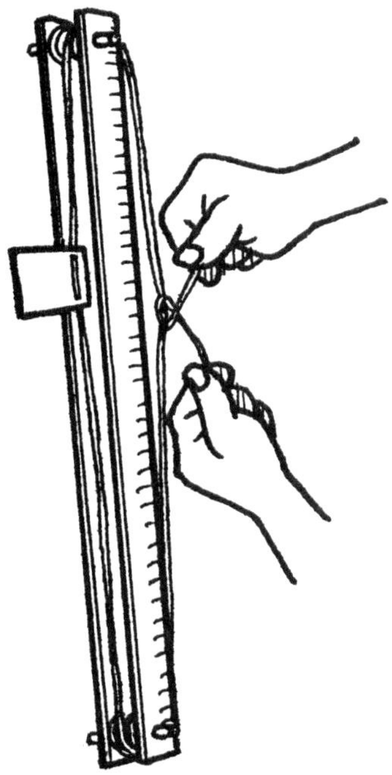

5. Loop one end of the string over the top spool and the other end over the bottom spool. Bring the ends of the strings together until they meet. Pull them tight and tie them together in a knot. The yardsticks, pencils, spools, and string form a fixed pulley. The two pulley wheels (the spools) are fixed—that is, they do not move up or down.

6. With your flag at the bottom of your "flagpole," pull the empty string down. In which direction does your flag move?

7. Record what happened in your log book.

CONCLUSION: Record in your log book.

BRAIN BUSTER

Using more than one pulley wheel spreads the weight of a load over more rope. That makes it even easier to lift such heavy loads as cars. Can you design a fixed pulley assembly using three or more wheels?

TIPS TO MAKE IT TOPS!

Window shades are usually raised by a small pulley. Find a way to include a pint-sized, homemade window shade as part of your display design.

Mix It Up

(Demonstration)

PURPOSE: To show the difference between a solution and a suspension.

KEY WORDS

chemical, element, evaporate, mixture, sediment, solute, solution, solvent, suspension

RESEARCH: Go to the library and research solutions and suspensions. Call a local college or university and arrange an interview with an expert in chemistry. If you live near a body of water, such as an ocean, river, or lake, ask an adult to take you there. Then obtain a water sample so you can evaporate the sample and examine any residue left behind. Call your local water company and ask for a list of the elements or chemicals found in your town water supply.

MATERIALS

- four small canning jars
- labels
- marking pen
- measuring cup and spoons
- hot tap water
- four stirring spoons
- sugar
- salt
- ground nutmeg
- ground allspice

PUT IT TO A TEST

1. Label the first jar "#1—sugar." Pour ½ cup of hot tap water into the jar and stir in ½ teaspoon of sugar.

2. Label the second jar "#2—salt." Pour ½ cup of hot tap water into the jar and stir in ½ teaspoon of salt.

3. Label the third jar "#3—nutmeg." Pour ½ cup of hot tap water into the jar and stir in ½ teaspoon of nutmeg.

4. Label the fourth jar "#4—allspice." Pour ½ cup of hot tap water into the jar and stir in ½ teaspoon of allspice.

5. Observe the solution or suspension in each jar. Do the jars containing sugar and salt look the same as the jars containing nutmeg and allspice? Record your observations in your log book.

6. Wait 10 minutes. Now what do you see? Are the sugar and salt still in jars #1 and #2? Dip a clean finger in jar #1 and taste. Do the same with jar #2. How do jars #3 and #4 look?

7. Record what happened in your log book.

CONCLUSION: Record in your log book.

TIPS TO MAKE IT TOPS!

Two solutions you made in this project are solids dissolved in a liquid. For your science fair project, make a list of other types of solutions or suspensions, such as:

- **club soda—a gas dissolved in a liquid**
- **river or seawater—the sand is suspended in water**

BRAIN BUSTER

You can go one step further with your project by observing what happens when you place jars #1 and #2 on a sunny windowsill and allow the sugar water and salt water to dry up.

Think about what other substances you can make into a solution or suspension in water. Are there some things that do not mix with water at all? Try a teaspoon of cornstarch, flour, or oil and observe what happens. Next try ½ teaspoon of cream of tartar and let it sit undisturbed overnight. What do you observe in the morning?

Anchors Away

(Experiment)

PROBLEM: What hull shape makes a boat go the fastest?

KEY WORDS

boat design, hull, seamanship, sailing, surface tension

RESEARCH: Go to the library and research different hull designs. Ask an adult to take you to a marina or a boat show to see various hulls up close. Arrange an interview with a boat owner who can help you with any questions you may have.

HYPOTHESIS: Record in your log book.

MATERIALS

- aluminum foil
- glue
- three craft sticks
- three 4-inch-by-4-inch pieces of lightweight paper
- marking pen
- modeling clay
- scissors
- plastic wading pool (for infants) or large plastic tub
- stopwatch (or watch with a second hand)

PUT IT TO A TEST

1. Tear off three 6-inch-wide sheets of aluminum foil and fold each into a boat with a different hull shape. For example, make one flat on the bottom (like a raft), one rounded on the bottom, and one with a V-shaped bottom.

rounded **V-shaped** **flat**

2. Glue a craft stick to the center of each square of paper to make three sails. So you don't mix the sails up later, write a name or a number on each one.

3. Form three small, marble-sized balls of clay. Be sure they are all the same size.

4. Press a ball of clay into the inside center of each boat. Push the end of a craft stick (sail) into each one.

5. Outside, fill the wading pool with water. You can also use a pond or other small body of water if it is available. Place the first boat in the water near the edge, and mark the time you begin. You can do this experiment on a windy day by using a battery-powered fan or by blowing hard on the sail. Whatever you choose, try to make the amount of wind blowing on each boat the same. Try to keep the boat going straight, and time how long it takes it to get across to the other side. Repeat the experiment with each boat.

6. Record what happened in your log book.

CONCLUSION: Record in your log book.

BRAIN BUSTER

Are there other ways besides shape to overcome surface tension? Try sprinkling pepper across the surface of a small bowl of water. Then plop one droplet of dish soap right into the center of the bowl. What happens?

For your science fair project, you can also explore ways that nature puts surface tension to good use. For example, it allows tiny insects called pond skaters to actually walk on water!

TIPS TO MAKE IT TOPS!

Since your project is about boats, come up with a sailing theme for your display. Blue and white background colors and a rope border around the display board can set the tone.

Dueling Diapers
(Research)

PURPOSE: To discover which brand of disposable diapers holds more liquid.

KEY WORDS
absorbency,
biodegradable,
capillary action,
diaper,
disposable

MATERIALS
- samples of three different brands of disposable diapers
- marking pen
- paper towels
- food coloring
- measuring cup
- warm water

RESEARCH: Go to the library and look up diapers in a consumer guide or magazine. Talk to new parents and ask which type of diaper works best for their baby and why. Interview someone from a diaper service and a local environmental group to get different viewpoints on cloth versus disposable diapers.

PUT IT TO A TEST

1. Label each diaper brand by name or number to help you keep track of each one. Then place diaper #1, plastic side down, on a paper towel.

2. Add several drops of food coloring to 1 cup of warm water. Slowly pour the water into the first diaper. Keep checking for

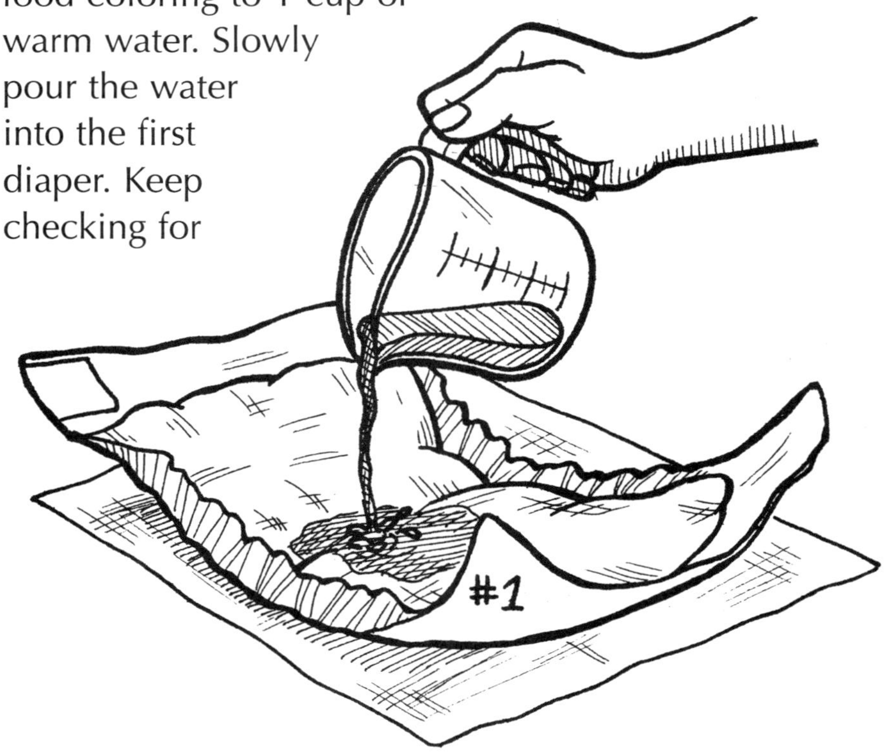

leaks on the paper towel. If you are able to pour the entire cup without a leak, prepare and pour more colored water. Make a note of how much the diaper holds before it leaks onto the towel.

3. Repeat the product test for diapers #2 and #3.

4. Record what happened in your log book.

CONCLUSION: Record in your log book.

BRAIN BUSTER

What are the advantages to using disposable diapers instead of cloth diapers? What are the disadvantages? Are any of the brands you test better for the environment (biodegradable) than others?

TIPS TO MAKE IT TOPS!

Gather photographs and pictures from magazines of adorable babies wearing different kinds of diapers. Those cute little faces are sure to brighten up your display!

Pucker Power!

(Demonstration)

PURPOSE: To show how the first battery was made and how it works.

KEY WORDS

battery, charge, chemical reaction, current, electricity, electron, proton, voltage

MATERIALS

- scissors
- blotting paper (found at stationery stores)
- aluminum foil
- knife
- fresh lemon
- small bowl
- adhesive tape
- two 3-inch-long electrical wires with ends stripped ½ inch
- ten pennies
- LED (a light-emitting diode, available at hobby stores)

RESEARCH: Go to the library and research different kinds of batteries. Ask an adult to take you to a battery recycling factory, or interview someone from a battery manufacturing plant.

PUT IT TO A TEST

1. To build a battery, cut ten penny-sized circles each from blotting paper and aluminum foil.

2. Ask an adult to cut the lemon in half and squeeze out all of the juice into a small bowl. Soak the blotting paper circles in the juice for about 30 seconds.

3. Tape one end of one electrical wire to an aluminum circle. With the wire on the bottom, place a juice-soaked circle of blotting paper on top of the aluminum circle. Place a penny on top of that.

4. On top of the first penny, build more layers: aluminum, more blotting paper, then a penny; aluminum, blotting paper, penny; and so forth. End with a penny.

5. Tape one end of the second piece of electrical wire to the top penny. You have now completed your battery.

6. Connect the loose ends of both wires to the LED. The LED should light up.

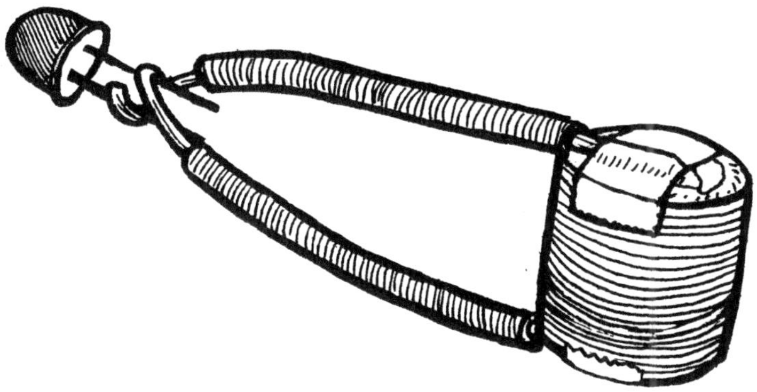

7. If you're still in the dark, make your battery taller (with more blotting paper, aluminum, and pennies), or substitute warm salt water or vinegar for lemon juice.

8. Record what happened in your log book.

CONCLUSION: Record in your log book.

A SHOCKING HISTORY

In the year 1800, an Italian scientist named Alessandro Volta discovered that he could produce a weak current of electricity by sandwiching together pieces of salt-water-soaked paper, silver, and zinc into a pile. As he touched a wire from the top of the pile to a wire from the bottom of the pile, sparks of electricity were generated. This was the first battery, and it is known as a voltaic pile. The electrical terms *volt* and *voltage* are named after Alessandro Volta.

TIPS TO MAKE IT TOPS!

Make a display of the various ways people use batteries. Include samples of different kinds of modern batteries.

Hello! Hello! Hello!

(Experiment)

PROBLEM: What types of surfaces help to create an echo?

KEY WORDS

acoustics, echo, echolocation, reverberation, sound waves

MATERIALS

- marking pen
- two paper towel tubes
- watch or small timer that ticks softly
- book (about 8 inches by 10 inches)
- dish towel
- plate
- sweater
- sheet of aluminum foil
- flat rock

RESEARCH: Go to a library and look up echoes. Ask an adult to take you to a concert hall or a theater. Ask questions about the importance of acoustics in a theater. (For example, can echoes ruin a performance?) Check out the materials engineers use to reduce echoes. Interview a scientist at a zoo or a marine life preserve to find out how animals use echolocation. Sailors also use a type of echolocation to find schools of fish. Find out how it works.

HYPOTHESIS: Record in your log book.

PUT IT TO A TEST

1. Mark an A on one end of tube #1, and a B on the other end. Lay tube #1 down on a flat surface, such as a desk or a tabletop. Slip the watch or the timer into the end of the tube marked A.

2. Stand the book upright at the end of the tube marked B as shown. Leave about a 1-inch gap between the tube and the book.

3. Place one end of tube #2 to your ear, then aim the other end toward any part of the book. What do you hear? Move the "ear tube" around to face any point on the book.

4. Now throw the dish towel over the book and repeat the experiment. Does the ticking get louder or softer? Take off the dish towel and carefully wrap a sheet of aluminum foil around the book, covering the area facing you. Is there a change in the echo? Remove the book. One by one, put the other materials in front of point B. What do you observe?

5. Record what happened in your log book.

CONCLUSION: Record in your log book.

BRAIN BUSTER

Many animals, such as bats, dolphins, and whales, use a method called echolocation to locate food. Find out how they use echolocation in this way.

Magnetic Attraction

(Experiment)

PROBLEM: Can some nonmagnetic materials be magnetized?

KEY WORDS

attraction,
compass,
electromagnet,
magnet,
magnetic field,
magnetic poles

MATERIALS

- iron nail
- needle
- aluminum foil
- quarter
- steel screwdriver
- butter knife
- scissors
- rock
- paper
- bar magnet
- paper clips

RESEARCH: Go to the library and research magnets and electromagnets. Ask an adult to take you to a metal scrap yard to see an electromagnet at work. Interview someone who works in a stereo-speaker factory to find out how magnets are used there.

HYPOTHESIS: Record in your log book.

PUT IT TO A TEST

1. Line up the following materials to magnetize: the nail, the needle, the piece of foil, the quarter, the screwdriver, the knife, the scissors, the rock, and the paper. Place the bar magnet near the paper clips, only to prove to yourself that they are attracted to it. Then remove the magnet.

2. Begin your experiment with the nail. Place it near the paper clips. Does the nail attract the clips? Now stroke the nail fifty times along one end of the bar magnet, always in one direction. Lift the magnet away from the nail after each stroke.

3. Test the nail with the paper clips once again. Does it attract the clips this time?

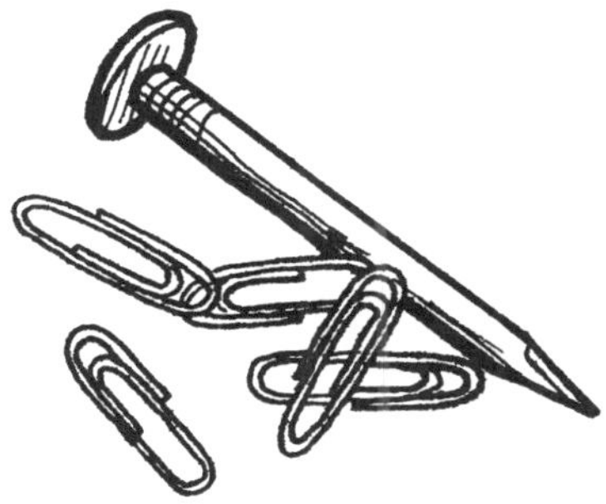

4. Repeat steps 2 and 3 to test each material. Which ones could be magnetized by the magnet?

5. Record what happened in your log book.

CONCLUSION: Record in your log book.

TIPS TO MAKE IT TOPS!

Instead of cutting plain squares of paper to display your written material, cut each piece in the shape of a bar magnet.

BRAIN BUSTER

Make your project more "attractive" by creating your own compass for display. Rub a bar magnet across a sewing needle at least thirty times in one direction. Fill a small bowl with water and place a drop of dish soap in the center. Float a quarter-sized slice of cork on the dish soap, then place the needle across the center of the cork (tape it if necessary). Spin the cork gently. When it stops, the needle will point north.

Good Conduct
(Experiment)

PROBLEM: Which materials are good conductors of electricity?

KEY WORDS

circuit, conductor, electricity, hydroelectric dam, insulator, terminal

MATERIALS

- wire cutters
- plastic-coated electrical wire
- flashlight bulb screwed into free-standing socket-type bulb holder (available at hobby or hardware stores)
- screwdriver
- duct tape
- 1.5-volt battery
- aluminum foil
- sample materials (see step 5)

RESEARCH: Go to the library and research the ways people produce and use electricity. If you live near a hydroelectric dam, ask an adult to take you there. Talk to the people who work there and take pictures. Interview a local electrician. The electric company may be able to send you information that would be useful in your display.

HYPOTHESIS: Record in your log book.

PUT IT TO A TEST

1. Ask an adult to help you cut three 3-inch lengths of electrical wire and strip ½ inch of plastic off each end.

2. Wrap one end of one wire around a terminal in the bulb holder. Screw the terminal in place. With the duct tape, tape the other end of the wire securely to either end of the battery.

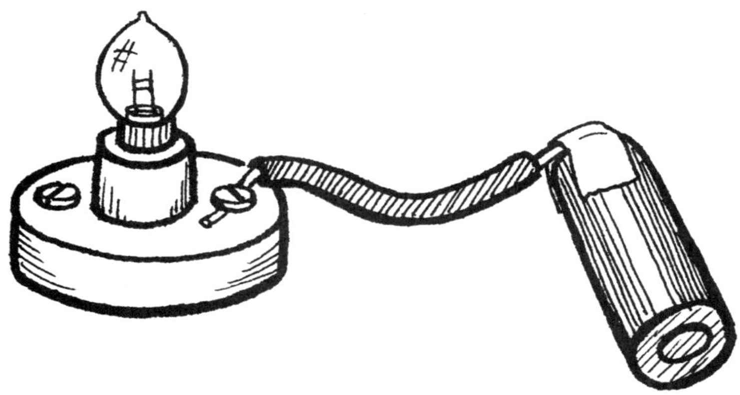

3. Tape one end of a second wire to the other end of the battery. Tightly wrap a pea-sized ball of aluminum foil around the loose end of this second wire.

4. Wrap one end of the third wire around the other bulb-holder terminal. Screw it in place. Tightly wrap the bare end of the third wire with a pea-sized ball of aluminum foil.

5. Line up your sample materials: a wood block, a quarter, a glass marble, a candle, a shell, a penny, and a butter knife. Pick up the two loose wire ends, one in each hand. (Hold the wires by the plastic coating, so the aluminum balls are free.) Touch the aluminum balls to each sample material. With what materials does the bulb light up? Try other materials, too.

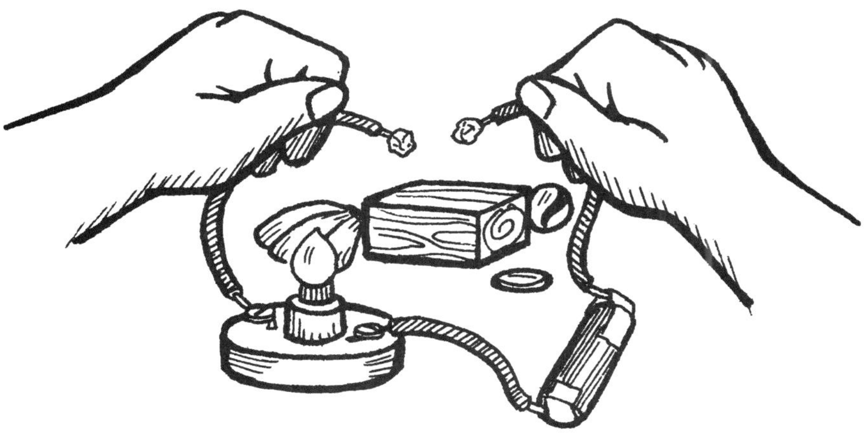

6. Record what happened in your log book.

CONCLUSION: Record in your log book.

BRAIN BUSTER

Try this same experiment, but alternate links of paper clips, copper wire, and a pencil (sharpened at both ends). Will electricity flow through one of the conductors into another?

Heat Stroke
(Experiment)

PROBLEM: Does the color of an object affect its temperature?

KEY WORDS
absorption, color, energy conservation, heat, reflection, solar power, temperature, thermometer, variable

MATERIALS
- white, green, and black water-based paint
- paintbrush
- four paper cups (nonwaxed)
- knife
- four indoor/outdoor thermometers

RESEARCH: Interview an architect or a representative from the gas or electric company. Ask questions about the use of color in conserving energy. Interview a manufacturer or retailer of clothing. Ask how color affects body heat.

HYPOTHESIS: Record in your log book.

PUT IT TO A TEST

1. Paint the outside and bottom of three cups. Use a different color for each cup and let them dry. Even if your paper cup is already white, you still need to paint it white in order to keep your test materials the same. The thickness of the paint could be a variable.

2. Turn the cups upside down. Ask an adult to help you by cutting a small opening in the bottom of each cup just large enough to fit a thermometer snugly.

3. Read the temperature on each thermometer and record it. Then insert a thermometer, bulb first, a few inches into each cup. Lift the cups and check to see that the thermometer bulbs are not touching anything.

4. Place the three cups outside in direct sunlight. Be sure they are all on the same kind of surface. Place the fourth thermometer on top of the fourth, unpainted cup. That is your control. Check the temperature of all four thermometers every 10 minutes for 30 minutes. Record your findings.

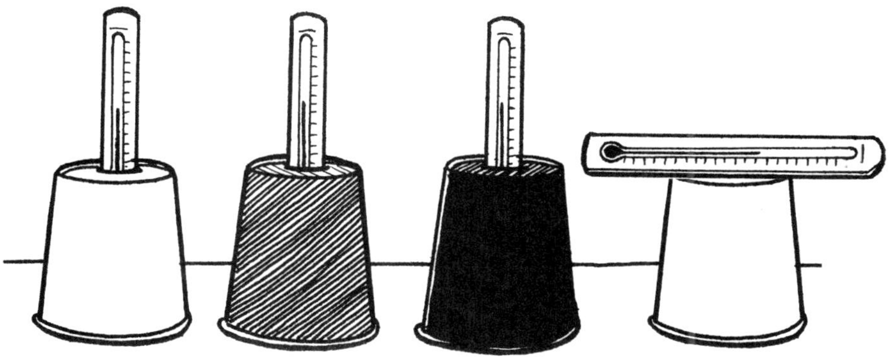

5. Record what happened in your log book.

CONCLUSION: Record in your log book.

BRAIN BUSTER

When your experiment is complete, move the cups and control thermometer indoors to a cool place. Once again, check the temperature of all four thermometers every 10 minutes for 30 minutes. Which cools down most quickly?

TIPS TO MAKE IT TOPS!

Use the same colors on your display as you used for your cups. Create a large sun shape as a background for your title and a giant cardboard thermometer for your display.

This Experiment Stinks!
(Experiment)

PROBLEM: How can I detect acid in food?

KEY WORDS
acid, base, chemical reaction, indicator, litmus paper

MATERIALS
- one-quarter head of red cabbage
- knife
- large bowl
- hot water
- strainer
- large canning jar with lid
- labels
- marking pen
- plastic egg carton
- measuring spoons
- test materials (see step 3)
- mixing spoon

RESEARCH: Go to the library and research acids. Call a local college or a university and arrange to interview a chemist. Call a dietician and find out how acidic foods affect your health. Visit your dentist and ask how acids affect the health of your teeth and gums.

HYPOTHESIS: Record in your log book.

PUT IT TO A TEST

1. Have an adult chop the cabbage into small pieces and place them in the bowl. Add enough hot water to cover the cabbage. Allow the cabbage to soak until the water is cool.

2. Strain the cabbage, collecting the cabbage water in the canning jar. Put the lid on the jar. Label the jar INDICATOR.

3. In each compartment of the egg carton, place about a tablespoon of each test material: lemon juice, milk, apple juice, smashed banana, and vinegar. Be sure to clean the measuring spoon after touching each material. Label each item.

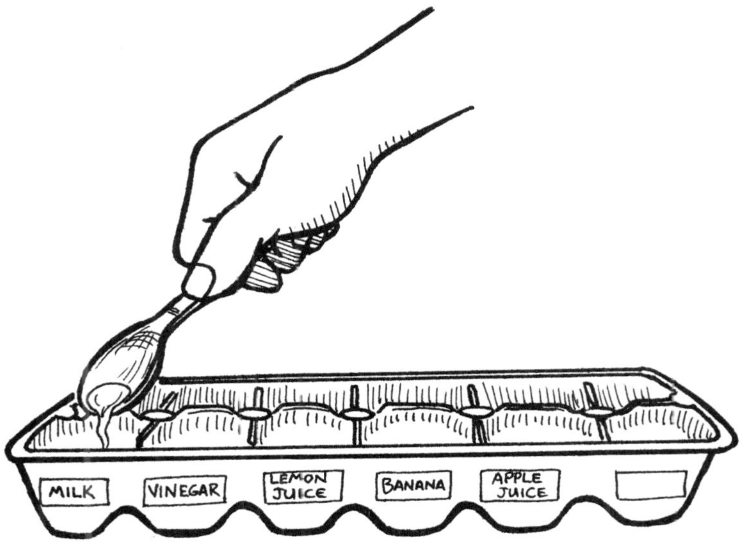

4. Carefully add a tablespoon of INDICATOR to each material and mix together with a mixing spoon. Again, carefully clean the spoon after touching each test material.

5. Check your INDICATOR for a color change in each egg-carton compartment. The INDICATOR turns red if the test material is acidic; it turns blue-green if the test material is a base (or basic). Write acid or base on each label.

6. Record what happened in your log book.

CONCLUSION: Record in your log book.

TIPS TO MAKE IT TOPS!

To include a truly impressive demonstration in your science fair project, use a cotton swab dipped in lemon juice to write a secret message on a piece of typing paper. Let dry. Then have a judge use your cabbage INDICATOR to make your message appear!

Skin Deep

(Demonstration/Experiment)

PROBLEM: Does the fat layer under the skin help keep people warm?

KEY WORDS

fat, insulation, skin

MATERIALS

- scissors
- two empty 1-quart milk containers
- marking pen
- two indoor/outdoor thermometers
- spoon
- measuring cup
- shortening (room temperature)

RESEARCH: Check out a chart on the human body to see where fat layers are. Talk to a dermatologist about how the fat layer under the skin affects you. Interview someone at a local zoo or an aquarium about how animals rely on body fat. Find out how sea mammals stay warm in cold waters.

HYPOTHESIS: Record in your log book.

PUT IT TO A TEST

1. Cut off the top half of each milk carton. Label the milk cartons #1 and #2. Check that both thermometers show the same temperature, then spoon 1 cup of shortening into milk carton #1. Slip thermometer #1 about halfway into the shortening so that the bulb is completely covered but doesn't touch the sides or bottom of the milk carton. Be sure you can read the temperature.

2. Place thermometer #2 in empty carton #2. Put both cartons in the refrigerator side by side. Be sure to mark them "experiment in progress."*

3. Record the temperatures on both thermometers every 15 minutes for 60 minutes.

4. For a variation on this experiment, try placing both cartons in bowls of ice water instead of in the refrigerator.

5. Record what happened in your log book.

CONCLUSION: Record in your log book.

*It's always a good idea to carefully label any experiment you store in the refrigerator or in a kitchen cupboard. If you don't, your experiment may end up in someone's stomach!

BRAIN BUSTER

Fat helps humans to stay warm. What are some other ways the human body uses fat? Find out how the body stores its food energy.

TIPS TO MAKE IT TOPS!

A model cross section of human skin will make your display stand out. Use the Baker's Clay recipe on page 77 to form your model. Be sure to label each layer of skin, including the fat layer. Add details such as sweat glands and hair. By the way, did you know that early settlers used animal fat to make soap? The average human body stores enough fat to make seven bars of soap!

Welcome to the Neighborhood

(Research)

PURPOSE: To create a Nature Guide of the main plants and animals in your neighborhood.

KEY WORDS

animal, ecology, ecosystem, environment, habitat, native plant, plant

MATERIALS

- local map
- backpack or knapsack
- pencils
- colored pencils or markers
- notebook
- camera
- plastic sandwich bags
- egg carton
- paper towels
- magnifying glass
- field guides (books) for plants and animals
- binoculars (optional)

RESEARCH: Interview members of local nature societies, such as bird, insect, or reptile societies. Ask what types of animals to look for in your area. Visit a local botanical garden to find out what plants are native to your area.

PUT IT TO A TEST

1. Choose a target area of about one city block, or about one-half square mile in your neighborhood. Mark it on the map. If you live in a major city, you might focus your study on a nearby park.

2. Make up a field research schedule. Try to fit in at least two 30-minute observation periods per week for at least 4 weeks. Pack your supplies into an easy-to-carry backpack or knapsack.

3. With an adult partner, walk slowly around your target area and look for signs of wild animals, including tracks, nests, and burrows. When you find an animal to

include in your Nature Guide, take a photo or make a sketch of it. Observe the animal's behavior and take plenty of notes, such as what it eats, how it reacts to other animals, and what sort of call or sound it makes, if any. Don't forget to look for spiders and insects. These are animals, too!

4. You have plenty of plant neighbors as well, including trees. Photograph or sketch as many plant varieties as you can. Include pictures of flowers and seeds, if possible. Note the type of soil each plant grows in, and whether it prefers shade or sun. Do you see any insects feeding on the plants?

5. If you want to collect samples for your display, such as feathers, a leaf, pinecones, or a flower, be sure no creatures are living on them. *Do not* pull out a plant by the roots. *Do not* touch a plant you do not recognize. Carry your samples in plastic sandwich bags or in the compartments of an egg carton. Use field guides to help you identify animals and plants. Label everything, including all the drawings in your log book and all your samples.

BRAIN BUSTER

You will often see different animals at night than you do in the daytime. For example, raccoons, opossums, bats, and owls are active at night. With an adult, plan three or four early-evening visits to your target area. Make a special "moonlight" section to go in your neighborhood Nature Guide.

6. Record your observations in your log book.

TIPS TO MAKE IT TOPS!

For your display, make a garden-in-a-bottle! Gather seeds from small plants you find growing in the shade in your target area. Turn an empty, 2-liter plastic soft drink bottle on its side. Have an adult cut a 2-inch flap in the top that can be opened and closed. Through the flap, place small pebbles in the bottom, then add a 1-inch-deep layer of soil. Sprinkle in the seeds you have gathered and keep the soil moist. In 2 or 3 weeks or less, some of your seeds should sprout.

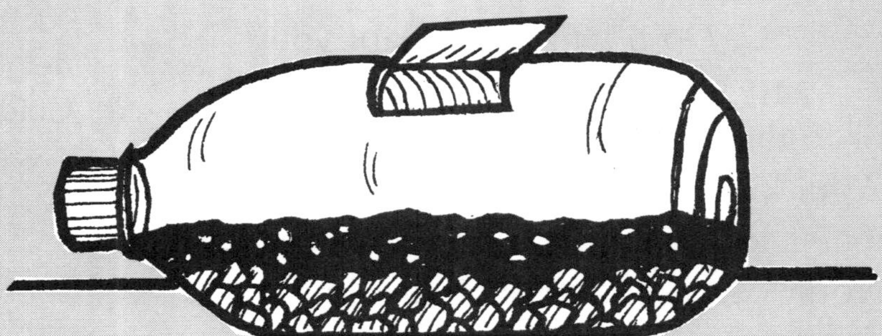

Nature's Landfill

(Experiment)

PROBLEM: What materials will decompose naturally?

KEY WORDS

bacteria, biodegradable, decomposition, enzymes, litter, organic, recycling

MATERIALS

- ½-gallon milk carton
- scissors
- small picture frame glass (3 inches by 5 inches)
- ruler
- masking tape
- pie tin
- handful of pebbles
- garden soil
- assorted litter (such as apple slices, grass, Styrofoam cup, plastic candy wrapper, newspaper, sandwich bag, and paper bag)

RESEARCH: Go to the library and research landfills. Then visit a landfill. Talk with the operator about what items decompose faster than others. Talk with a local farmer about creating a compost pile. Ask an adult to take you to an arboretum. Ask workers there how they dispose of their dead leaves and plants. Interview a biochemist at a laboratory or a university. Visit a local recycling center.

HYPOTHESIS: Record in your log book.

PUT IT TO A TEST

1. Wash out the milk carton and open its top all the way, as shown. Have an adult cut an opening in the side of the carton. Make the opening slightly smaller than the picture frame glass, and about 3 inches from the carton top. Punch a few holes in the bottom of the carton for drainage.

2. Tape the glass to the inside of the milk carton, creating a window out of the opening cut in step 1.

3. Place the milk carton inside a pie tin. Put pebbles in the milk carton, then fill the carton up to the bottom of the window with soil.

4. Cut or tear each kind of litter into small pieces. Spread a thin layer of one kind of litter in the milk carton, then cover it with about ½ inch of soil. Spread a thin layer of a second kind of litter, and cover that with ½ inch of soil. Continue to make layers of different kinds of litter, then soil. Record the different materials in order of their appearance. Make sure you can see the layers through your window. End with a final layer of soil. Put a little water in the carton and let it filter down. Do not soak the soil.

BRAIN BUSTER

Some plastic products are biodegradable. That means that they break down (degrade) when they are buried in a landfill. Test this for yourself. Ask an adult for permission, then dig two holes 6 inches deep in a garden. Bury a regular plastic sandwich bag in one, and a biodegradable sandwich bag in the other. With a waterproof marker, write "bio" on one craft stick and "regular" on the other. Mark each hole with the correct stick. Keep the area damp for 4 weeks, then dig up the bags and see if they have changed at all.

5. Close the top of the carton and put it in a warm, dark place. Keep the soil slightly moist. Over the next 3 or 4 weeks, observe the litter through the window.

6. Each week, record what happened in your log book.

7. Open the milk carton and remove some of each type of litter. Try not to disturb the sample directly in front of the "window." Note the changes that have occurred. Did everything deteriorate at the same rate? Be sure to save some "before" and "after" samples to display with your project.

CONCLUSION: Record in your log book.

TIPS TO MAKE IT TOPS!

Reuse some trash (aluminum cans, Styrofoam cups, and so forth) by making it into artwork! You can display your artwork as part of your science fair project.

Take a Little Off the Top

(Experiment)

PROBLEM: Does grass grow back no matter how short it is cut?

KEY WORDS

grass, growth point, leaves, phototropism, stems

RESEARCH: Go to the library and look up grass to find out about its growth patterns. Interview a gardener or someone from a local nursery. Find a box of grass seed and write to the manufacturer printed on the box. Ask if the company has information it could send you.

HYPOTHESIS: Record in your log book.

MATERIALS

- three plastic margarine containers with several small holes in the bottom
- potting soil
- measuring spoons
- rye grass seed
- misting bottle filled with water
- marking pen
- ruler
- scissors

PUT IT TO A TEST

1. Fill one margarine container with soil, nearly to the rim. Sprinkle about a teaspoon of grass seed evenly across the top. Cover the seed with slightly more soil, and mist it lightly until it is moist.

2. Prepare the other two containers in the same manner. Label all three containers.

3. Place all three containers in a warm, bright place. Keep the soil moist and allow the grass to sprout and grow for 1 week.

4. Measure and record the average length of the grass in each container. Using scissors, cut the grass in container #1 by half. Cut the grass in container #2 to within ¼ inch of the soil. Cut the grass in container #3 as even with the soil as possible.

5. Continue to mist the grass for another week. Observe and record the growth in all three containers. Then repeat step 4. Do a third and fourth trial of your experiment.

6. Record what happened in your log book.

CONCLUSION: Record in your log book.

BRAIN BUSTER

Find the growth point for other fast-growing plants, such as alfalfa and radish.

You've Been Fingered

(Demonstration)

PURPOSE: To show how fingerprints can be "lifted" from other materials.

KEY WORDS

crime scene, criminologist, Federal Bureau of Investigation (FBI), fingerprints

MATERIALS

- various test materials (such as a glass jar, a doorknob, paper, an apple, and a desktop)
- talcum powder
- soft ¼-inch paintbrush
- clear cellophane tape
- black shiny paper (from a craft store)

RESEARCH: Go to the library and research fingerprints. Ask an adult to take you to a local police department. Ask police officers how they find and save fingerprints from a crime scene. Interview a detective or someone from a police science lab.

PUT IT TO A TEST

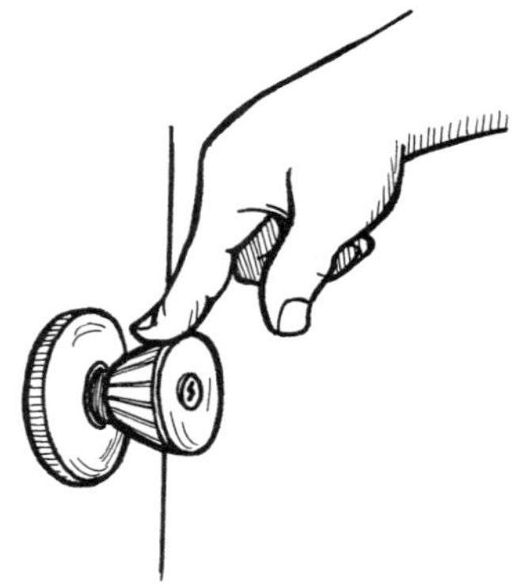

1. Don't wash your hands for a couple of hours, then touch each of your test materials in different places.

2. Sprinkle the talcum powder lightly over each test material. Wait a moment, then blow away any excess powder. The powder will stick to any greasy or oily areas, including your fingerprints.

3. Using the soft paintbrush, lightly brush the powdered areas to reveal the fingerprints. Take your time. You don't want to damage the prints. (You might have to practice this step a few times.)

4. Press a piece of clear tape over each fingerprint. Then carefully lift each one by pulling up the tape and sticking it onto the shiny black paper. You will see the powdered pattern of the fingerprint. Label what test material each print was lifted from.

5. Record your results in your log book.

Brain Buster

The process of detecting and lifting prints was created by Sir Francis Galton in the mid-nineteenth century. Today, fingerprints give police a helping hand in fighting crime, and computers store the fingerprints of many criminals. Find out how such law enforcement agencies as the FBI use fingerprints to identify a criminal.

Tips to Make it Tops!

Somewhere in your display, be sure to mention that people are not the only ones to have one-of-a-kind prints. Cows have one-of-a-kind nose prints! When an owner enters a cow into certain contests, the owner must send in the cow's nose print. When it's time to pick the best heifer, the judge takes the contestant's nose print and compares it to the one on file. This prevents cheating through "cow switching." It's a moo-velous process, wouldn't you say?

Red Sky at Night

(Demonstration)

PURPOSE: To show why the sky becomes red at sunset.

KEY WORDS

atmosphere,
spectrum,
sunlight

MATERIALS

- rectangular clear glass or plastic container (a small aquarium works well)
- water
- marking pen
- clay
- flashlight with fresh batteries
- measuring cup
- milk
- spoon

RESEARCH: Go to the library and research sunlight. Visit a local planetarium to see a model of how the sun's light strikes the earth. Interview a meteorologist or a sailor about how the color of the sky can tell you what weather may be coming.

PUT IT TO A TEST

1. Put the container on a flat surface, then fill it nearly to the top with tap water. Mark one of the short sides A, and the other short side B. Mark the long sides C and D.

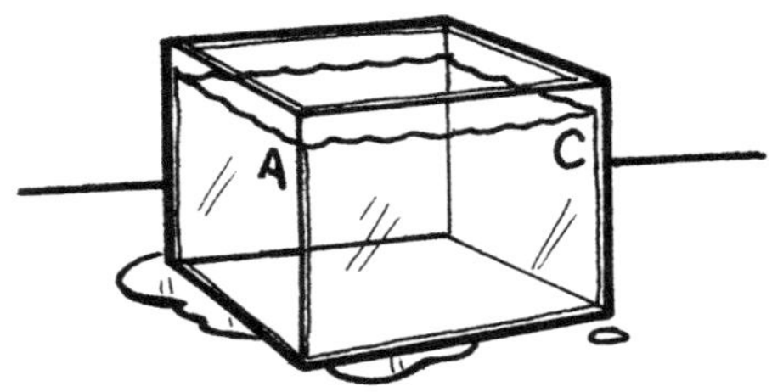

2. Make a ball of clay about the size of a baseball. Flatten one side of the ball a little so that it won't roll. Place it on the flat surface, about 3 inches from the edge of side A of the container.

3. Press the flashlight into the clay so that it stays in place. Adjust its position so that its light will shine right through the container. Be sure you are able to reach the switch easily.

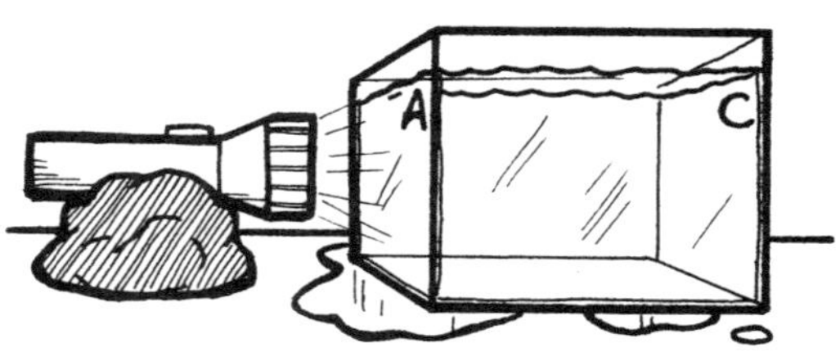

4. Pour ¼ cup of milk into the water and stir with the spoon. Allow the mixture to become still, then turn on the light.

5. Stand at side B and look through the milky fluid toward side A.

6. What do you see if you look through the container from side C to side D?

7. Record what happened in your log book.

CONCLUSION: Record in your log book.

BRAIN BUSTER

What happens if you use colored filters (or colored cellophane) on the flashlight?

TIPS TO MAKE IT TOPS!

You have all the colors of the rainbow at your fingertips. Use them to make the backdrop of your display a beautiful sunset. Or use paper in rainbow colors to accent your texts.

Create a drawing showing how the sun's rays travel through less atmosphere when the sun is overhead than when it is low on the horizon.

Under Pressure
(Experiment)

PROBLEM: Does water pressure increase with depth?

KEY WORDS
force,
water pressure

RESEARCH: Go to the library and research water pressure. Visit a local scuba-diving shop and ask how water pressure affects the human body. Interview an engineer and ask how water pressure is used to move heavy objects.

HYPOTHESIS: Record in your log book.

MATERIALS
- nail
- empty 1-quart milk carton
- ruler
- masking tape
- 10 inches of heavy string
- scissors
- aluminum foil
- double-sided tape
- several small paper cups (bathroom dispenser size)
- marker

PUT IT TO A TEST

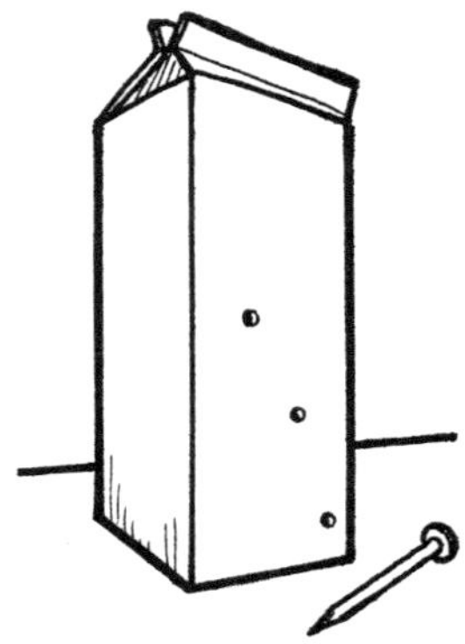

1. Have an adult use the nail to punch three holes of the same diameter in one side of the milk carton. Make the first hole 1 inch from the bottom and ½ inch from the right edge. Make the second hole 2 inches above that and ½ inch to the left of the first hole. Make the third hole 2 inches higher and ½ inch to the left of the second hole. Place a strip of masking tape over each hole.

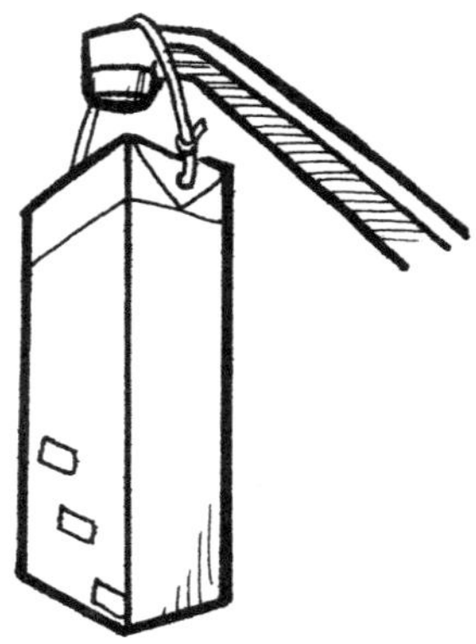

2. Open the top of the carton all the way. Ask an adult helper to punch two more holes, one on either side of the opening about an inch from the rim. Tie one end of the string

through one hole and the opposite end of the string through the other hole. Loop the string handle over the faucet of your kitchen sink so that the water runs into the carton.

3. Create a target in the bottom of the sink with a strip of aluminum foil 1 foot across. Place three long strips of double-sided tape over this foil. Place the tape strips ½ inch apart, just the way the holes in the carton are ½ inch apart.

4. Press the small paper cups side by side onto the strips, creating three rows. With a marking pen, label the cups in each row, with #1 being closest to the milk carton.

5. Fill the carton with water. Remove the strips of masking tape to allow water to shoot out of the holes. Keep filling the carton slowly from the faucet. Which stream shoots farthest? Check the cups to see which ones have water in them.

6. Record what happened in your log book.

CONCLUSION: Record in your log book.

BRAIN BUSTER

Would your experiment turn out differently if you used salt water? Would the water pressure be greater on a scuba diver in the salt water of an ocean or in the freshwater of a lake?

Water, Water Everywhere

(Demonstration)

PURPOSE: To show how rain forms.

KEY WORDS

atmosphere,
clouds,
evaporation,
precipitation,
rain, steam,
water vapor

MATERIALS

- water
- tea kettle
- stove or hot plate
- metal pie plate
- ice
- oven mitt

RESEARCH: Go to the library and research the water cycle. Interview a meteorologist about how rain forms. Also ask about cloud-seeding and how it works.

PUT IT TO A TEST

1. Put about 3 inches of water in the tea kettle. Place it on a hot plate or a stove. Have an adult helper turn on the heat.

2. When the kettle begins to boil, fill the pie plate with ice.

3. Wearing a protective oven mitt, hold the plate about 6 inches above the kettle. Observe what

happens as the water boils. What do you see? What happens to the bottom of the pie plate?

4. Record what happened in your log book.

CONCLUSION: Record in your log book.

TIPS TO MAKE IT TOPS!

To jazz up your demonstration, gather photographs and cut out pictures from magazines of various kinds of precipitation, such as rain, hail, snow, sleet, dew, and fog.

BRAIN BUSTER

Here is a way to measure the size of raindrops on a rainy day. Fill a baking pan with about ½ inch of flour. Run outside in the rain for a few seconds and catch a few drops of rain in the pan. The drops will form little balls of dough. Let the balls dry for a couple of hours until they harden. Strain the hardened drops from the flour and measure the diameter of each one. They will be approximately the size of the raindrops that made them.

Rock On

(Demonstration/Collection)

PURPOSE: To show how the rock cycle works.

KEY WORDS

erosion, igneous rock, metamorphic rock, molten, sedimentary rock, weathering

MATERIALS

- your rock collection
- rock and mineral identification guide
- poster board
- marking pens
- sturdy pegboard for display
- small hooks and shelves for use with the pegboard
- labels
- index cards
- flip card file

RESEARCH: Visit a local rock store and check out samples of different kinds of rock. Go to the library and research rocks and minerals. Obtain a field guide to rocks and minerals. Have an adult accompany you on a collecting trip, then try to identify what you find. Interview a geologist from a local university.

PUT IT TO A TEST

1. Prepare a poster to show the rock cycle. Draw a large circle using arrows as shown on the next page. At the bottom of the circle, write IGNEOUS ROCK. Below this heading, write something like: "Rocks carried deep within the earth become molten. Molten rock travels to the surface and hardens." (Use your own words.) Your arrow should point toward the text described in the next step.

2. Keep moving left around the circle. A third of the way around the circle, write SEDIMENTARY ROCK. Include a description. Your arrow should point toward the text described in the next step.

3. Two-thirds of the way around the circle, write METAMORPHIC ROCK. Include a description. Your arrow should point toward the text below IGNEOUS ROCK. The circle is now complete.

4. Insert shelves on the pegboard to display your rock collection. Keep in mind that if the collection is too heavy, your display could tip over!

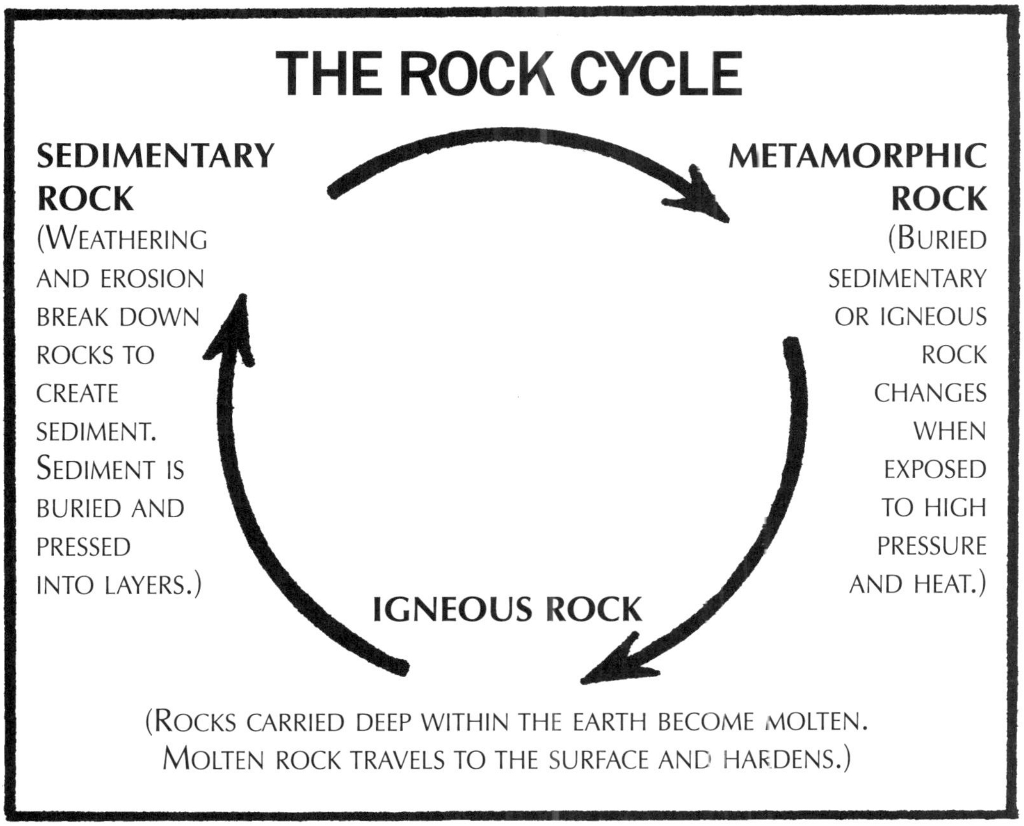

5. Label each rock with a number. Provide a flip card file that corresponds with the numbers and gives detailed information about each rock. For instance, you might include such information as the type of rock it is, where it was found, and its identifying features.

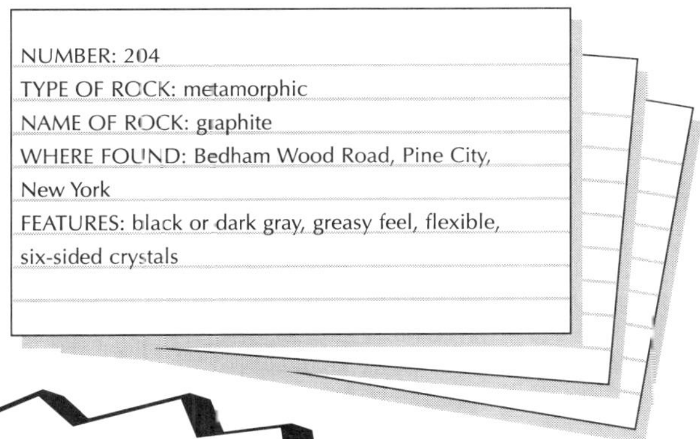

TIPS TO MAKE IT TOPS!

Use the space in front of your display to exhibit large rocks and the tools you use when rock hunting. When preparing your poster of the rock cycle, include illustrations or maps of where the sample rocks might be found.

The Root of the Problem

(Experiment)

PROBLEM: Do plants help prevent soil erosion?

KEY WORDS

conservation, erosion, root, soil

MATERIALS

- two 1-inch-deep baking trays
- measuring cup
- small pebbles or gravel
- potting soil
- rye grass seed
- misting bottle filled with water
- newspaper
- two 1-inch blocks of wood
- aluminum foil
- watering can

RESEARCH: Go to the library and research the parts of a plant, particularly the roots. Interview a local farmer about methods of soil conservation. Interview someone from your fire department and ask how a fire affects hillsides burning away plant material. Write to the Department of Forestry for information on how plants help to preserve soil.

HYPOTHESIS: Record in your log book.

PUT IT TO A TEST

1. Prepare both baking trays at the same time. Spread out 1 cup of small pebbles or gravel in each, then add enough potting soil to cover the pebbles and fill each tray to the rim. Don't add seeds to tray #1.

2. Sprinkle ½ cup of grass seed evenly over tray #2. Cover the seed lightly with soil, then mist it until it's moist. Place the tray in a warm, sunny spot. Allow the seed to sprout and grow until the grass is 1 inch high (1 or 2 weeks). Be sure to keep the soil moist but not soaked.

3. Once you have a growth of grass, spread newspaper on a flat surface outside. Place the two trays side by side on the newspaper. Put a wood block under each tray so they are tilted upward. Place aluminum foil under the bottom edge of the trays, and crimp the edges to catch any soil that washes away during the experiment.

4. With the watering can, pour ½ cup of water over each tray. Check the aluminum foil at the bottom. Which tray loses the most soil? Repeat the watering procedure once a day for one week. How does each tray look at the end of the experiment?*

5. Record what happened in your log book.

CONCLUSION: Record in your log book.

*Be sure to label your experiment, even at home. One sad science fair participant reportedly worked very hard on her plant experiment for a week. On coming home from school one day, she found that the gardener had thrown it away!

TIPS TO MAKE IT TOPS!

Grow a sample of grass in a glass jar. Display the jar in your exhibit section to show how roots spread throughout the soil and help to hold it in place.

Shake and Quake
(Demonstration)

PURPOSE: To show how a seismograph works.

KEY WORDS
earthquake,
epicenter,
seismic wave,
seismograph

MATERIALS
- cardboard box (approximately 12 inches square) with an open top
- marking pen
- knife
- roll of adding machine paper
- small paper cup
- 23-inch-long piece of string
- adhesive tape
- scissors
- ruler
- pebbles or gravel

RESEARCH:
Call a local university and interview a geologist. Go to the library and research earthquakes. Interview an engineer about how buildings are constructed to survive earthquakes.

PUT IT TO A TEST

1. Label the four sides of the box A, B, C, and D. Side A should be opposite side C, and side B should be opposite side D. Label the bottom E.

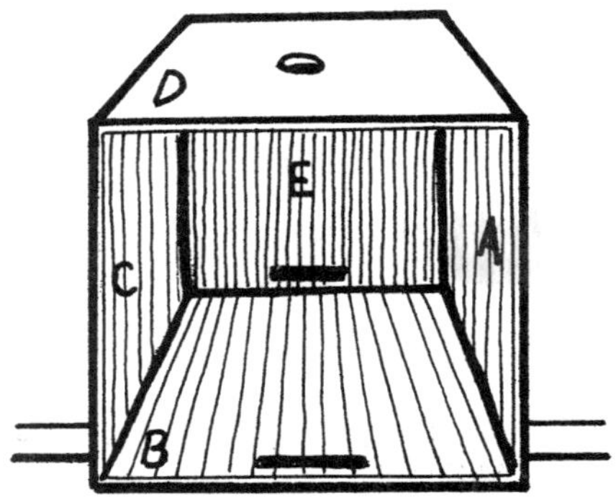

2. Have an adult punch a small hole in the center of side D. Then put the box at the edge of a table, side B down, so the opening is in the front and the side D hole is on top. Ask your adult helper to cut two slits large enough for the adding machine paper to slide through. Make slit #1 near the open edge of side B as shown. Make slit #2 at the lower edge of side E also as shown.

3. Place the adding machine paper behind the box. Slip the loose end through slit #2 into the box, then through slit #1 out of the box. Let the loose end hang freely in front of side B.

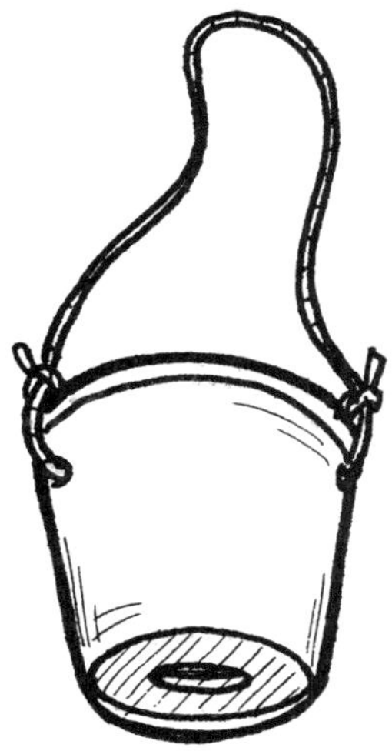

4. Punch two holes just below the rim of the paper cup. In the bottom of the cup, punch one more hole just large enough for the marking pen to fit in snugly.

5. Tie the string through the holes at the cup rim as shown. Pinch the string together and pass the center of it through the hole in side D of the box. Tape it in place. The opening of the cup should be facing upward. The bottom of the cup should be about an inch above the bottom of the box.

6. Push the uncapped marking pen through the bottom of the cup until the tip just touches the adding machine tape. Fill the cup with pebbles or gravel.

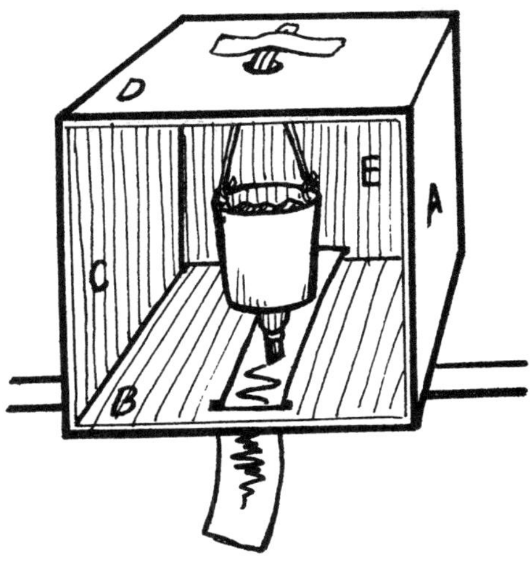

7. As you shake the box from side to side, hold the loose end of the adding machine tape and pull it toward you slowly. You don't need to lift the box. Just put one hand on the side and shake it.

8. Record what happened in your log book.

CONCLUSION: Record in your log book.

BRAIN BUSTER

The apparatus you have made is a horizontal seismograph. It records movement from side to side. What if the movement is up and down? Design a piece of equipment that could record such movement.

Natural Beauty

(Demonstration)

PURPOSE: To show how crystals grow.

KEY WORDS

crystal, gem, geode, solution

MATERIALS

- water
- measuring cup and spoons
- stainless steel pan
- three glass jars
- cream of tartar
- mixing spoon
- labels
- marking pen
- camera
- alum (found at grocery stores)
- sugar
- scissors
- lightweight string
- paper clip
- pencil
- paper towel
- magnifying glass

RESEARCH:

Go to the library and research crystals. Look through the phone book for a local geologist or gemologist to interview. Have an adult take you to a local rock shop or a county fair that has a rock display. Check out exhibits at a local museum.

PUT IT TO A TEST

1. Pour ½ cup of water into the pan. Ask an adult to heat it almost to boiling, then carefully remove it from the heat.

2. Rinse one of the glass jars with hot water to warm it up. Have an adult helper fill the jar with the heated water from the pan.

3. Add ¼ teaspoon of cream of tartar and stir until dissolved. Label the jar, and place it in a protected spot where it won't be disturbed.

4. Check the jar in 2 hours to see if any crystals have begun to form. Let the solution sit undisturbed for a week. Without disturbing the jar, check it every day and draw or photograph what you see.

5. For giant crystals, follow the same directions, but this time use 3 tablespoons of alum. Label the jar, and leave the solution undisturbed for 2 weeks. Check it every day for signs of crystals.

6. For crystals you can eat, again follow the same directions, but this time add ½ cup of sugar. After making the solution, cut a piece of string that's an inch shorter than the height of the jar. Tie a paper clip to one end of the string. Tie the other end of the string to a pencil. Place the pencil across the rim of the jar so that the string and paper clip dangle into the solution as shown. Cover loosely with a paper towel. Leave the solution undisturbed for 2 to 4 days, then check to see if crystals have formed on the string.

7. Using a magnifying glass, compare the different crystal formations you make. Draw the crystals and record the information in your log book.

CONCLUSION: Record in your log book.

TIPS TO MAKE IT TOPS!

To add extra interest, create a geode as described above, but coil a small piece of clean, lightweight string inside each eggshell before adding the sugar solution. Crystals will form all along the string.

BRAIN BUSTER

Have you ever seen a geode? It is a hollow rock with crystals inside. To create your own geode, carefully crack open a few eggs. Save the contents to use for cooking or baking. Rinse out the eggshell halves that have no cracks, and place them in an egg carton. Pour the cooled sugar solution into the eggshell halves, filling them almost to the top. (If you like, add food coloring to the solution before pouring it.) Leave the egg carton undisturbed for 2 weeks.

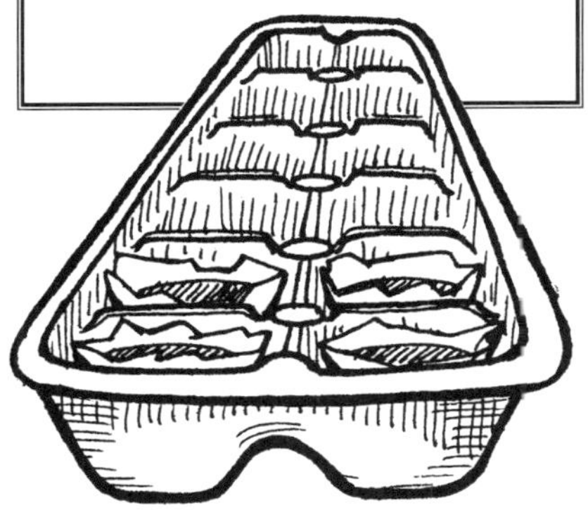

Solar Still
(Demonstration)

PURPOSE: To use solar power to distill freshwater.

KEY WORDS
condensation,
distillation,
evaporation,
solar energy,
solar power

MATERIALS
- old aluminum pan (9 inches by 13 inches and 4 or 5 inches deep)
- flat black paint
- paintbrush
- small glass bowl
- measuring cup
- salt
- hot tap water
- three small rocks
- clear plastic wrap
- large rubber band

RESEARCH: Go to the library and look up distillation. Ask an adult to take you to a backpacking or camping store, where you can interview a person about survival information. Call a local college or university and talk to someone in the atmospheric sciences department about solar power. Visit a planetarium that has a telescope with a solar filter.

PUT IT TO A TEST

1. Paint the inside and outside of the aluminum pan with black paint. Let it dry.

2. In the small bowl, mix ¼ cup of salt and 2 cups of hot tap water. Stir until the salt dissolves.

3. Pour the salt water into the aluminum pan. Place the bowl in the center of the pan. (The bowl needs to be at least 1 inch shorter than the pan.) If the bowl floats, put a clean rock in it to hold it in place.

4. Cover the whole pan with plastic wrap and secure it with a rubber band.

5. Carefully place a small rock or two on the plastic wrap, creating a dip. The dip should be centered over the bowl, and about ½ to 1 inch above the bowl's rim.

6. Place the pan in bright sunlight for several hours.

7. Record what happened in your log book.

CONCLUSION: Record in your log book.

BRAIN BUSTER

Does it make a difference if you cover the pan with foil instead of plastic wrap? Would you collect more water if the pan were painted white instead of black? Why can't people survive by drinking salt water?

How They Work

Below, you'll find explanations of how each of the science fair projects work. Did you come to the same conclusions?

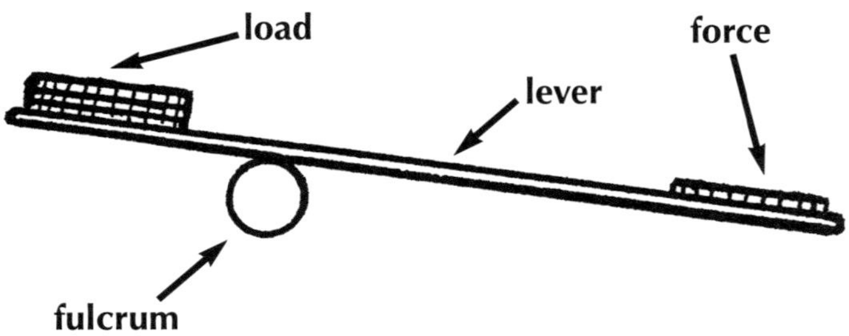

BALANCING ACT **(Page 20):** A lever can be any board, stick, or bar (or in this case, a tongue depressor or a craft stick) that turns freely on a fixed point of support. The fixed point is called the fulcrum. In this experiment, the pencil is your fulcrum. The closer the fulcrum is to the load, the less force is needed to lift it. A lever is known as a simple machine.

RUN IT UP THE FLAGPOLE **(Page 22):** With a fixed pulley, the pulley wheels (the spools) do not move with the load (in this case, the flag). A fixed pulley is a simple machine made up of one or more wheels, with a string (or a rope, a belt, or a chain) moving around them. When you pull down on the rope, the load goes up. It is easier to pull a weight down than to lift a load straight up, so a fixed pulley helps you do the work with less effort. Just think how tired you would be if you had to scurry up the flagpole every morning and evening!

MIX IT UP **(Page 24):** The sugar and salt seem to disappear when they dissolve in the hot water. They are still there. You cannot see them, but you can taste them. The tiny particles (called molecules) that make up the sugar and salt move between the tiny molecules that make up the water. They form what is known as a *solution.* The salt and sugar are called *solutes.* The water is the *solvent.* If you allow the water to evaporate, what remains of the salt and sugar is called a *residue.*

The molecules of the nutmeg and allspice do *not* interact with the molecules in the water, and they do not change how they look. Instead of dissolving, they are *suspended* in the water. The water and spices are called a *suspension.* Over time, some of the spice slowly settles to the bottom of the jars. The settled layer is known as *sediment.* If you stir the jar, the spices and water form a suspension again.

ANCHORS AWAY (Page 26): At its surface, water forms a sort of stretchy "skin." This is called *surface tension.* Surface tension is what causes water to form into droplets. It can also slow down a boat cruising across water. Certain hull designs are more effective than others in cutting surface tension, which is strongest at the front of the boat.

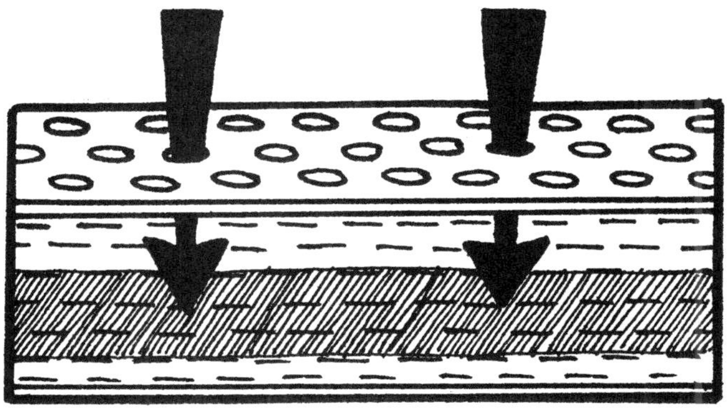

DUELING DIAPERS (Page 28): The pads in baby diapers are made up of lots of tiny fibers that absorb (soak up) liquid through a process called *capillary action.* The fibers have spaces between them. The water slowly creeps into these spaces. Once the spaces are all filled, the diaper leaks.

PUCKER POWER! (Page 30): The copper pennies and aluminum work together to create electricity when exposed to an acid-soaked (lemon juice) disc of blotting paper. A chemical reaction between the metals and the acid causes tiny particles in the materials, called electrons, to gather at one end of the battery. The electrons have a negative (–) charge. Protons gather at the other end. The protons have a positive (+) charge. This charge difference from one end of the battery to the other creates an electrical *current.* When the current passes through the LED, the LED lights up.

HELLO! HELLO! HELLO! (Page 32): An echo is formed when sound waves are bounced, or reflected, off a hard surface. In your experiment, sound waves bounce off the book cover toward you. The "ear tube" boosts the sound. Soft surfaces, such as a towel or a sweater, soak up (absorb) sound waves.

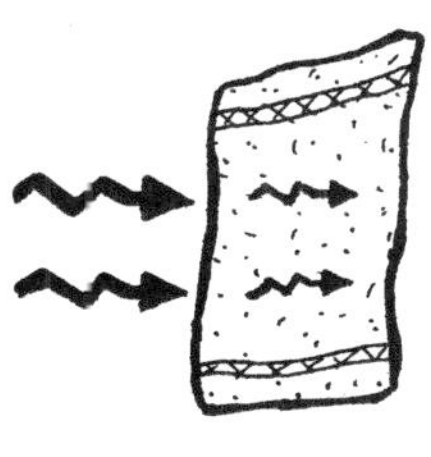

MAGNETIC ATTRACTION (Page 34): Many materials contain tiny bits of nonmagnetized iron. Each bit of iron has its own north pole and south pole, but the poles are scattered in all different directions. When you stroke a bar magnet across test materials that contain iron, you force the like poles to all line up in the same direction. With the poles now lined up, the material becomes magnetized.

GOOD CONDUCT (Page 36): Electricity does not flow through all materials. Those that it will flow through are called conductors. Those that it will not flow through are called insulators. When you touch the two aluminum balls to a conductor, you complete the circuit and the bulb will light.

HEAT STROKE (Page 38): The sun's rays heat the earth. Light-colored materials reflect the sun's rays, so the inside of the white-painted cup stays cooler than the other cups. Dark-colored materials absorb rays quickly, so the insides of the green and black cups warm up. Which color absorbs the sun's rays quickest of all?

THIS EXPERIMENT STINKS! (Page 40): Acids usually taste sour and can eat away other substances. Many foods contain weak acids. The cabbage water (INDICATOR) reacts with the acid in food in a chemical reaction. This reaction changes the color of the INDICATOR from purple-blue (no reaction) to pink or red (meaning acid is present), or a greenish-blue if a base is present.

A base is a chemical substance that reacts with an acid to form a salt. Bases, such as baking soda, taste bitter. Your INDICATOR turns blue-green in the presence of a base. Try your INDICATOR on baking soda, then other materials.

SKIN DEEP (Page 42): The shortening you use in this experiment is a kind of fat similar to the fat in a human body. Fat acts as an insulator to slow the rate at which heat leaves the body. All mammals, including humans, have a layer of fat beneath their skin. The fat layer helps to keep them warm when it is cold outside. Even so, over time, body heat will eventually be lost.

WELCOME TO THE NEIGHBORHOOD (Page 44): Ecology is the study of how living things interact with their home, or *environment.* If you live in the country, the living things that make up the local environment might be trees, flowering plants, rabbits, deer, and plenty of insects and birds. The nonliving things include soil, water, and air. All living and nonliving things that exist in an environment make up what scientists call an *ecosystem*.

NATURE'S LANDFILL (Page 47): Some items break down, or decompose, faster than others due to bacteria and enzymes. Food and plant materials usually rot away very quickly. Under the right conditions such as those in your experiment, paper products also decompose fairly quickly. (Remember that paper is made from wood, a plant product.) Plastic items can take hundreds of years to break down. That means the plastic things you throw away today might still be around for your great-great-great-great-great-great-great-great-grandchildren to deal with.

TAKE A LITTLE OFF THE TOP (Page 50): Young plants usually have a growth point—the point from which new leaves are produced. If you cut away the growth point, the plant will die. The growth point of rye grass is at soil level. That is why it continues to grow even after it's cut with a lawn mower or chewed on by a hungry plant eater.

YOU'VE BEEN FINGERED (Page 52): Your skin has tiny openings called pores. Oil and perspiration flow up through the pores to the skin surface. When you touch something, the ridges (prints) on your hands leave deposits of oil and perspiration. Fine powder sticks to these deposits, revealing the fingerprints of the person who left them.

Your fingerprints are unique. They form two months before you are even born, and no one in the world has the same print pattern as you do!

RED SKY AT NIGHT (Page 54): The sunlight we see is made up of different colors that move at slightly different speeds. As sunlight passes through the atmosphere, it hits particles that break it up and scatter the different colors. During the day, the rays of the sun are direct. You

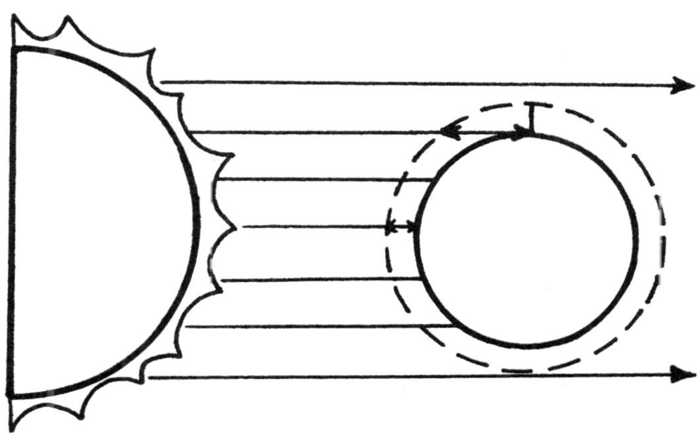

see the scattered blue light, so the sky appears blue. When the sun is low on the horizon, the rays strike the atmosphere at a low angle. Sunlight must pass through more atmosphere, which means it is scattered more. Only red light reaches your eye, so the evening sky appears red.

When the light from the flashlight passes through the liquid in the container, it strikes tiny milk particles that break it up into different colors and scatter it. When you look through the container from side B to side A, the light rays you see have been scattered a lot. You see only the longer, slower red light rays. When you look through the container from side C to side D, the light rays are less scattered, and the milk has a bluish tint.

UNDER PRESSURE (Page 56): Pressure is a force that one material exerts on another. The water at the surface of the milk carton exerts pressure on the water below it. The pressure of water increases with depth because of the weight of water pushing down from above. That's why the water from the lowest hole shoots out farthest.

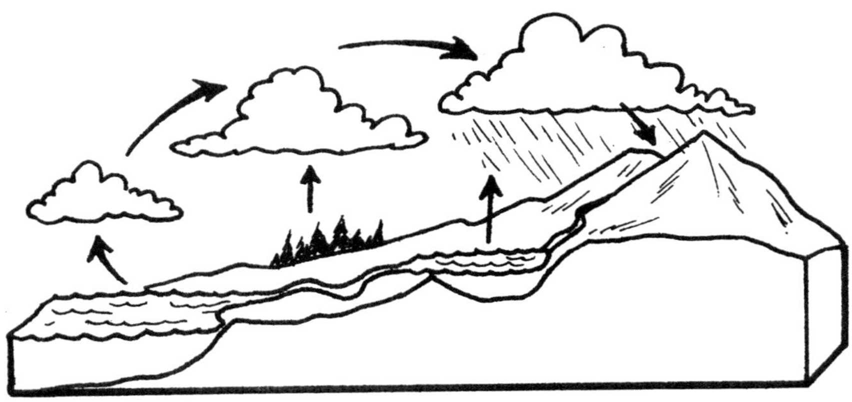

WATER, WATER EVERYWHERE (Page 58): In this experiment, the water boils, turning to steam (or water vapor). The water vapor condenses on the bottom of the cold pie plate and forms drops that "rain" down. One of the biggest recycling projects on earth is nature's own water cycle. Water is always evaporating from the oceans and other bodies of water. The water vapor rises high into the atmosphere, where it cools, condenses, and forms clouds. The condensed water eventually falls back to earth again as rain.

ROCK ON (Page 60): No explanation needed.

THE ROOT OF THE PROBLEM (Page 62): Soil is a layer of loose material that blankets much of the surface layer of the earth's dry land. Soil is made up of particles of rocks, minerals, and other materials, such as rotted leaves. Most plants cannot grow without soil. Loose soil can be washed away by water, or blown away by wind. Plants help to shield the soil from wind, and plant roots hold the soil in place.

SHAKE AND QUAKE (Page 64): The cup stays steady while the paper underneath it moves, so the pen draws a zigzag line on the paper. The cup stays in place due to *inertia,* the tendency an object has to stay in the same state (at rest or moving) unless a force changes that state. A real seismograph works the same way.

NATURAL BEAUTY (Page 66): A crystal is a solid substance with flat surfaces. The surfaces always meet at the same angle. Almost all minerals are made up of crystals. Crystals can form from a solid, a liquid, or a gas. The atoms that make up a particular crystal arrange themselves, layer after layer, in a pattern. As more material is added to the outer surface, the crystal grows. There are seven crystal categories, or systems, based on shape. Look up crystal systems in the encyclopedia to see how each is shaped.

SOLAR STILL (Page 68): In this demonstration, you use the sun's energy to separate the water from the salt. The sun heats up the salt water. The water gradually *evaporates* into water vapor. The vapor then *condenses* onto the plastic wrap. The salt is left behind in the pan. The dip in the plastic channels the water down into the bowl, where it collects as distilled water. If you taste it, you will discover that it is no longer salty.

Some arid desert countries use solar energy to obtain drinkable distilled water from sea water.

Make It Yourself!

Models and handmade displays can make your science project stand out. The recipes below might come in handy when you're designing your presentation.

PAPIER-MÂCHÉ MODEL

1. Tear old newspapers into 1-inch-wide strips.

2. Make a form for your model by molding recycled aluminum foil or crumpled paper into the shape you want. You can also use an inflated balloon. Cover the form with masking tape.

3. Mix ½ cup of flour and 2 teaspoons of salt in a bowl. Add 1 cup of warm water. Mix this paste with your hands until it is thick and creamy.

4. To finish the model, dip newspaper strips into the paste and hold them over the bowl until they stop dripping. Cover the form with overlapping strips of paper. Continue until it is covered with two or three layers. Finish with a final layer of blank paper strips.

5. Give your model several days to dry completely. Drying it on a rack will allow air to circulate and prevent mold from forming. After it's dry, it's ready to paint!

BAKER'S CLAY

1. In a bowl, mix together 1½ cups of flour and ½ cup of cornstarch. In a separate bowl, mix ¼ cup of salt and ¾ cup of hot water, then add that to the flour and cornstarch. Blend with a spoon. The "clay" should stick together.

2. Form the clay into a ball and squash it in your hands for 5 or 10 minutes, until it's smooth and satiny. Now the clay is ready to form into any design you choose.

3. When you have finished your model, place it on an ungreased cookie sheet. Have an adult put it in the oven at 200°F for 1½ to 2 hours, or until it is completely hardened. A large piece may take as long as 4 hours. Don't overcook it! Once it has cooled, it's ready to paint.

DISPLAY CARDS

1. Gather plant materials, such as seeds, leaves, and flowers. Arrange them as you like on a piece of colorful construction paper.

2. Cut a piece of clear, adhesive plastic (available at craft stores) the same size as your construction paper. Carefully place it, sticky side down, over your arrangement. Press the final product between newspaper and under a heavy book for several days before displaying.

Resources

The following are good sources of information on various scientific subjects.

SOCIETIES AND MUSEUMS

Chemistry

American Chemical Society
Science Office (K-8)
1155 16th Street, NW
Washington, DC 20036
phone: (800) ACS-5558
(When the voice menu prompts you, press # for the education department.)

Insects

Young Entomological Society
1915 Peggy Place
Lansing, MI 48910-2553
fax and phone: (517) 887-0499
E-mail: YESbugs@aol.com

Spaceflight

NASA Goddard Space Flight Center
Educational Office
Greenbelt Road
Greenbelt, MD 20771
Attn: Code 130
phone: (301) 286-7205

Weather

American Meteorological Society
45 Beacon Street
Boston, MA 02108
phone: (617) 227-2425

Geology

American Geological Institute
4220 Kings Street
Alexandria, VA 22302
phone: (703) 379-2480

Environment and Wildlife

U.S. Fish and Wildlife Service
Main Interior Building
1849 C Street, NW
Washington, DC 20240
phone: (800) 344-WILD
Web site: http://www.fws.gov

National Audubon Society
700 Broadway
New York, NY 10003
phone: (212) 979-3000
Web site: http://www.audubon.org

National Wildlife Federation
8925 Leesburg Pike
Vienna, VA 22184-0001
phone: (800) 822-9919

The Sierra Club
85 2nd Street, 2nd Floor
San Francisco, CA 94105
phone: (415) 977-5653
E-mail: information@sierraclub.org
Web site: http://www.sierraclub.org

General Science

Field Museum
Roosevelt Road at Lake Shore Drive
Chicago, IL 60605
phone: (312) 922-9410

Fort Worth Museum of Science and History
1501 Montgomery Street
Fort Worth, TX 76107
phone: (817) 732-1631

WEB SITES

National Hurricane Center
http://www.nhc.noaa.gov/

National Climatic Data Center
http://www.ncd.noaa.gov/ncdc.html
(Forecasts, information on the Tropical Storm Prediction Center, and satellite and radar imagery)

Kennedy Space Center
http://www.kscvisitor.com
(Historical spaceflight information, space news, space theater, and more)

SCIENTIFIC EQUIPMENT AND SUPPLIES

(Write or call for catalogs, books, or kits.)

Edmund Scientific Co.
101 East Gloucester Pike
Barrington, NJ 08007
phone: (609) 573-6250

Fisher Scientific Co.
4901 West Lemoyne Street
Chicago, IL 60651

The Science Eye
18241 SW 52nd Court
Fort Lauderdale, FL 33331
phone: (954) 680-7077

Science Kit, Inc.
777 East Park Drive
Tonawanda, NY 14150

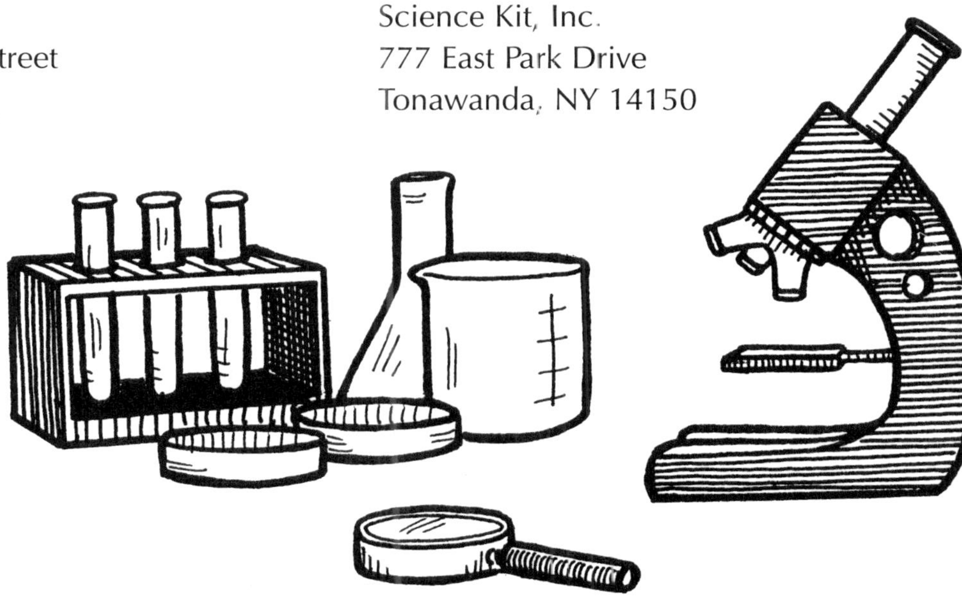

Timetable

Use this handy timetable to help you organize your time for any science fair project. Just photocopy this page, or copy it onto a separate piece of paper.

Science fair date:

Science fair location:

TASK	BEGIN	DEADLINE	WHEN COMPLETED
Get a copy of the rules			
Choose a topic and write a purpose			
Do research			
Gather materials			
For experiment: • Choose a problem • Design an experiment • Draw conclusions • Perform experiment (or build model, prepare collection, design a demonstration, and so forth)			
First draft of written report			
Final draft of written report			
Prepare display			

Glossary

absorb: to take in. A paper towel absorbs liquids.

angle: the amount of space between two lines (or planes) that meet at a point or intersect each other. An angle is measured in degrees.

biodegradable: able to be broken down by natural agents, such as bacteria.

chlorophyll: a chemical in plants that is used during photosynthesis. Chlorophyll gives plants their green color.

classify: to arrange information in logical order.

condensation: the changing of a gas or a vapor into a liquid by cooling or by a lowering in pressure.

data: information collected during an experiment and used to find patterns or relationships.

decompose: to break down into a simpler form.

evaporation: the changing of a liquid into a gas by heating. A liquid doesn't necessarily need to reach the boiling point in order to evaporate.

force: the energy or power exerted on an object that makes the object move, change shape, or change direction.

hypothesis: an educated guess.

inertia: the tendency of an object to keep doing what it's doing (whether that's resting or moving) unless it is acted upon by a force.

load: the material being moved by a machine.

molecule: the smallest amount of a substance that has the properties of that substance. Molecules are made up of two or more atoms.

observe: to use the senses to obtain information.

photosynthesis: the process by which green plants produce food from carbon dioxide, water, and sunlight.

precipitation: any form that water takes when condensing and falling to earth. Rain, fog, snow, and dew are all forms of precipitation.

pressure: the amount of steady force applied to an area.

temperature: the measure of how hot or cold a material is.

water vapor: water that has become gas due to evaporation or boiling.

Index

Part Two:
Science Experiments

Contents

To Parents and Teachers

Children are naturally curious about the world and love to explore it. This section provides children with fascinating and rewarding experiments they can do themselves. Each activity begins with a question you may have heard your child ask, for example, "Where does the wind come from?" Next is a simple description that gives some background about the experiment. The description and question at the beginning of each activity will motivate your child to complete the experiment. An explanation of what happened in the experiment immediately follows.

The activities in *Part Two: Science Experiments* are fun and safe to do. Instructions are kept as simple as possible. Performing these experiments will give a child a sense of accomplishment and an appreciation of how science works. Some activities require the assistance of an adult, for example, those using heat or a flame. You may help your child learn new vocabulary, too. All Key Words from the activities are defined in the Glossary at the back of this section. Join your child as he or she discovers excitement and success through science.

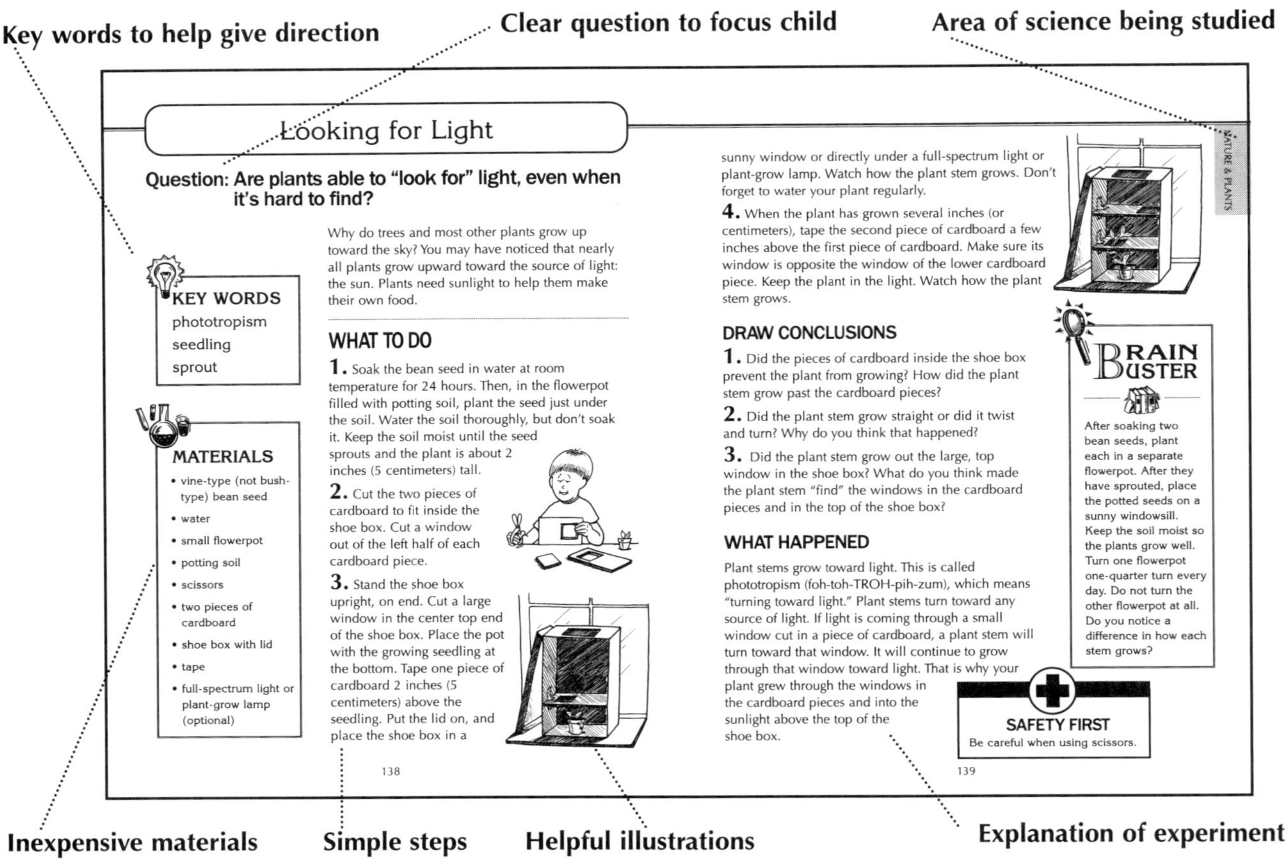

Looking for Light

Question: Are plants able to "look for" light, even when it's hard to find?

KEY WORDS
phototropism
seedling
sprout

MATERIALS
- vine-type (not bush-type) bean seed
- water
- small flowerpot
- potting soil
- scissors
- two pieces of cardboard
- shoe box with lid
- tape
- full-spectrum light or plant-grow lamp (optional)

Why do trees and most other plants grow up toward the sky? You may have noticed that nearly all plants grow upward toward the source of light: the sun. Plants need sunlight to help them make their own food.

WHAT TO DO

1. Soak the bean seed in water at room temperature for 24 hours. Then, in the flowerpot filled with potting soil, plant the seed just under the soil. Water the soil thoroughly, but don't soak it. Keep the soil moist until the seed sprouts and the plant is about 2 inches (5 centimeters) tall.

2. Cut the two pieces of cardboard to fit inside the shoe box. Cut a window out of the left half of each cardboard piece.

3. Stand the shoe box upright, on end. Cut a large window in the center top end of the shoe box. Place the pot with the growing seedling at the bottom. Tape one piece of cardboard 2 inches (5 centimeters) above the seedling. Put the lid on, and place the shoe box in a sunny window or directly under a full-spectrum light or plant-grow lamp. Watch how the plant stem grows. Don't forget to water your plant regularly.

4. When the plant has grown several inches (or centimeters), tape the second piece of cardboard a few inches above the first piece of cardboard. Make sure its window is opposite the window of the lower cardboard piece. Keep the plant in the light. Watch how the plant stem grows.

138

NATURE & PLANTS

DRAW CONCLUSIONS

1. Did the pieces of cardboard inside the shoe box prevent the plant from growing? How did the plant stem grow past the cardboard pieces?

2. Did the plant stem grow straight or did it twist and turn? Why do you think that happened?

3. Did the plant stem grow out the large, top window in the shoe box? What do you think made the plant stem "find" the windows in the cardboard pieces and in the top of the shoe box?

WHAT HAPPENED

Plant stems grow toward light. This is called phototropism (foh-toh-TROH-pih-zum), which means "turning toward light." Plant stems turn toward any source of light. If light is coming through a small window cut in a piece of cardboard, a plant stem will turn toward that window. It will continue to grow through that window toward light. That is why your plant grew through the windows in the cardboard pieces and into the sunlight above the top of the shoe box.

BRAIN BUSTER

After soaking two bean seeds, plant each in a separate flowerpot. After they have sprouted, place the potted seeds on a sunny windowsill. Keep the soil moist so the plants grow well. Turn one flowerpot one-quarter turn every day. Do not turn the other flowerpot at all. Do you notice a difference in how each stem grows?

SAFETY FIRST
Be careful when using scissors.

139

All the materials used in these experiments are safe, inexpensive, and easy to find. Most are common household objects or substances. Here are some types of stores where you may find the materials you'll need:

Supermarket
food coloring, scissors, straws, glass jars and glasses, measuring cups and spoons, baking soda, vinegar, soda bottles, waxed paper, plastic bags, food items, wooden spoon, birdseed, paper towels, dishwashing liquid, cornstarch, lightbulbs, balloons, notebook, food scale, crayon

Drugstore
eyedropper, iodine, rubbing alcohol

Hardware Store
thumbtacks, ruler, compass, scissors, glue, window screening, cardboard, tape, string, flashlight, grease pencil, magnets, magnifying glass (hand-held lens), rubber bands, watch, cardboard tubes

Arts and Crafts Store
clay, colored paper or poster board, small mirror, balloons, yardstick, colored plastic sheets, rubber bands

Flower Shop or Garden Center
flowerpots, potting soil, sand, flowers, plants, plant sprayer

Photo Shop
photographic paper

If additional equipment is wanted, try contacting a scientific supply company, such as Edmund Scientific at 101 East Gloucester Pike, Barrington, NJ 08007 (609) 573-6250. Their catalog is extensive and prices are reasonable.

Introduction

Let's Experiment!

One day many years ago, Isaac Newton was sitting under an apple tree. Newton was a very curious fellow. He was always asking questions about the world and how it worked. He wanted to know about everything. One thing he had wondered about was why people and animals stay fixed to the earth and don't go flying off into space. While Newton was dozing under the tree, it is said, an apple fell off a branch and hit him on the head. Newton had two thoughts. The first was "Ouch!" The second was "Whatever force made that apple fall off the tree is what keeps people from flying off into space!" So Newton decided to find out what that force was.

Newton went off—rubbing the bump on his head, no doubt—and began doing experiments to discover what made the apple fall to the ground. After lots of experimenting and thinking, Newton discovered and explained what we today know as the force of gravity.

You probably ask a lot of questions about how the world works, just as Isaac Newton did. Isaac Newton was one of the world's greatest scientists. Like all scientists, he asked a lot of questions. All science begins with a question: Why is the sky blue? What is the wind? How does something work? One of the best ways to answer questions like these is to do an experiment and see what happens.

BEING A SCIENTIST

Being a scientist means thinking of ways to answer interesting questions. Science is really just a matter of common sense, logical thinking, and careful observation. To be a scientist, you must

- **LOOK.** Notice things you would like to know about. Looking carefully at things gives you ideas about them and raises questions about how they work.
- **QUESTION.** When you look closely at things around you, you may have questions about them. Scientists ask lots of questions. They don't know all the answers, but they plan on finding out.

- **TEST.** An experiment is simply a test. Scientists design tests that will give them answers to their questions.
- **OBSERVE.** During an experiment, scientists look very carefully at what happens. You also need to look carefully at what happens during and at the end of an experiment. This may give you clues that help you answer your question.

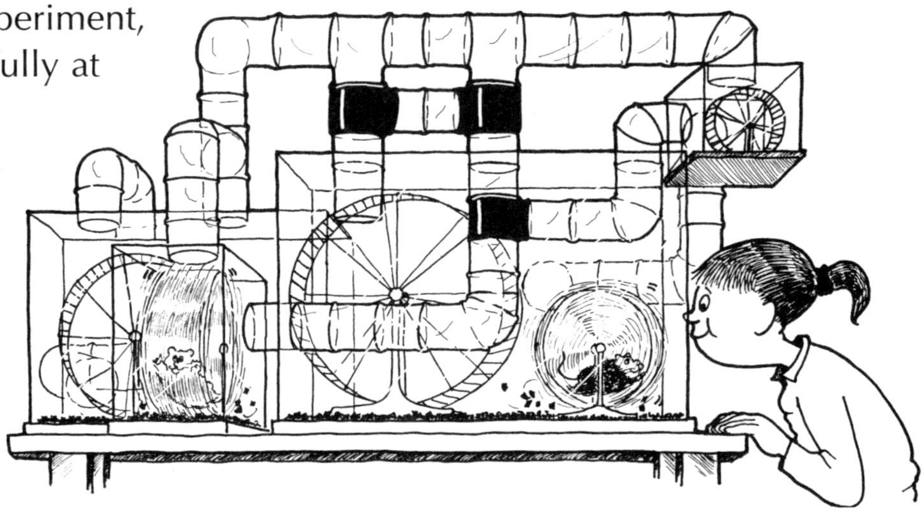

- **RECORD.** Write down what you see. Write down what happens during and at the end of an experiment. Writing everything down helps scientists understand the results of the experiment.

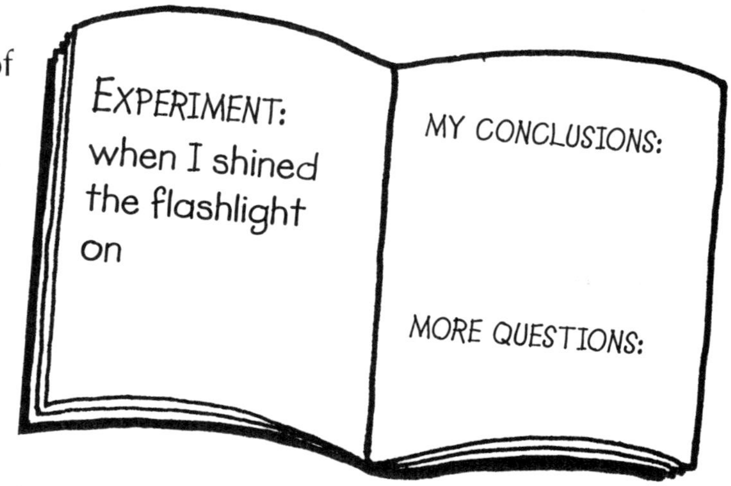

- **THINK.** Think about the results of your experiment. What do the results tell you? Do they answer your question? Very often, the results of an experiment raise more interesting questions.
- **CONCLUDE.** Decide what the test results are "telling" you, and draw conclusions. What have you learned from your experiment?

Remember, "doing science" is asking questions about things you don't know. Sometimes an experiment answers your question. Other times an experiment does not answer your question but instead makes you think of more questions! Experiments don't always turn out exactly the way you think they will. Let the results of your experiments lead you to new ideas and new questions.

BEFORE YOU DO AN EXPERIMENT

When doing the experiments in this section, be sure to do the following things first:

1. Get a parent's or another adult's permission to do the experiment.
2. Read the list of materials. Gather everything you will need.
3. Read the instructions. Make sure you understand what you have to do and how long the experiment will take.
4. Write down what you observe.

Remember, too, that there is no such thing as failure. If an experiment does not turn out as you planned, you can always do it again. Making mistakes can be useful in science. Sometimes a mistake leads to a very interesting result—and maybe even a great scientific discovery.

SAFETY FIRST!

You should be smart and safe when doing your science experiments. Some experiments use materials that only adults should handle. Have an adult be your "lab assistant." Follow these simple rules for safe science.

1. Have a grown-up present when you do experiments.
2. Plan ahead—know what materials you'll need and have them ready. Read the experiment instructions.
3. Only an adult should use anything hot or anything on or near a flame.
4. Be careful when using sharp objects, such as scissors, or have an adult use them.
5. Never taste, eat, or swallow anything you make during a science experiment. Do not touch

your eyes, lips, or mouth when working with experiment materials. Always wash your hands after doing an experiment.

6. It's smart to label all the concoctions you make when you do your experiments.
7. Keep small children and pets away from your "science lab" experiment area. Tie up or pin back long hair and loose clothing.
8. Keep your science lab clean. Start on a clean surface and then clean it thoroughly when you're done.

KEEPING RECORDS

Sometimes it's difficult to remember everything that you did and everything that happened during an experiment. For this reason, it's helpful to write down what you do and what you observe. It's a good idea to keep a science notebook handy so you can write things down. Writing things down helps you remember. It also helps you analyze the results of your experiment and answer your question. Your notes may help you link something you did during an experiment with the results you got. Your notes may lead you to ask more interesting questions about your experiment.

Writing down your observations is called keeping a record of what happens during a science experiment. Get a notebook, a pad, or some paper. For each experiment, write down what you do and what you observe. You may also write down the conclusions you draw from the results of your experiments—and any new questions the results make you think of. See the next page for an example from a science notebook.

EXAMPLE OF A SCIENCE NOTEBOOK PAGE

Date:

Description of Experiment:

What is happening during the experiment?

What happened when the experiment was over?

Why do you think you got the results you did?

More questions that you have now:

The Weight of Air

Question: Does air have weight?

Is air heavy? Do things weigh more when they're full of air than when they have little or no air? Find out.

KEY WORD

balance

MATERIALS

- yardstick OR long, thin piece of wood and ruler and pencil
- string, 6 to 12 inches (15 to 30 centimeters) long
- tape
- thumbtacks
- two equal-size balloons
- pen

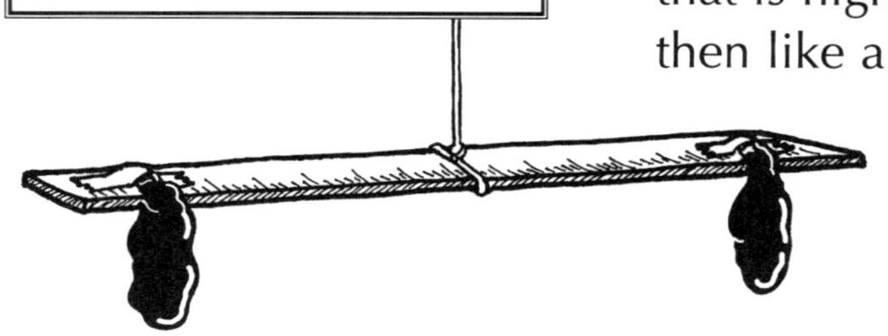

WHAT TO DO

1. If you are not using a yardstick, mark inches on the stick of wood, using the ruler and pencil.

2. Find the center of the yardstick or wooden stick. Tie approximately 6 to 12 inches (15 to 30 centimeters) of string around this center point and knot it. Tape the string in place if necessary. Leave enough string to dangle the stick from as you hold on to the free end of the string. Hanging there from the string, the stick should be balanced. If it is not, press thumbtacks on the side of the stick that is higher, until both sides are even. The stick is then like a balance scale.

3. Tape one empty balloon to one end of the stick. Tape the other empty balloon to the other end of the stick.

Make sure that you use equal lengths of tape and that the stick is still balanced. If not, move one balloon slightly until the stick is balanced and parallel to, or even with, the floor. Dangle the stick from the string to see that it is balanced.

4. With a pen, mark the places where the balloons are taped. Now that you know the empty balloons are balanced, take one balloon off the stick. Blow this balloon up until it is full of air. Tie the end of the balloon tightly so no air escapes.

5. Tape the inflated balloon back on the stick in the same spot. Dangle the stick from the string. What do you see?

DRAW CONCLUSIONS

1. Why did the stick "scale" have to be well balanced for this experiment?

2. What happened to the stick when you attached the inflated balloon? Why do you think this happened?

WHAT HAPPENED

You saw that both balloons were balanced—were the same weight—when they had no air. When you blew up one balloon, you added air to it. The air you blew into the balloon made it get "fat." When you attached the inflated balloon to the stick, it was no longer balanced. It was weighted down by the inflated balloon because the air in that balloon made the balloon heavier.

BRAIN BUSTER

Do you weigh more when you're full of air? Get an accurate bathroom scale (a digital scale, if possible). Breathe out until there is no air in your lungs. Keep the air out and look to see how much you weigh. Write down how much you weigh with no air in your lungs. Then take a deep breath, filling your lungs. Hold the air in and step on the scale. Is there a difference in your weight with and without air in your lungs?

Balloon in a Bottle

Question: Does air take up space?

KEY WORD

inflate

MATERIALS

- balloon
- glass soda bottle

Try to blow up a balloon in a bottle and find out if an empty bottle is really empty.

WHAT TO DO

1. Hold on to the open end of the balloon as you push the closed part into a clean, dry soda bottle.

2. Stretch the open end of the balloon over the lip of the bottle. Make sure the balloon end fits tightly on the mouth of the bottle.

3. Try to blow up the balloon. Blow into the balloon as hard as you can. Does the balloon inflate, or expand with air?

DRAW CONCLUSIONS

1. What do you think prevented the balloon from inflating inside the bottle?

2. What was stronger, the pressure inside the bottle or the air you were blowing out of your lungs into the balloon?

WHAT HAPPENED

Though the bottle looked empty, it really was full—of air! Air takes up space. As you tried to inflate the balloon, it began to take up more space in the bottle. The balloon wouldn't inflate because of the air trapped inside the bottle. The air in the bottle was trapped there when you sealed the bottle top with the balloon. The "bottled air" pressed hard on the balloon you tried to inflate. You couldn't blow up the balloon in the bottle because the air had no space in which to expand.

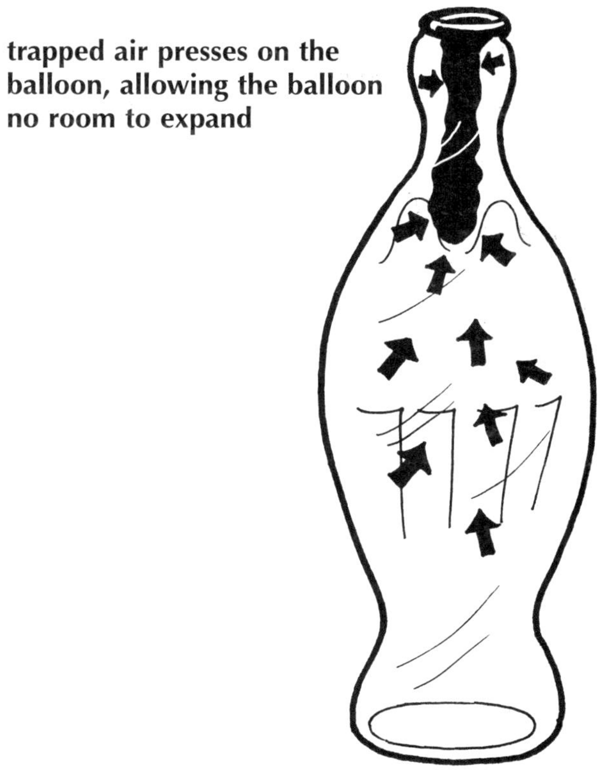

BRAIN BUSTER

Air space can keep an underwater paper towel dry. Stuff a paper towel securely into an empty juice glass. Make sure the towel doesn't fall out when you turn the glass over. Fill a large pot with cool water. Hold the glass straight upside down and plunge it into the pot of water. Wait a few seconds. Then carefully lift the glass out of the water. If you held the glass perfectly straight throughout this experiment, the paper towel in the glass will be dry. The air in the glass (between the paper towel and the glass rim) kept the water out—so the paper towel stayed dry.

Seeing Some Sound

Question: Can the effects of sound vibrations be seen?

KEY WORD

vibration

MATERIALS

- heavy-duty black plastic garbage bag
- small plastic bowl (margarine container, for example)
- scissors
- rubber band (to fit around bowl)
- tape
- uncooked rice or orzo pasta
- large pot, 2–3 quarts (2–3 liters) size
- wooden spoon

You hear sound when something causes the air to vibrate, or move rapidly. There is a way you can "see" sound vibrations that are moving through the air. Just try it!

WHAT TO DO

1. Place the plastic bowl facedown on the plastic bag. Cut the bag around the bowl, a bit larger than the outline of the bowl.

2. Turn the bowl right side up, and place the plastic over the opening. Stretch the plastic tightly and secure it with the rubber band. Tape all the edges of the plastic bag to the bowl.

3. Carefully place some rice grains or orzo pasta in the middle of the firmly stretched plastic.

4. Set the large pot on its side with the opening close to the bowl, but not touching it. Hit the bottom of the pot with the wooden spoon. Watch what happens to the grains on the plastic stretched over the bowl.

DRAW CONCLUSIONS

1. What caused the grains on the plastic to jump?

2. How might the grains move differently if you hit the bottom of the pot more softly? If you hit it much harder?

WHAT HAPPENED

When you hit the bottom of the pot with the spoon, the air began to vibrate. This vibration traveled to the plastic-covered bowl. The moving air (the vibration) caused the stretched plastic to move, too. When the stretched plastic moved, the grains that were on it moved as well. The moving grains showed you that the air was moving—that sound is a vibration in air.

SAFETY FIRST

Be careful when using scissors.

BRAIN BUSTER

Make bottle music! Get several bottles of the same kind and size (soda bottles, for example). Fill one bottle with water to within 1 inch (2.5 centimeters) of the top. Leave 2 inches (5 centimeters) of air in the second bottle, 3 inches (8 centimeters) of air in the next bottle, and so on. Each bottle should have 1 inch (2.5 centimeters) less water than the previous bottle. Line the bottles up and blow across the top of each to make a different sound. That's because a different amount of air is vibrating in each bottle. Play a tune on the bottle instrument you made.

Make Light Photos

Question: How are images made on photo paper without using a camera?

KEY WORDS

light-sensitive

silhouette

MATERIALS

- scissors
- heavy black construction paper
- black-and-white photographic paper
- assorted objects (leaf, feather, hair clip, etc.)
- lamp

When you take a photograph, the light entering the camera makes a picture on the light-sensitive film. The image on the film makes a picture when light shines through it onto special light-sensitive paper. But did you know that you can make "light photos" without a camera?

WHAT TO DO

1. Cut the black construction paper until it is about half the size of a sheet of photographic paper. Then cut any interesting shapes you like out of the black construction paper. You should first punch a hole in the paper, then cut out your shape, keeping all edges of the paper intact.

2. Darken the room as much as possible. Take out one sheet of photographic paper. Very quickly, put the black construction paper with the shapes cut out of it on one-half of the photo paper and the assorted objects on the other half. Do not move anything once it's on the photo paper. Turn on the lamp so the light shines directly on the photo paper. Leave the lamp on for about 1 minute. Then turn it off.

3. Take the black construction paper and the assorted objects off the photo paper. You will see that a "light picture" is left on the photo paper. (But not for long!)

DRAW CONCLUSIONS

1. In what way are the images in the "light picture" like a photograph? In what way are they different?

2. What do you think caused the "light picture" images to form on the photo paper?

3. After several minutes, the "light pictures" you made will begin to disappear. The photo paper starts to turn black. Why do you think this happens?

WHAT HAPPENED

Light-sensitive chemicals on photographic paper turn black when exposed to light. Your "light images" were made because the black construction paper and assorted objects you put on the photo paper blocked the light, preventing it from reaching the paper. The images you made were silhouettes—like shadows—of the objects that blocked the light. Several minutes after the experiment, light in the room made the light-sensitive paper turn black and the "light pictures" disappear.

BRAIN BUSTER

Can you make a "light picture" of your hand? How would you do it? Use what you learned in this activity to make a silhouette image of your hand on a piece of light-sensitive photographic paper.

SAFETY FIRST

Be careful when using scissors.

Rainbow in Your Room

Question: What colors is sunlight made of?

The sunlight that's all around you makes everything bright and easy to see. It seems to be white—or colorless. But sunlight is really made up of many different colors of light. In this experiment, you will separate sunlight into its many colors. You will make a rainbow.

KEY WORDS

prism
rainbow
refract
spectrum
wavelength

MATERIALS

- shallow bowl (wide, shallow soup bowl, for example)
- water
- small mirror
- flashlight

WHAT TO DO

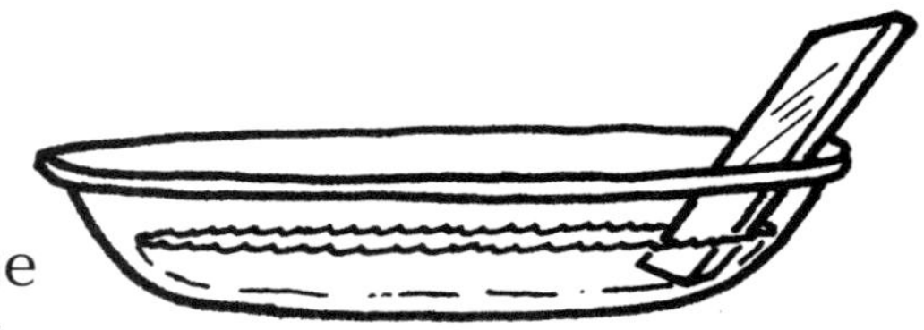

1. Fill the shallow bowl about two-thirds full with water. Place the mirror in the bowl, resting it on the side of the bowl, so it is angled.

2. Make the room as dark as possible. Then shine the flashlight toward the mirror.

3. Look at the ceiling. What do you see?

DRAW CONCLUSIONS

1. How do you think the water helped in producing the rainbow?

2. What colors did you see in your ceiling rainbow? In what order did they appear?

WHAT HAPPENED

A prism is anything that can separate white light, such as sunlight or light from a flashlight, into its different colors. The seven different colors that make up white light are called a spectrum. Each color has a different wavelength. For example, red has a long wavelength; blue has a short wavelength. In this case, water acted as a prism. The water refracted, or bent, the light according to each color's wavelength. Each color making up white light is bent in a slightly different way, so the colors appeared separated on the ceiling. You probably saw up to seven colors—red, orange, yellow, green, blue, indigo (a dark blue), violet (purple)—reflected on the ceiling. The colors you saw are all part of sunlight.

A rainbow is sunlight refracted through water vapor in the air. Water droplets float in the air after a rainstorm. Sunlight strikes the droplets and, if the angle is right, the light is refracted and reflected off the droplets in such a way that the light is separated into an arc of colors—a rainbow.

BRAIN BUSTER

You can buy a small prism and make your own rainbows without water. Hold the prism in the sun and make rainbows on the wall. In what order do you see the colors in the spectrum? Why do you think the colors of the spectrum are always in the same order?

All From One, One From All

Question: What colors can you make from red, yellow, and blue?

The white light you experience as sunlight really contains many colors, including red, blue, and yellow. You can mix and match these three colors, called the primary colors, to make lots of different colors. See how many colors you can make.

KEY WORDS

primary colors

MATERIALS

- three transparent plastic sheets: one each of red, yellow, and blue
- scissors
- sheet of white paper

WHAT TO DO

1. Cut each plastic sheet into 2-inch (5-centimeter) strips. Place a yellow strip on the paper. Cover it with a blue strip. What color do you see? Cover these two strips with another yellow strip. What happens to the color?

2. Place a red strip on the white paper. Cover it with a blue strip. What color do you see? Cover these with a yellow strip or another red strip. What happens to the color?

3. Use the color strips, one over the other, to make as many colors as possible. How many colors did you make? Which ones?

DRAW CONCLUSIONS

1. What two colored strips make the color green? What strips together make the color orange?

2. What did you do to make a color lighter or darker? For example, how would you turn a dark green into a light green?

3. Why might there be no limit to the number of colors you can make out of red, blue, and yellow?

WHAT HAPPENED

All colors we can see are made from combinations of many colors, including red, blue, and yellow. By adding or taking away different color strips, you saw how colors combine to make many different colors.

SAFETY FIRST

Be careful when using scissors.

BRAIN BUSTER

You know you can make colors out of red, blue, and yellow. But did you know that white is a color that contains all other colors? Cut a circle out of cardboard or heavy art paper. Have an adult make a hole exactly in the center of the circle. Color exactly one-third of the circle red, one-third of the circle blue, and one-third of the circle yellow. Make a top by pushing a pencil, point down, through the hole in the circle's center. Be sure that the colored side of the circle is on top. Spin your top quickly and watch what happens to the colors. If your top spins fast enough, all the colors will blend together and become white.

Thar' She Blows!

Question: What chemical reaction causes a home-made volcano to erupt?

Have a volcano explode in your own home! Use chemistry and build your own volcano that erupts with red flowing lava. Your erupting volcano will look like the real thing—but it's not dangerous.

KEY WORDS

acid

base

carbon dioxide

erupt

lava

MATERIALS

- sand or potting soil
- large flat metal tray (like a cookie sheet with sides)
- small container with one end removed (soup can, for example)
- baking soda
- measuring cup with pitcher or spout
- red food coloring
- white vinegar

WHAT TO DO

1. Form the sand or soil into a mound on the flat tray. Set the small container, closed side down, on top of the soil.

2. Put ½ cup (118 milliliters) baking soda in the small container through the open top, and press the container into the top of your "mountain." Then pile the sand or soil up around the container until it is hidden (but don't cover the open top).

3. In the pitcher, add enough red food coloring to ½ cup (118 milliliters) vinegar to make it look like lava, the superhot material that oozes out of real volcanoes.

4. Quickly pour the red vinegar into the container in the top of your "mountain." Then stand back and watch what happens.

DRAW CONCLUSIONS

1. Did you hear a hissing or bubbling sound as the vinegar hit the baking soda? Did you see any bubbles? What do you think caused the sound and the bubbles?

2. What two substances do you think were involved in this chemical reaction?

WHAT HAPPENED

Baking soda is a substance called a base. Vinegar is a substance called an acid. When this acid and this base come into contact, a chemical reaction occurs. In this experiment, carbon dioxide gas is produced (that's where the hissing and bubbles came from). The gas bubbles forced the red vinegar out of the container and down the sides of your "volcano." The volcano erupted, or exploded.

DID YOU KNOW?

Inside a real volcano is a long tube, or chamber, that extends deep down into the earth. The inside of the earth is so hot, rocks and metals melt and flow there like liquids. Many hot gases are also inside a volcano. When the pressure of the hot gases gets too high, the volcano erupts. The gases under pressure force the melted rock out of the volcano. The melted rock, called lava, may shoot out the top of the volcano or may ooze down the sides of the mountain. Burning hot gases may explode hundreds of feet into the air.

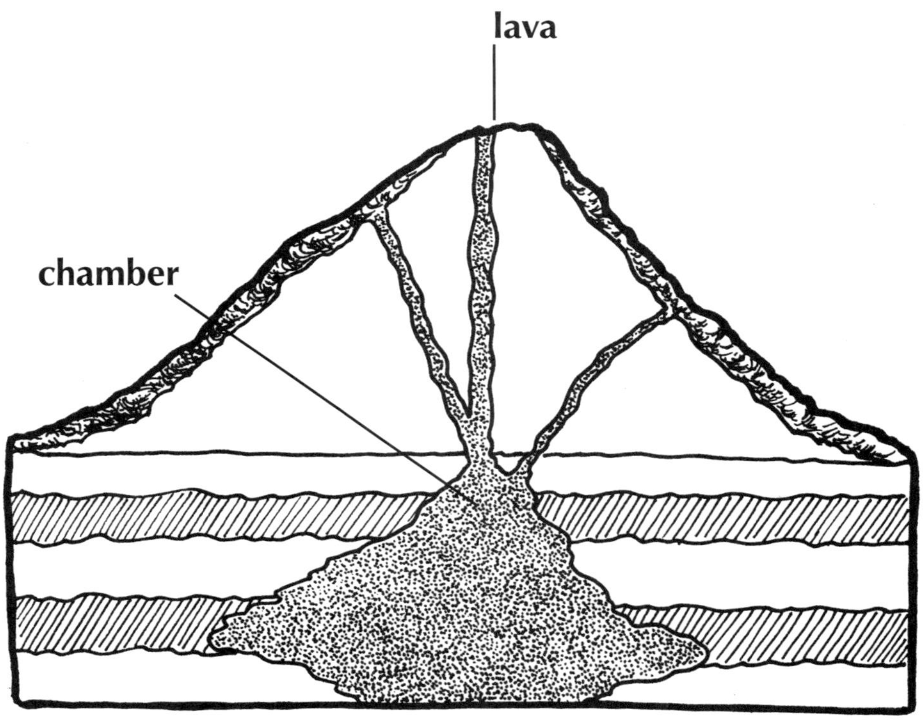

Leaky Limestones

Question: Are some rocks in my neighborhood made out of limestone?

KEY WORDS

acid
base
calcium
chemical reaction
compound
limestone
vinegar

MATERIALS

- tool for digging
- paper bag
- running water
- liquid soap
- plates (one for each rock dug up)
- white vinegar
- tablespoon

You have probably seen lots of rocks in your backyard or in the park. Have you ever wondered what the rocks are made of? Some rocks may be made of a kind of stone called limestone. In this experiment, you will test rocks to see if they contain limestone.

WHAT TO DO

1. Take the digging tool and the paper bag to the park or your backyard. Collect as many different kinds of rocks as you can. If necessary, use the tool to dig up some small rocks. Place the rocks in the paper bag to carry them home.

2. Carefully wash each rock under running water, using the liquid soap. Rinse them thoroughly and let them dry.

3. Place one rock on each plate. Spoon 1 tablespoon (15 milliliters) vinegar over the rock. Watch what happens. Write down in your science notebook what you see. Did you see any bubbly "fizz" on the rock?

4. Repeat step 3 for all the rocks you collected. Did any of the rocks bubble and fizz?

5. Place together all the rocks that bubbled and fizzed.

DRAW CONCLUSIONS

1. Did any of the rocks you tested have limestone in them? How do you know?

2. Were there more rocks with limestone or without limestone in your rock collection?

3. Do you think there are lots of limestone rocks or few limestone rocks in your area? Explain your answer.

4. Do the rocks that contain limestone look similar in some way? What might you look for in other rocks that would tell you if they contain limestone?

WHAT HAPPENED

Limestone contains a calcium compound that is a base. The calcium in limestone comes from the shells of shellfish that died millions of years ago. Vinegar is a substance that is a mild acid. The scientific name for vinegar is *acetic* (uh-SEE-tik) *acid*. When an acid is added to a base, a chemical reaction takes place. In this case, acid in the vinegar reacted with the calcium base in the limestone to form bubbles, or "fizz."

SAFETY FIRST

Don't touch your eyes if your fingers are wet with vinegar. Wash your hands first.

BRAIN BUSTER

Find out about acids and bases. Learn why a chemical reaction sometimes occurs when acids and bases come into contact with each other. You will learn more about acids and bases in the experiments "Thar' She Blows!" and "Etch an Egg," and in the food-testing experiments (such as "Now You 'C' It") in this section.

Etch an Egg

Question: How can an eggshell be etched?

KEY WORDS

acid

base

calcium

carbon dioxide

etch

MATERIALS

- egg
- small pan
- water
- crayon or grease pencil
- clear glass jar (big enough to fit an egg)
- white vinegar

You can "print" your name or make a design on an egg. And you won't break the egg either. The secret is using chemistry.

WHAT TO DO

1. Have an adult hard-boil an egg in the small pan of water. Allow the egg to cool to room temperature.

2. Use a crayon or a grease pencil to write your name or draw a simple picture or design on the egg's shell.

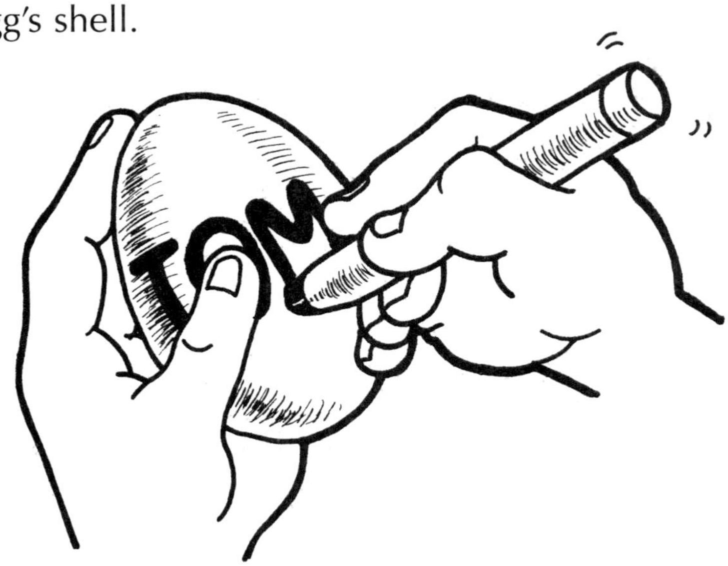

3. Fill the jar about three-fourths full with vinegar. Place the egg gently in the jar. The vinegar should cover the egg.

4. Every few hours, gently touch the egg to see if the crayon marks feel slightly raised above the rest of the eggshell. When you feel the raised crayon marks, remove the egg from the jar and rinse the egg. Carefully wipe off the crayon marks. You will see that the eggshell is etched, or eaten away, everywhere except around the raised markings.

DRAW CONCLUSIONS

1. Why do you think you had to use a waxy crayon or grease pencil for your design or name?

2. Did you see bubbles in the jar while the egg was in the vinegar? What do you think they were?

3. What do you think the vinegar does to the substance the eggshell is made of?

WHAT HAPPENED

An eggshell is made out of calcium, a mineral also found in milk. Eggshell material is called a base. A base is a substance that reacts chemically with any substance that is an acid. In this experiment, vinegar was the acid. The chemical reaction between the eggshell and the vinegar produced a gas: carbon dioxide. This gas was produced as vinegar "ate away" at the eggshell during the chemical reaction. The waxy crayon or grease pencil markings protected the marked parts of the shell from the effects of the vinegar.

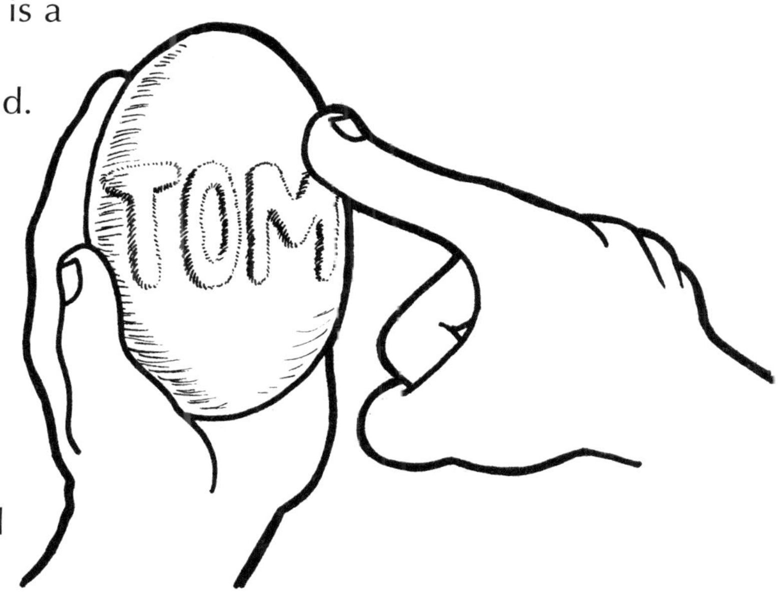

So these marked parts of the shell were not eaten away. That's why you felt them raised above the rest of the shell.

DID YOU KNOW?

Many public statues are made out of a stone called limestone, which contains a substance that is a base. What happens when acid rain, a kind of air pollution that comes from factory smokestacks, falls on the statues? The acid in the rain eats away at the statues—because the stone they are made from is a base. In many cities, such as Rome, in Italy, beautiful old statues and sculptures are being destroyed as the acid in rain reacts with limestone. (See the "Leaky Limestones" activity on page 109.)

FIRST-TIMER'S TIP!

Avoid household poisons. Have an adult tell you which substances are safe to test.

BRAIN BUSTER

Litmus paper changes color, depending on whether it touches a substance that is a base (the litmus paper turns blue) or an acid (the litmus paper turns red). Buy some litmus paper at a hardware store. Use the litmus paper to test various substances around your house to see if they are acids or bases. For example, test orange juice, milk, detergent, and other safe substances.

Now You "C" It

Question: How can food be tested to see if it contains vitamin C?

KEY WORDS

indicator

vitamin C

MATERIALS

- water
- small pan
- spoon
- cornstarch
- iodine
- eyedropper
- various juices (orange, tomato, apple, grape, etc.)
- clear juice glasses (one for each juice)

You need vitamin C to stay healthy. But how do you know what foods contain vitamin C? This activity will show you how to test foods to learn which contain the most vitamin C.

WHAT TO DO

1. Have an adult boil 1 cup (237 milliliters) water in a small pan. Then stir 1 teaspoon (5 milliliters) cornstarch into it. Allow to cool.

2. Draw up some iodine into the eyedropper. Slowly add drops of iodine, one at a time, to the water until it is blue. The blue water is your indicator, a substance that will show you, or indicate, how much vitamin C different kinds of juices have. Once your indicator is made, rinse the eyedropper with running water.

3. Pour about 1 inch (2.5 centimeters) of one of the juices into a clear, clean juice glass.

4. Draw up some indicator into the clean eyedropper. Start dropping the indicator, one drop at a time, into the juice. Count the number of drops needed to make the blue indicator color disappear into the juice. Record the number of drops in your science notebook.

5. Repeat steps 3 and 4 with each juice you wish to test. Use fresh indicator for each juice tested.

DRAW CONCLUSIONS

1. Which juice contained the most vitamin C? How many drops of indicator did you use for this juice?

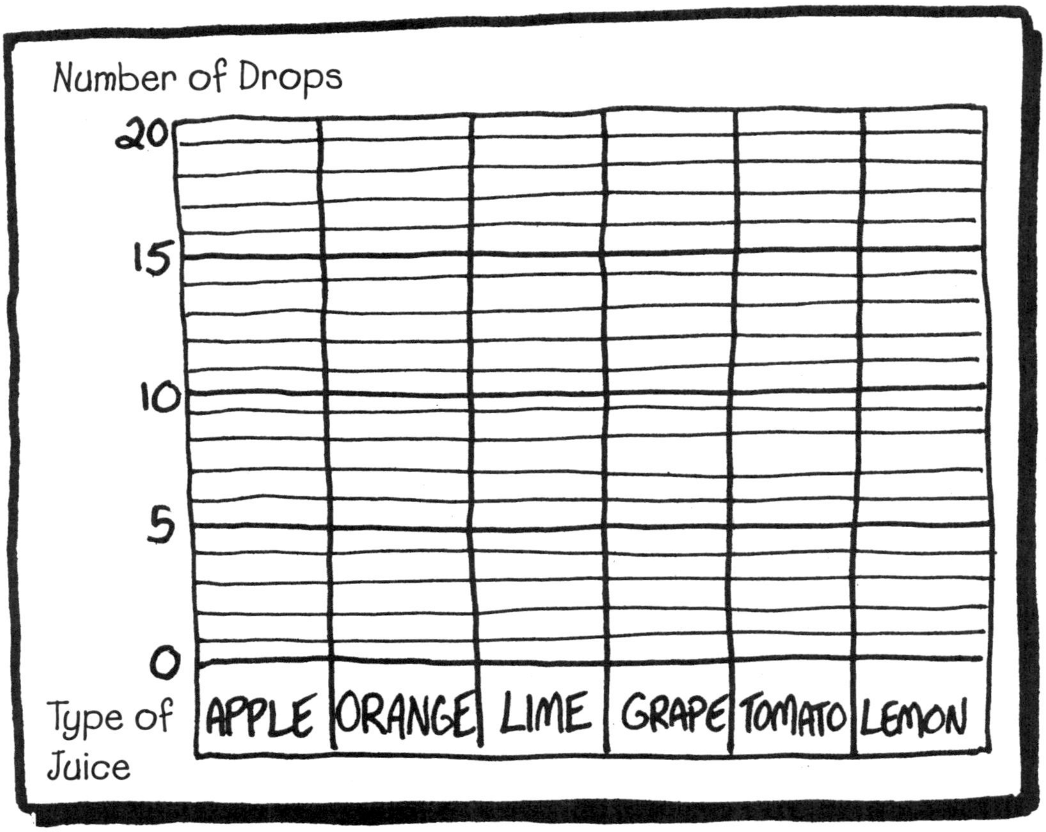

SAFETY FIRST

Have an adult boil the water for you.

Do not swallow iodine or put it in your mouth.

Do not drink the indicator or the juices you tested with the indicator.

2. Which juice contained the least vitamin C? How many drops of indicator did you use for this juice?

3. Why did you need to use fresh indicator for each juice tested?

4. Make a graph of your test results, based on the results you recorded.

WHAT HAPPENED

The indicator reacted chemically with vitamin C. The more vitamin C a juice had, the more quickly the chemical reaction occurred. That is why juices needing many drops of indicator had less vitamin C than juices needing only a few drops of indicator.

BRAIN BUSTER

What effect does heat have on the vitamin C in juice? Use fresh indicator to test for vitamin C. After you do the steps on pages 115 and 116, have an adult put one of the juices in a pot and boil it. With an adult's help, remove the pot from the stove and let it cool for 1 minute. Then test the boiled juice with indicator. How many drops did you need before the blue disappeared? Does heat increase or destroy the vitamin C in juices?

FIRST-TIMER'S TIP!

The more drops of indicator it takes before the blue color disappears, the less vitamin C the juice contains.

Sweet Scents—Make Your Own Perfume

Question: How is perfume made?

What is your favorite perfume scent? Is it rose or jasmine or vanilla? Perfume can be made from many different kinds of plants. In this activity, you will learn how perfume is made by creating your own.

KEY WORDS

dissolve
fragrance
solute
solution
solvent

MATERIALS

- plant part for scent (clove, vanilla bean, rose petals, lavender, lilac, etc.)
- black plastic film canister
- rubbing alcohol
- tablespoon

WHAT TO DO

1. Place about 2 tablespoons (30 milliliters) rose petals (or 1 clove or ½ vanilla bean), or the equivalent amount of the "scent" plant you are using, into the film canister. (Note: If you don't have a film canister, use the smallest clean covered container you can find. Paint the outside of the container black or cover it with heavy black plastic, like a heavy-duty garbage bag, to prevent light from affecting the perfume.)

2. Add about 2 tablespoons (30 milliliters) rubbing alcohol to the canister, enough to cover the "scent" plant.

3. Cover the canister tightly. Shake it. Leave it in a cool, dark place.

4. Shake the canister briskly once a day for seven days (do not open it!). After one week, test the perfume you made by opening the container and dabbing a bit of the solution on your wrist. Take a whiff. You smell great!

DRAW CONCLUSIONS

1. Where did the scent of your perfume come from?

2. What do you think the function of the rubbing alcohol was?

WHAT HAPPENED

Perfume is a solution, a mixture in which one substance disappears into another. For example, salt water is a solution in which salt dissolves, or mixes into, water. Science calls salt the solute and water the solvent. When making the perfume, the sweet-smelling plant part was the solute and the rubbing alcohol the solvent. The rubbing alcohol drew the sweet-smelling chemicals out of the plant part. These fragrant chemicals mixed with the alcohol to form a perfume solution.

DID YOU KNOW?

It takes 1,100 pounds (500 kilograms) of rose petals to make less than 1 ounce (about 500 grams) of rose essence for perfume. No wonder perfume is so expensive!

BRAIN BUSTER

You can make your perfume smell stronger by removing the original solute (the plant part) after one week and adding fresh solute to the same rubbing alcohol. The alcohol then absorbs new chemicals from the fresh solute. You can also experiment with different scents by adding different sweet-smelling plants to the same alcohol each week.

Here and Gone

Question: What makes invisible ink appear?

Write secret messages with invisible ink! Find out how something that is in the air you breathe can make invisible writing appear like magic.

KEY WORDS

invisible

oxidation

oxygen

MATERIALS

- juice glass or small glass bowl
- sugar
- water
- matchstick or cotton-tip swab
- white writing paper
- lamp with incandescent lightbulb

WHAT TO DO

1. In the glass or bowl, mix 1 tablespoon (15 milliliters) sugar in about 2 inches (5 centimeters) of water. Stir well until the sugar is dissolved. The sugar water is your ink.

2. Dip the wooden end of the matchstick or tip of the cotton swab in the sugar water, and write your name or a message with this ink on the white paper. Let the ink dry completely. Your message will be invisible.

3. Set up a lamp with no lamp shade. Turn it on.

4. Have an adult hold up the paper near the heat of the lightbulb. In a little while, you will see your name or your message appear on the paper.

DRAW CONCLUSIONS

1. Why was your sugar and water "ink" invisible?

2. Why do you think the heat of the lightbulb made your message appear on the paper?

WHAT HAPPENED

The sugar and water solution was invisible—it couldn't be seen—because the sugar disappeared when it dissolved in the colorless water. But when the sugar was heated by the lightbulb, some chemicals in the sugar combined with the oxygen in the air. This chemical reaction, called oxidation, caused those chemicals in the sugar to turn brown. When heat made the sugar on your paper turn brown, you could then read your secret message.

SAFETY FIRST

Do not drink your invisible ink solution.

Be careful around the heat of the lightbulb.

BRAIN BUSTER

You can make invisible ink with other liquids. Try writing your secret message using lemon juice, milk, or vinegar. (You don't have to mix these with water.) Have an adult hold your messages up to the heat of a lightbulb and see what happens. Heat causes oxidation of many substances.

Stringing Water Along—Shocking Shoelaces

Question: How do we know that water molecules move?

Water is always on the move. Tiny bits of water, called molecules (MAH-luh-kyoolz), are forever bumping around and into each other. Molecules also love to travel. Find out how.

KEY WORDS

fiber

molecule

MATERIALS

- measuring cup
- water
- four small bowls or cups
- food coloring (four colors)
- long piece of white string (preferably cotton) or a long white shoelace

WHAT TO DO

1. Put about ½ cup (118 milliliters) water into each bowl or cup. Add a different color of food coloring to each bowl of water. (The more food coloring you add, the deeper the color will be.)

2. Wet the string or shoelace with water and "snake" it from one bowl to the other. Do not push it deep into the water. Only one "bend" in the string should be below the surface of the water in each bowl. There should be white string visible between the bowls.

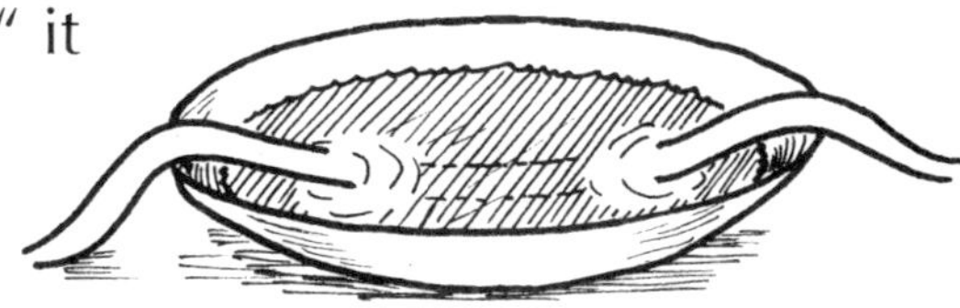

3. Watch what happens to the string or shoelace. Is it picking up color? Leave it for a while, checking on it until it has absorbed all the color it can. Then remove the string or shoelace and let it dry. (If you want, repeat these steps to make a matching, colorful shoelace.)

DRAW CONCLUSIONS

1. Did the whole string or shoelace absorb color?

2. Bits of water stick to one another (that's why water forms "drops") and help one another move. Why, then, do you think this experiment works best if the string or shoelace is wet, not dry?

WHAT HAPPENED

String is a fiber, a material that contains many threads with lots of tiny tubelike spaces in between. Water molecules can move up these tubelike spaces and are then absorbed by the fiber. These molecules (small units of matter) stick to one another—as some water molecules move up into the fiber, the water molecules below stick to them. So the lower molecules are also dragged up into the fiber and absorbed. That's how the water molecules moved through the string or shoelace. Water molecules are so strong, they continually drag more and more water molecules up behind them.

BRAIN BUSTER

Watch water molecules on the move. Fill a clear glass jar three-fourths full with water. Add a few drops of food coloring. DO NOT STIR! What do you see? Notice the way the food coloring first sinks to the bottom, leaving a trail of color behind it. The food coloring drops are breaking up because they are being hit constantly by water molecules. If you keep watching the jar, you will see the food coloring spread evenly throughout the water. The water molecules bounce the food coloring around until it mixes thoroughly all through the water in the jar.

Multicolored Carnations

Question: How does water move through a plant?

All plants need water. But how does a tall tree get water to its top leaves? Plants have a special way of moving water from their roots, through their stems, to all their parts.

KEY WORDS

capillary action
cell
molecule

MATERIALS

- two glasses
- water
- food coloring (two colors)
- white carnation
- ruler
- knife or scissors

WHAT TO DO

1. Fill the glasses about three-fourths full with water. Add one food coloring to one glass of water, and the other food coloring to the other glass. Add enough food coloring to get a good, strong color. Place the glasses next to each other in a warm room.

2. Have an adult cut the stem of the carnation to about 8 inches (20 centimeters) long. Remove any leaves from the stem. Then have the adult carefully cut the lower 5 inches (13 centimeters) of the stem in half lengthwise. Be careful the stem is not crushed.

3. Gently place one split stem in one glass of colored water, and put the other split stem in the other glass of different-colored water. Adjust the glasses to make sure the split stems stay in the water and the flower stands upright between

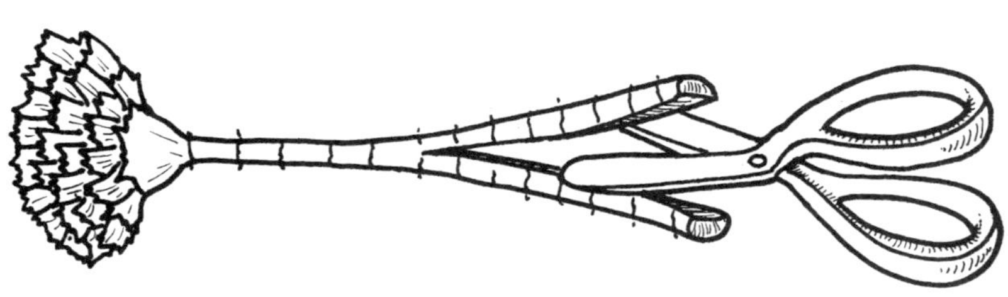

the two glasses. Let the flower absorb the water for several hours, until you see the petals changing color. Check on the flower every hour to see how it changes.

DRAW CONCLUSIONS

1. Did the carnation's petals change color? What colors did the petals become?

2. What part of the plant "drank up" the colored water and carried it to the flower?

3. If you had split the stem into three parts and put each part in a glass with different food coloring, how many colors do you think the flower would then have?

WHAT HAPPENED

Water moves through a plant's stem by a process called capillary (CAP-ih-leh-ree) action. In this experiment, you saw that the colored water traveled all the way to the flower petals. Inside the plant stem are long, thin tubes made of tiny structures called cells. Tiny units of water, called molecules, "climb" the narrow stem cells. Water molecules tend to stick to each other (that's why water forms drops). As water molecules climb into the stem cells, more water molecules follow. The water molecules are so tightly packed in the stem cells, they become strong enough to pull more water molecules up behind them. In this way, the water molecules move up through the cells and draw more water after them. The water moves up and up until the whole plant has had enough to drink.

BRAIN BUSTER

Does temperature affect capillary action? Cut about 1 to 2 inches (2.5 to 5 centimeters) off the bottom of two stalks of celery. Mix glasses of water with food coloring, and place one stalk of celery in each glass. Place one glass in a warm room. Place the other glass in the refrigerator. Observe both for several hours. What can you conclude about the effect of temperature on the capillary action that draws water up a celery stalk?

SAFETY FIRST

Be careful when using scissors.

Water Ball Race

Question: Why does water "race" over certain surfaces?

Forget your favorite game—it's time to have a water ball race. Make your own water drop racer and see if you can win.

KEY WORDS

adhere

cohere

MATERIALS

- waxed paper
- ruler
- grease pencil
- measuring cup
- water
- three cups
- food coloring (three colors)
- eyedropper
- three straws

WHAT TO DO

1. Prepare the "race course" on a piece of waxed paper, 12 inches (31 centimeters) long. Use the ruler and grease pencil to mark off the "starting line" and the "finish line" on opposite sides of the paper. Then connect these two lines with three "tracks" (each about 3 inches, or 8 centimeters, wide), which each water drop will race on. (This experiment is based on three water racers, but you can adjust it to have fewer or more.)

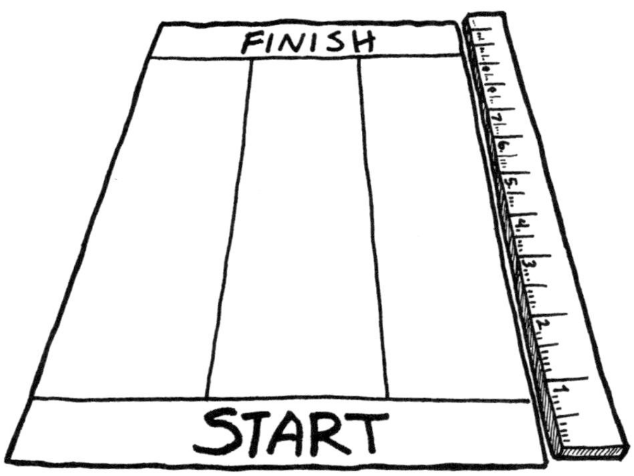

2. Put ½ cup (118 milliliters) water into each of three cups. Mix a different color of food coloring into each cup. Draw water into the eyedropper, and then release a few drops onto the waxed paper

at the starting line on one of the tracks of the race course. This will make your "racing drop." Repeat this for the other racers. Each racer has a different color drop, but all water drops should be the same size.

3. At the word *go,* each racer puts the straw to his or her lips and begins blowing a water drop across the race course toward the finish line. Do not blow too hard, or the water drop may break up. Make sure the drop stays in its track. If the drop breaks up or leaves the track, make a new drop and begin again at the starting line. The water drop that crosses the finish line first wins.

DRAW CONCLUSIONS

1. Why do you think it was important to use waxed paper for your race course?

2. What do you think would have happened if you had used a paper towel? (Try it—drop water on a paper towel and see what happens.)

3. Why do you think the water drop stayed together as you blew on it and it moved along the track?

WHAT HAPPENED

Water adheres to, or stays on, many surfaces. In science, the word *adhere* means "to stick to a substance that is different." For example, water adheres to the slippery surface of waxed paper. But water coheres to itself. *Cohere* means "to stick to something that is the same." Water molecules stick to—or cohere to—other water molecules. That's why your racing ball (drop) of water stayed together. Sometimes, though, if a force is powerful enough, it can separate water molecules. If you blew on your water drop too hard, the force of your breath may have separated the molecules of water. If you blew with just the right amount of force, the water drop stuck to itself and to the surface of the waxed paper as you moved it toward the finish line.

A paper towel is a fiber that has many tubelike threads, as do some cloth fabrics. These tubes absorb the water, so the water does not remain as a drop on top of the fiber.

BRAIN BUSTER

Stretch water with air. Mix together in a container: 2 cups (500 milliliters) water, 1 tablespoon (15 milliliters) sugar, and ¼ cup (59 milliliters) dishwashing liquid. Put the cap on the container and shake well. After the liquid settles and the foam is gone, pour it into a bowl. Bend the end of a hanger into a ring. Dip the ring into the liquid, and then blow on one side of it. You're blowing bubbles! Your breath pushes on the water molecules that are sticking together (cohering), and expands them to make a colorful bubble. If they expand too much (if you blow too hard), the molecules separate and your bubble bursts!

Grapes Lose Weight

Question: What happens to grapes when they "lose weight"?

KEY WORDS

evaporation

grape

MATERIALS

- scissors
- cardboard
- grapes
- tape
- two plastic window screens
- food scale
- two long strings

Sometimes people go on a diet to lose weight. People may also make certain kinds of fruits "lose weight." Do you know what grapes that lose weight are called? By the end of this experiment, you will!

WHAT TO DO

1. Have an adult help you cut a hole out of the center of the cardboard. The hole should be large enough to enclose ⅛ pound (2 ounces, or .07 grams) grapes.

2. If necessary, have an adult cut the screens to fit over the cardboard hole. Use tape to attach one plastic screen over the hole.

3. Copy the chart below in your science notebook.

WEIGHT OF GRAPES BEFORE DRYING	WEIGHT OF GRAPES AFTER DRYING

4. Put the grapes on the food scale. Write in the chart how much the grapes weigh.

5. One by one, place the grapes on the screen taped to the cardboard. Then cover the grapes with the second screen. Tape this screen in place over the grapes to secure them.

6. Tape the strings to the bottom of the cardboard, so the cardboard can hang evenly from them. Hang the cardboard outside, above the ground, in a place that is sunny during the day.

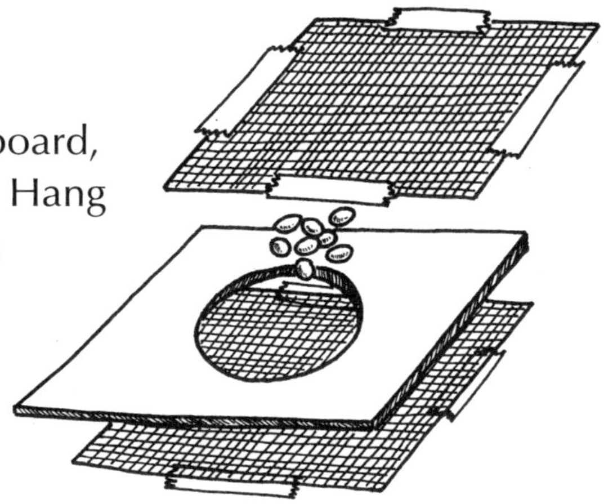

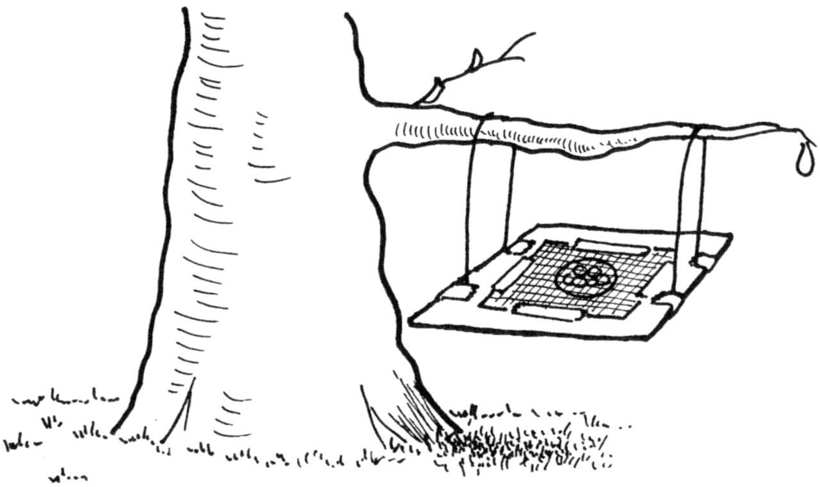

7. Leave the cardboard outside during the day, for about 7 days, until the grapes look dried up. (Don't leave the cardboard out at night or on rainy days.)

8. When the grapes look wrinkled and dry, bring them inside and remove them from the screened cardboard. Weigh the wrinkled grapes, or raisins, on the food scale. Record the weight in your chart.

DRAW CONCLUSIONS

1. What do you think caused the grapes to "lose weight"? How much weight did the grapes lose?

2. What substance in the grapes do you think the grapes lost as they dried up?

WHAT HAPPENED

The grapes "lost weight" when they lost some of the water that made them plump and juicy. The heat of the sun caused the water in the grapes to evaporate. During evaporation, heat caused the water to expand and leave the grapes through tiny holes in the skin of the fruit. The water then entered the air as a gas. Evaporation is a process in which water changes from a liquid to a gas. When you climb out of a swimming pool, the water on your skin evaporates into the air and cools you.

BRAIN BUSTER

People like to eat raisins and many other dried fruits. Try using the above experiment to make your own dried apricots, plums, apple or banana slices, or other fruit you may like. You may want to put an additional screen covering over the sliced fruits to keep away insects.

SAFETY FIRST

After you have weighed the raisins, make sure you wash them thoroughly in running water before you eat them.

Sail Away

Question: Can the force of magnetism work through a dish of water?

The wind makes sailboats move over the sea. Engines make speedboats zoom over the water. You know that the force in magnets—magnetism—attracts metals such as iron. Can magnetism extend through a dish of water so you can race boats you make yourself?

KEY WORDS

magnet
magnetism

MATERIALS

- two small pieces of flat Styrofoam
- scissors or knife
- metal thumbtacks
- newspaper
- large shallow glass or plastic dish
- pitcher
- water
- tape
- two bar magnets
- two 12-inch (30-centimeter) rulers

WHAT TO DO

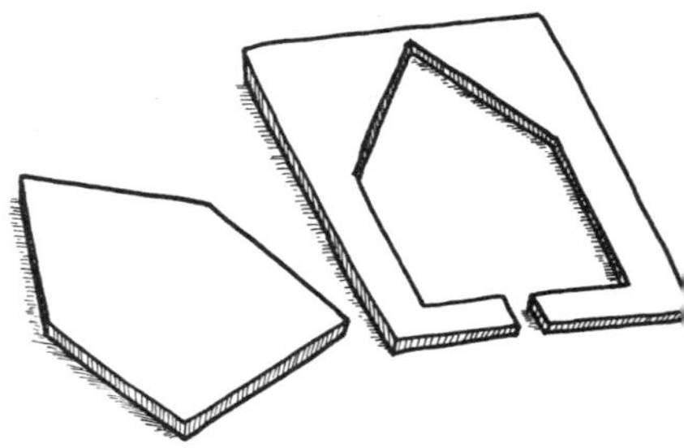

1. Have an adult help you cut each small piece of flat Styrofoam into a boat shape with the scissors or knife. Carefully stick two thumbtacks firmly into the bottom of each "boat."

2. Make two stacks of newspapers. The stacks should be the same height, at least 3 inches (8 centimeters) high, and close enough to set the shallow dish on top of both.

3. Lay the dish across the stacks of newspaper. The center part of the dish should be exposed between the newspaper stacks. With a pitcher, pour water into the dish until it is about half full.

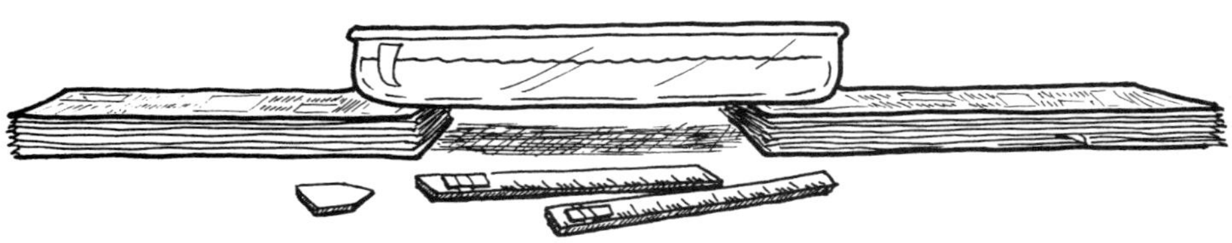

4. Tape one bar magnet to the end of each ruler. You and a friend each use one ruler to race your boats.

5. Place the boats (thumbtack side down) in the water at the starting line. Guide your boat across the dish to the finish line by moving the ruler and its magnet beneath the dish.

DRAW CONCLUSIONS

1. Can the force of magnetism pass through a dish of water? How do you know?

2. What part of the boats was attracted to the magnets?

WHAT HAPPENED

Magnetism is the force a magnet has on certain metal objects—for instance, on thumbtacks. Magnetism can pass through materials such as water. Thumbtacks are made from a metal that is attracted by the force of magnetism. That's why you could move your boat across the water. The magnet attracted the metal thumbtacks and "pulled" them (and the boat) in the direction you moved the ruler.

SAFETY FIRST

Have an adult use the scissors or knife.

Be careful not to stick yourself with the thumbtacks.

BRAIN BUSTER

Can magnetism pass through cardboard? Get some iron filings or have an adult cut up a steel wool pad for you. Lay a piece of cardboard on top of two equal stacks of newspaper. Sprinkle the filings or the steel wool pieces on the cardboard. Move the magnet around underneath the cardboard to move the filings. Sketch a picture or a design. Does magnetism pass through cardboard? How do you know?

Ironing Out Your Cereal

Question: How can the iron be removed from cereal?

Many breakfast cereals contain iron, a nutrient that you need to stay healthy. In this experiment, you will find out how iron—a metal that is attracted to magnets—can be removed from cereal.

KEY WORDS

magnet
magnetism

MATERIALS

- packet of uncooked instant hot cereal (e.g., iron-reinforced oatmeal)
- plastic zip-top sandwich bag
- magnet
- handheld lens (magnifying glass)

WHAT TO DO

1. Make sure the instant cereal you use has iron added (this should be stated on the front of the box or on the nutrition label). Open the packet and pour the cereal contents into a plastic zip-top sandwich bag.

2. Place the small magnet in the bag, too. Seal the bag and shake it well, for about 2 minutes.

3. Carefully, take the magnet out of the bag. Look at it closely with the handheld lens. What do you see?

DRAW CONCLUSIONS

1. What did you see clinging to the magnet?

2. Why do you think the iron specks stuck to the magnet?

WHAT HAPPENED

A magnet contains a kind of force that affects some substances, particularly iron. Iron is a metal that is attracted to the force of a magnet. That is why the tiny specks of iron in the cereal stuck to the magnet. They were attracted to the magnet's force. A magnet's force is called magnetism.

SAFETY FIRST

Do not eat the iron specks separated from the cereal.

BRAIN BUSTER

A magnet will attract any object that contains iron. How many objects in your house contain iron? Test your magnet by holding it near various objects: hair clips, nails, screws, jar lids, and so on. If iron objects are small, they may move toward the magnet. If iron objects are too large, you may just feel a "pull" between the magnet and the object. What objects in your house contain iron?

For the Birds

Question: What kinds of seeds do different birds like to eat?

KEY WORDS

feeder

field guide

millet

seed

sunflower

thistle

MATERIALS

- five flat plastic dishes
- anchors for dishes (such as stones, clay, nails, or hooks)
- measuring cup
- birdseed (sunflower seeds, shelled unsalted peanuts, millet mix, cracked corn, thistle seeds)
- field guide to birds (available at a local library)

Have you seen birds around a bird feeder? Do all the birds like to eat the same kind of food? In this activity, you will find out.

WHAT TO DO

1. Place the flat dishes outside, about 4 to 5 inches (10 to 13 centimeters) apart. Make sure the plates are held in place well, using a stone, clay, nail, hook, or other anchor.

2. Measure 1 cup (237 milliliters) of each kind of birdseed you are using and place it on a plate. Make sure each plate has only one kind of seed.

3. From a window, watch the birds that come to each plate to eat. Notice the color of the birds' feathers. Notice the shape of the birds' beaks. In your science notebook, write or draw a description of each kind of bird.

4. Use the bird field guide to find the picture and name of each kind of bird that comes to your bird feeder. If necessary, have an adult help you. Write the bird's name in your science notebook, next to its description and drawing.

5. In your science notebook, write down

- how many of each kind of bird you see
- the kind of seed each type of bird likes to eat

DRAW CONCLUSIONS

1. What kinds of birds came to your bird feeders? How many of each kind came to eat? Did the same kinds of birds all eat the same seed?

2. What kinds of seeds did the different birds that you observed like to eat best?

WHAT HAPPENED

Different kinds of birds like to eat different kinds of seeds. Very often, large birds, such as blue jays with large, strong beaks, prefer to eat large seeds, like peanuts. Smaller birds, like sparrows, have smaller beaks and may prefer to eat smaller seeds, like sunflower seeds or thistle seeds. The size and shape of a bird's beak often gives you a hint about the kind of food that bird likes to eat.

blue jay

sparrow

SAFETY FIRST

Do not touch leftover birdseed.

Do not touch or bother the birds that come to your feeder.

Looking for Light

Question: Are plants able to "look for" light, even when it's hard to find?

KEY WORDS

phototropism
seedling
sprout

MATERIALS

- vine-type (not bush-type) bean seed
- water
- small flowerpot
- potting soil
- scissors
- two pieces of cardboard
- shoe box with lid
- tape
- full-spectrum light or plant-grow lamp (optional)

Why do trees and most other plants grow up toward the sky? You may have noticed that nearly all plants grow upward toward the source of light: the sun. Plants need sunlight to help them make their own food.

WHAT TO DO

1. Soak the bean seed in water at room temperature for 24 hours. Then, in the flowerpot filled with potting soil, plant the seed just under the soil. Water the soil thoroughly, but don't soak it. Keep the soil moist until the seed sprouts and the plant is about 2 inches (5 centimeters) tall.

2. Cut the two pieces of cardboard to fit inside the shoe box. Cut a window out of the left half of each cardboard piece.

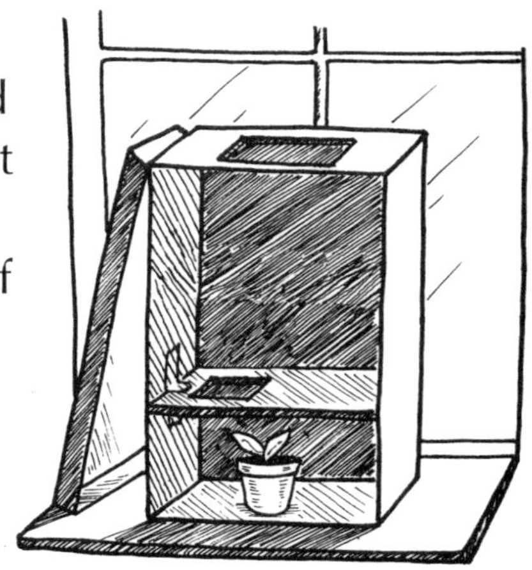

3. Stand the shoe box upright, on end. Cut a large window in the center top end of the shoe box. Place the pot with the growing seedling at the bottom. Tape one piece of cardboard 2 inches (5 centimeters) above the seedling. Put the lid on, and place the shoe box in a sunny window or directly under a full-spectrum light or plant-grow lamp. Watch how the plant stem grows. Don't forget to water your plant regularly.

4. When the plant has grown several inches (or centimeters), tape the second piece of cardboard a few inches above the first piece of cardboard. Make sure its window is opposite the window of the lower cardboard piece. Keep the plant in the light. Watch how the plant stem grows.

DRAW CONCLUSIONS

1. Did the pieces of cardboard inside the shoe box prevent the plant from growing? How did the plant stem grow past the cardboard pieces?

2. Did the plant stem grow straight or did it twist and turn? Why do you think that happened?

3. Did the plant stem grow out the large, top window in the shoe box? What do you think made the plant stem "find" the windows in the cardboard pieces and in the top of the shoe box?

WHAT HAPPENED

Plant stems grow toward light. This is called phototropism (foh-toh-TROH-pih-zum), which means "turning toward light." Plant stems turn toward any source of light. If light is coming through a small window cut in a piece of cardboard, a plant stem will turn toward that window. It will continue to grow through that window toward light. That is why your plant grew through the windows in the cardboard pieces and into the sunlight above the top of the shoe box.

BRAIN BUSTER

After soaking two bean seeds, plant each in a separate flowerpot. After they have sprouted, place the potted seeds on a sunny windowsill. Keep the soil moist so the plants grow well. Turn one flowerpot one-quarter turn every day. Do not turn the other flowerpot at all. Do you notice a difference in how each stem grows?

SAFETY FIRST

Be careful when using scissors.

Rooting Right

Question: Do plant roots always grow in the same direction?

You know that plant roots grow down into the earth. But how do they "know" how to do that? Will plant roots *always* grow down, even if a seed is planted sideways? In this experiment, you will find out.

KEY WORDS

geotropism
seed
seedling
tropism

MATERIALS

- about eight fresh bean seeds
- bowl
- water
- paper towels
- two medium-sized wide-mouth clear glass jars
- plant sprayer (optional)

WHAT TO DO

1. Soak the beans overnight in a bowl with room-temperature water.

2. Stuff crumpled paper towels into each glass jar to fill each nearly to the top. Use the plant sprayer or flick water from your fingers to thoroughly soak the towels in each jar. Pour out any excess water.

3. Place four beans about 1 to 2 inches (2.5 to 5 centimeters) from the top of each jar, on different sides. You should be able to see each bean between the paper towels and the glass. Each bean should be in a different position: pointed down, pointed up, on its side, on an angle.

4. Place the jars in a shady place, where you can watch them for several days. Each day, carefully feel the paper towels, which should be damp, not wet. If they're dry, use the plant sprayer or flick water from your fingers onto the paper towels until they are moist.

5. In a few days, the seeds will sprout. Roots will begin to grow from one part of the seed. Notice in what direction the seed's roots are growing. Do the roots grow in the same direction no matter what position the seed is in?

6. When the "baby" roots are 1 to 2 inches (2.5 to 5 centimeters) long, place one of the glass jars on its side. Watch both jars for several more days. Do the roots of the seedlings in each jar grow in the same direction?

DRAW CONCLUSIONS

1. Does the position of the seed have any effect on the direction its roots grow?

2. When you turned one jar on its side, in what direction did the roots grow?

3. What conclusion can you draw about how roots grow?

WHAT HAPPENED

Plant roots contain a chemical that makes them grow down toward the earth and the pull of gravity. The response of plant roots to gravity is called geotropism (from the word *tropism* meaning "turning toward" and the prefix *geo* meaning "earth"). Geotropism (JEE-oh-TROH-pih-zum) is very important for plants. Geotropism makes sure that plant roots grow into the soil to hold the plant securely in the earth.

BRAIN BUSTER

Do the roots of older, mature plants also show geotropism? Find a clear plastic flowerpot, or a clear plastic container, and a houseplant that will fit in it and still have room enough to grow. Make sure you can see the roots through the plastic. Place the potted plant on a windowsill, but *put the pot on its side.* (You may have to place something around the pot to keep it from rolling.) Observe the direction in which the roots grow.

Wear Plant Colors

Question: How can we get dyes from plants?

For thousands of years, people have used plants to dye clothing. Certain plant chemicals give plants their color. Some of these plant chemicals can be removed from plants and used to dye fabric such as cotton.

KEY WORDS

dye
fabric
pigment
simmer

MATERIALS

- white cotton cloth (an old T-shirt, for example)
- plant used for dyeing
  red: berries, beets
  brown: onion skins
  green: parsley, spinach
- measuring cup
- medium to large pot
- water
- strainer
- large clear glass bowl
- wooden spoon

WHAT TO DO

1. Decide what color you want to dye the cotton cloth. Get the necessary plant and chop or tear it up into small pieces. You should have about 1 cup (237 milliliters) plant material. Put all the pieces in the pot, and add water to just cover them.

2. Have an adult put the pot on the stove, boil the water, and simmer it for 15 to 20 minutes, stirring occasionally. When the water looks strongly colored, have an adult remove the pot from the heat and pour the "dye stew" through a strainer to strain the dye water into the glass bowl. Allow the water to cool.

3. When the water is room temperature, gently place the white cotton cloth in the bowl of dye water. Swirl the cloth in the bowl to make sure it is thoroughly wet with dye. Let the cloth remain in the bowl until it is the color you want it to be. You may "stir" the cloth from time to time with a wooden spoon. When the cloth is dyed, carefully remove it from the bowl. Squeeze out the extra dye water. Hang the cloth up to dry.

DRAW CONCLUSIONS

1. If you had wanted a deeper color dye, what might you have done to make the color stronger?

2. What do you think is the relationship between a plant's (or fruit's or flower's) color and the color dye it might give you?

FIRST-TIMER'S TIP!

Be careful with the dye water—it will stain any cloth or clothing it touches!

WHAT HAPPENED

Plants contain chemicals called pigments, which help them use different kinds of light. Many plants contain lots of green pigment—that's why they appear green. The plants used in this activity contain pigments that are easily separated out of the plant. They are easily absorbed and held by cloth such as cotton. Cotton is a "fuzzy" kind of fabric. Cotton threads are made up of many, many tiny threads. Each tiny thread can absorb dye, so in this activity, the whole fabric became dyed.

SAFETY FIRST

Stay away from heat. Have an adult boil, simmer, and strain the "dye stew."

An adult should also handle the heavy pot of water.

BRAIN BUSTER

Do all fabrics absorb dye in the same way? Find another piece of white cotton and also a piece of white polyester fabric. Use the dye water you made. Soak each piece of cloth in the dye water for 15 minutes. Remove each piece of cloth and compare the two colors. Did the cotton and the polyester absorb the same amount of dye? Repeat this experiment to find out how well other fabrics, such as felt, burlap, or wool, absorb dye.

Under Pressure

Question: How can air pressure be measured?

KEY WORDS

barometer

humid

Sometimes you may notice that the air seems "heavy" and that it "feels like rain." You are right. Air may feel heavy when the air pressure changes. And sometimes, changes in air pressure do indicate a change in the weather. A barometer (buh-RAH-muh-tuhr) is a device that indicates air pressure. In this activity, you will make your own barometer so you can predict the weather.

MATERIALS

- glass jar
- water
- light-colored food coloring
- straw
- centimeter ruler
- grease pencil or marker
- clay
- eyedropper
- tape

WHAT TO DO

1. Fill the jar two-thirds full with water and add the food coloring.

2. Put the straw up against the ruler and, with the grease pencil, mark centimeters on the straw. Using small print, number each centimeter.

3. Close one end of the straw with a ball of clay, making sure it is airtight. Use the eyedropper to fill the straw two-thirds full with colored water.

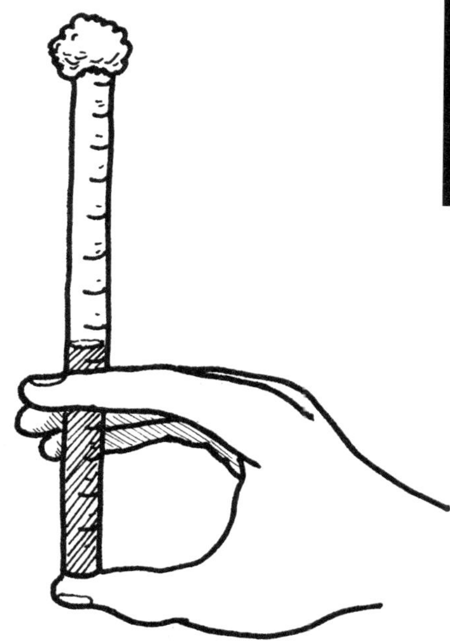

4. Cover the open end of the straw with one finger. Turn the straw upside down, with the clay end up. Tap the straw gently with your other hand until all the air in the straw is at the top of the straw.

5. With your finger still on the open end of the straw, carefully lower it into the jar of water. The bottom of the straw (with your finger on it) should be about 2.5 centimeters below the surface of the water. Once the straw is 2.5 centimeters under the water, remove your finger from the end. Tape the straw to the side of the jar.

6. The lower end of the straw must always be under about 2.5 centimeters of water. Because water evaporates, look at the water level every day and add water to the jar as needed. You may also add a bit of food coloring if necessary.

7. Keep a record of your barometric readings—the level of the water as indicated by the centimeter marks on the straw. Begin your record on a mild, sunny day.

Date	Time	Weather	Barometric Reading

Read the barometer at about the same time each day for a month.

DRAW CONCLUSIONS

1. What relationship, if any, did you notice between the weather outside and the readings you took on your barometer?

2. How might air pressure pushing down on the water have caused the change in the water level in your barometer?

3. How might you use your barometer to predict the weather?

WHAT HAPPENED

Air has weight. When air is "heavy," it may contain lots of water vapor. Then the weather feels humid, or damp. The barometric reading is low, indicating that rainy or stormy weather is ahead. When the air is not heavy and air pressure is low, the water level in the straw rises, and you know that fair weather is on the way.

BRAIN BUSTER

Low barometric readings indicate that a storm may be on the way. Sometimes thunderstorms bring dangerous lightning. Here's a way you can figure out how far away from you lightning is during a thunderstorm. Simply compare the speed of light with the speed of sound!

When you see a flash of lightning, begin counting off seconds (one thousand one, one thousand two, and so on). Stop counting as soon as you hear thunder. Every second you count indicates that the storm is one-fifth of a mile away. In other words, if you count 5 seconds between the flash of lightning and the roll of thunder, the lightning storm is 1 mile away from you. When thunder follows lightning immediately, take cover, because the storm is right around you.

You can calculate a storm's distance because of the different speeds at which light and sound travel. You can use these speed differences to locate a thunderstorm, since thunder is the sound produced by air heated by the lightning bolt you see.

Whipping Winds

Question: How can wind direction be determined?

Sometimes you can predict the weather if you know what direction the wind is blowing from. In this activity, you will make your own wind vane, which will tell you the wind's direction and help you make predictions about your weather.

KEY WORDS

vane

wind

MATERIALS

- small plastic container or pot
- pencil with eraser at the end
- grease pencil or marker
- scissors
- colored paper
- straw
- ruler
- long thumbtack
- compass
- clay

WHAT TO DO

1. Set the container bottom side up on a table. Have an adult use the pencil point to make a hole in the center of the bottom of the plastic container. Push the pencil into the hole, with the eraser end up.

2. Mark the four directions on the bottom of the container with the grease pencil or marker. You may indicate east with the letter *E*, west with *W*, north with *N*, south with *S*.

3. Use the scissors to cut out two equal-sized triangles from the colored paper. Then cut two short slits in each end of the straw. (The slits should be made in the same direction.) Put the base of one paper triangle firmly into two slits. Put the point of the second triangle firmly into the other slits. The triangles should be pointing in

the same direction. You have made a vane to move with the wind.

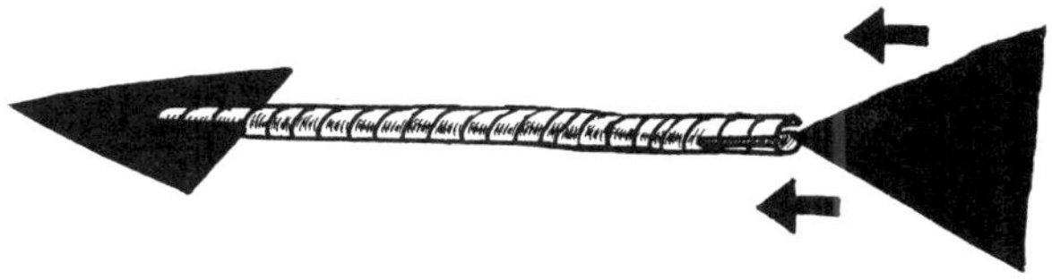

4. Use the ruler to find the exact center of the straw (not including the triangles). Mark the center, and at this point, carefully push the long tack all the way through the straw. The tip of the tack should come out the side of the straw. Press the tip of the tack into the pencil eraser. The tack should hold your vane securely, but the vane should be able to spin freely. Twirl it to test it out. If it's too tight, loosen the tack a little.

5. Put your wind vane outside. Use a compass to set your wind vane so that the directions on the container point correctly. After it is positioned, secure the container with a ring of clay around its base.

6. Record wind direction and a description of the weather every day or even several times a day for one month. *Note that wind direction is the direction from which the wind comes.* For example, in a wind that blows from east to west, the vane will be pointing east.

Date	Wind Direction	Weather

DRAW CONCLUSIONS

1. When you had the fairest weather, what direction did the wind generally blow from?

2. From what direction did the wind bring rain and storms?

3. Why did you have to use the compass to position your wind vane?

WHAT HAPPENED

Winds form when the sun heats the earth's atmosphere. Heated air expands and rises. Cooler air sinks beneath the rising warm air. As air is alternately warmed and cooled, the air moves. We call this air movement the wind. Sometimes air moves over an area in a predictable pattern. Huge currents of air may normally move in a certain direction. In some places, for example, people know that air currents moving in from the west bring rain. So, knowing the wind direction—in this case, westerly—can help predict rain. Find out about the course of your weather by keeping records of wind direction and weather for several months.

SAFETY FIRST

Be careful when using scissors.

BRAIN BUSTER

See how heat causes wind. Turn an ordinary lightbulb into a wind generator! First remove the shade from an incandescent (regular) lightbulb. Let the bulb heat up for a minute or two. Then carefully sprinkle a tiny bit of talcum powder or baby powder an inch above the bulb. What happens? The powder "flies" up because the lightbulb's heat warmed the surrounding air, causing a current of air to rise all around the hot bulb. This current of air, which is like the wind, carried the powder up with it.

Considering Clouds

Question: How does the form of a cloud help people predict weather?

You have probably noticed that there are different kinds of clouds. Some are thin and wispy; others are big and look a lot like cotton balls. Did you know that you can often predict the weather from clouds? In this activity, you will learn how clouds may tell you about the weather ahead.

KEY WORDS

cirrus clouds

cumulus clouds

stratus clouds

WHAT TO DO

1. In your science notebook, create a chart in which you can record the kinds of clouds you see and the accompanying weather.

Date	Time	Cloud Type	Weather

MATERIALS

- weather record (see "What to Do," step 1)

2. Look at the pictures on pages 152 and 153 of the different kinds of clouds. Learn what each kind of cloud indicates about the weather:

Cirrus clouds are thin and wispy, like white feathery streaks across the sky. Cirrus clouds are generally high in the air—usually about 20,000 feet (6,100 meters) above the earth's surface. Because they are so high, the water drops in cirrus clouds are frozen into tiny ice crystals. A "mackerel sky" has cirrus clouds that have become puffy, like tiny cotton balls. Cirrus clouds may sometimes create what looks like a halo around the moon or sun.

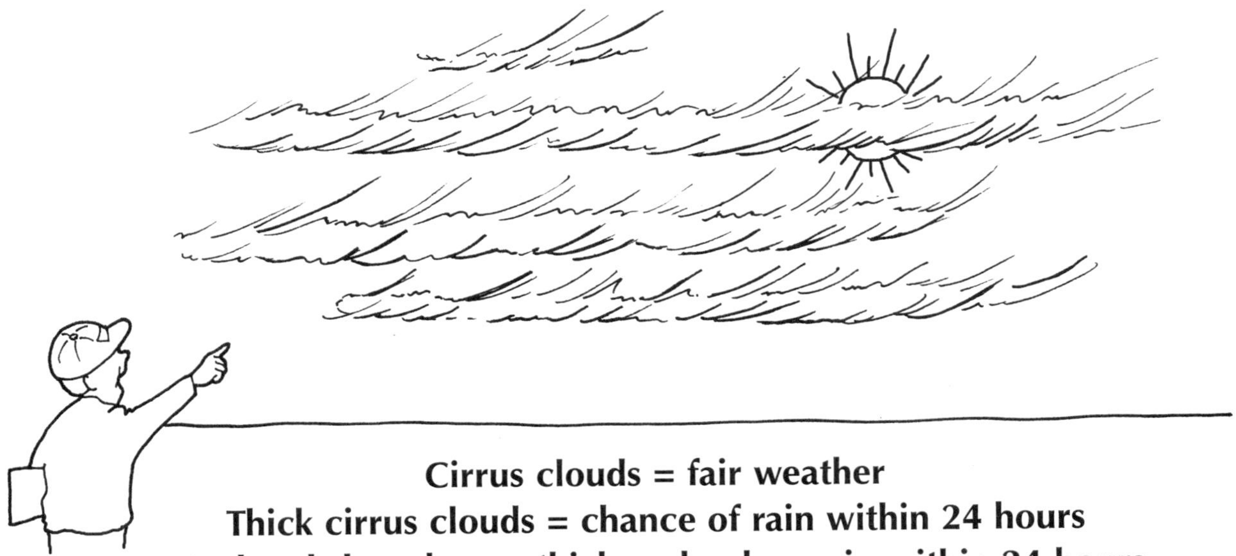

Cirrus clouds = fair weather
Thick cirrus clouds = chance of rain within 24 hours
Mackerel sky + lower, thicker clouds = rain within 24 hours
"Halo" around moon or sun = rain (or snow) within 24 hours

Stratus clouds occur nearer the ground in flat layers that often extend over large areas of sky. Fog is really stratus clouds that are very near the earth's surface.

Stratus clouds or fog = drizzle or rain
Thick stratus clouds = heavy, steady rainfall

Cumulus clouds resemble large tufts of cotton piled up in the sky. Often cumulus clouds occur in a clear blue sky. Sometimes, though, cumulus clouds may grow upward, swelling into dark gray storm clouds.

Low cumulus clouds in blue sky = fair weather
Upward-growing, dark cumulus clouds (thunderheads) = advancing thunderstorm

3. Keep your cloud record chart for several weeks. Check the sky for clouds as often as you can to see if clouds really do help you predict weather.

DRAW CONCLUSIONS

1. How accurately did cloud formation predict the weather that was ahead?

2. What other factors do you think affect the weather?

DID YOU KNOW?

Clouds are made of tiny droplets of water or ice. A cloud forms when water vapor or moisture in the air is condensed by cold temperatures above the surface of the earth. If a cloud forms very high above the earth where the temperature is very cold, the cloud will be made of water vapor that has condensed into ice crystals. If a cloud forms nearer the surface of the earth where the temperature is warmer, the water vapor will condense into water droplets.

Weather Wizard—Putting It All Together

Question: How can tomorrow's weather be accurately predicted today?

KEY WORD

thermometer

MATERIALS

- your homemade barometer (see page 144)
- your homemade wind vane (see page 148)
- outdoor thermometer
- record chart
- pencil

Use what you have learned to be a weather forecaster. See if you can predict the weather better than the weatherperson on TV or radio.

WHAT TO DO

1. Create your own outdoor Weather Center. After becoming an expert at using your barometer and wind vane, get an outdoor thermometer to tell you the temperature outside. Attach it securely in a suitable spot outdoors, where you can read it easily. Try to keep it in the same area as your wind vane and your barometer.

2. Keep a daily record of your weather readings:

Date	Time	Temperature	Cloud Form	Barometer	Wind Direction

3. Use the following weather "clues" to help you predict tomorrow's weather:

FAIR WEATHER IS COMING IF . . .

- wind is coming from the west or north
- barometric pressure is going up
- clouds break up and blue sky appears
- the base of the clouds in the sky rises

FAIR WEATHER WILL CONTINUE IF . . .

- high barometric pressure continues
- temperature is steady and seasonal
- there is a clear sky at sunset
- fog disappears in the morning
- there is dew or frost in the morning

A STORM IS APPROACHING WHEN . . .

- wind is from the east and the barometric pressure is falling
- winds shift from south to north or west and the barometer falls
- the moon or sun has a "halo"
- the barometric pressure falls
- clouds get thicker, deeper, and darker
- low clouds move in quickly from the south or east
- the wind shifts to the south or east
- the temperature rises as humid air sweeps in from the south or east

THE WEATHER WILL BECOME COLDER IF . . .

- winds start to blow from the north or northwest
- the sun sets in a clear sky and a west wind dies down at night
- the northern sky looks greenish and clouds break up

THE WEATHER WILL BECOME WARMER WHEN . . .

- the night is cloudy
- wind direction changes from the northwest to the south

With this information, you should become a first-rate weather forecaster. But don't feel bad if sometimes your weather predictions aren't exactly right. Remember that predicting the weather is a tricky business—even for grown-up scientists.

Glossary

acid: any chemical substance that reacts with a base to form a kind of salt; a substance that turns litmus paper red.

adhere: to stick to or stay attached to a material, especially to a material unlike the original.

balance: a state in which things are of equal weight or value.

barometer: a weather instrument that measures air pressure.

base: any chemical substance that forms a salt when it reacts with an acid; a substance that turns litmus paper blue.

calcium: an element of many bases; an important part of dairy products such as milk.

capillary action: a force that acts on liquids to move them up and through tiny tubes, such as the tiny capillary tubes that carry blood to all parts of the body.

carbon dioxide: a gas compound, made up of carbon and oxygen atoms, in which flames cannot burn.

cell: the smallest structure that, when combined with other cells, makes up all living things.

chemical reaction: the forming of new substances when two or more chemicals combine.

cirrus clouds: wispy, light clouds high in the air that usually indicate fair weather.

cohere: to stick to or stay attached to identical material.

compound: any substance made up of two or more elements; for example, water is a compound made up of hydrogen and oxygen.

cork: the tough outer cells of the bark of the cork oak tree.

cumulus clouds: large, cottony clouds that may occur on fair days or, if they build into thunderheads, may indicate storms ahead.

dissolve: to blend completely with a liquid; to form a solution with a liquid.

dye: any substance that gives color, usually permanently, to a material; pigment.

erupt: to explode, as a volcano.

etch: to create a picture or other design by using acid to eat away an unprotected (unwaxed) surface of an object.

evaporation: the process by which fluid, or flowing, water becomes invisible water vapor in the air; a change of state from a liquid to a gas.

extinguish: to put out; to destroy.

fabric: a woven cloth made of materials such as cotton or wool.

feeder: a structure, designed to hold seed for birds, at which birds can easily perch and feed.

fiber: any material that can be made into cloth; for example, yarn.

field guide: a book containing pictures as well as written descriptions and information about plants and/or animals that people may see in nature.

fragrance: an aroma or scent; the smell of an object.

geotropism: the growth of plant roots in response to the pull of gravity; plant roots growing down into the soil toward the center of the earth where the pull of gravity is greatest.

grape: the fruit of the grapevine; a berry.

humid: when there is a certain amount of moisture in the air that usually makes people feel uncomfortable; damp or wet.

incandescent bulb: a bulb that burns with bright light and produces a lot of heat.

indicator: any substance that clearly indicates, or shows, a change.

inflate: to blow or puff up; to make larger.

insulation: any material that prevents or slows great changes in temperature; a material that prevents the loss of heat or cold.

invisible: not able to be seen.

lava: the liquid, melted rock that spews from an erupting volcano.

light-sensitive: refers to any material that changes or reacts to light; for example, photographic material.

limestone: a kind of rock containing substances that are a base, particularly calcium.

magnet: a piece of metal that is able to attract other metals such as iron.

magnetism: the force of attraction between two materials, particularly metals.

millet: a grain grown for food, similar to rice and barley.

molecule: the smallest unit of a substance, so small it can't be seen (it consists of only a few atoms).

oxidation: the joining of oxygen to chemicals in a substance.

oxygen: a chemical element that occurs as a gas (in the air) and combines with many other elements to form compounds (hydrogen and oxygen combine to form water).

phototropism: the growth of plants toward a source of light.

pigment: a chemical substance in a living thing that gives it color; for example, the green in green plants. Pigments may be used as dyes to color fabrics and other nonliving things.

primary colors: colors (red, yellow, and blue) that are part of the spectrum and can be combined to make most other colors.

prism: a solid crystal whose shape separates light into the spectrum colors.

rainbow: water drops in the air, usually after rain, that are struck by sunlight in such a way that they show the colors of the spectrum in an arc or circle.

refract: to bend, as light bends when it passes through different substances including water and air.

seed: the reproductive "package" produced by flowering plants.

seedling: a very young, growing plant.

silhouette: an outline; usually a dark shape against a light foreground.

simmer: to boil lightly, with a gentle roll.

solute: the substance that dissolves when added to a liquid.

solution: a blend of a solute and a solvent.

solvent: the substance, often a liquid such as water, that dissolves certain other substances (like salt) that are added to it.

spectrum: the full range of colors that make up "white" light; the colors in light separated according to their wavelength by a prism.

sprout: the tiny new growth produced by a seed.

stratus clouds: gray sheetlike clouds that usually layer solidly over the sky.

sunflower: a large bright yellow or orange flower that often produces hundreds of seeds.

thermometer: an instrument for determining temperature.

thistle: the tiny seeds of the prickly thistle plant.

tropism: the response of plants to stimulus in their environment. Phototropism is response to light, while geotropism is response to gravity.

vane: a weather instrument that indicates wind direction.

vibration: a rapid rhythmic movement; a quiver.

vinegar: a food item that is an acid; acetic acid.

vitamin C: a nutrient that is an acid; vitamin C is found in citrus fruits, tomatoes, and leafy vegetables. A body needs vitamin C to be healthy.

wavelength: the speed of a vibration, particularly sound; the distance between the tops of the curves of two waves: the shorter the distance, the shorter the wavelength.

wind: air movement caused when cooler air sinks beneath rising warm air. As air warms and cools, it moves, creating wind.

Index